diabetes
meals by the plate

90 low-carb meals
to mix & match

Houghton Mifflin Harcourt
Boston • New York • 2014

Published by Houghton Mifflin Harcourt Publishing Company,
New York, New York

For information about permission to reproduce selections from this
book, write to Permissions, Houghton Mifflin Harcourt Publishing
Company, 215 Park Avenue South, New York, New York 10003.

www.hmhco.com

Library of Congress Cataloging-in-Publication Data

Diabetes meals by the plate : 90 low-carb meals to mix & match.
    pages cm
  Includes index.
  ISBN 978-0-544-30213-6 (paperback);   978-0-544-30234-1 (ebk)
  1. Diabetes --Diet therapy --Recipes. 2. Low-calorie diet --Recipes
  RC662.D524 2014
  641.5'6314 --dc23

                                2014033601

Meredith Corporation
Diabetic Living® Diabetes Meals by the Plate™

Editor: Martha Miller Johnson

Food and Nutrition Editor: Jessie Shafer, RD

Art Director: Michelle Bilyeu

Contributing Project Manager: Shelli McConnell,
Purple Pear Publishing, Inc.

Cover Photographer: Blaine Moats

Cover Food Stylist: Jennifer Peterson

Publisher: Natalie Chapman

Editorial Director: Cindy Kitchel

Executive Editor: Anne Ficklen

Senior Editor: Adam Kowit

Editorial Associate: Molly Aronica

Managing Editor: Marina Padakis Lowry

Production Editor: Jacqueline Beach

Design and Layout: Kathryn Finney

Illustration: Patti Smith-Lawrence

Production Director: Tom Hyland

Printed in the United States of America

DOW 10 9 8 7 6 5

4500556025

Fill your plate & enjoy!

There's an easy trick to healthful eating that can simplify your life—no more counting every gram of carbohydrate, no more measuring tools, and no more guesswork about meals that are both satisfying and nutritious.

The trick is all in how you fill your plate. Visually divide your plate in half and fill one of those halves with nonstarchy vegetables. Divide the remaining half of the plate in two and fill one quarter with a protein. Fill the last quarter with a serving of grains or other starchy food. That's it!

This simple formula is genius because the portions are built right in. What's more, there are countless ways to mix and match your healthful meals—check out pages 8 and 9. When you get a handle on the types of foods that fill each section of the plate, swap them to your liking. When you've mastered that, use the recipes in this book to create meals your whole family will love. Don't like one side dish? Swap it for one from another menu.

You'll notice that not all of recipes fit perfectly into the sections on the plate—you'll find casseroles, pizza, and even soup where one part of the meal might contain some vegetables and some protein, or some grains and some vegetables. That's where we've done the figuring for you—and if each ingredient were to be divided out, you'd still be filling your plate the right way.

We hope you'll find this book is both functional and fun. Not only will it help you get dinner on the table, but it can lead to better blood sugars, weight loss, and better health. Now that's a winning formula!

Jessie

Jessie Shafer, RD
Food & Nutrition Editor

On the Side
Dairy or Fruit

½ Plate
Nonstarchy Veggies

¼ Plate
Protein

¼ Plate
Starch or Grain

Contents

Discover the easiest way to eat healthy. All you have to do is learn how to fill your plate.

COVER RECIPES, page 137

Icon key

Identify easy ways to adapt the recipes to fit your schedule or please your taste buds by looking for these symbols scattered throughout the book.

Flavor Boost Add a burst of flavor with a sprinkle of this or a dash of that.

Make It Mine Swap out ingredients to customize the dish to your liking.

Time-Saver Shave time off meal prep with these shortcuts.

5

Plan Your Plate

Getting your eating on track (or fine-tuning your current meal plan) is a cinch if you use this visual guide to meals that offer the right mix of nutrients (including carbohydrate, protein, and fat) for better control of glucose and weight.

1. Start with a 9-inch plate

Portion control is easier when your plate is no more than 9 inches wide. If the actual plate size of your dinnerware is more than 9 inches, fill just inside the rim. A shallow rimmed bowl (like a pasta bowl) is also a good option, as long as it measures 9 inches wide. Along with a right-size plate, use a 1-cup glass for milk, a 1/2-cup dish for fruit or dessert, and a 1-cup bowl for cereal or soup.

2. Partition your plate

Mentally divide your plate into sections and fill it as follows:

1/4 protein: Choose a lean meat, such as poultry, lean beef or pork, fish, tofu, eggs, cheese, or nuts.

1/4 starch or grain: Choose a serving of bread, tortilla, pasta, rice, beans, or starchy vegetable, such as potatoes, corn, or peas. (Men may need two servings of starch.) Choose whole grains and beans to give meals a fiber boost.

1/2 nonstarchy vegetables: Choose from asparagus, broccoli, carrots, green beans, cauliflower, cucumbers, peppers, salad greens, tomatoes, zucchini, and many others. For variety, pick two nonstarchy vegetables per meal.

3. Plate extras

For at least one meal each day, and as your calorie allowance permits, enjoy a cup of low-fat milk or light yogurt and a small piece of fresh fruit or 1/2 cup cut-up fruit. When you pick low-fat options, a meal with these side items and each of the three plate components totals less than 50 grams of carbohydrate and less than 500 calories.

4. Measure the height

Don't fall into the trap of piling food too high on your plate to make up for the plate's smaller size. Foods should be no more than 1/2 inch high.

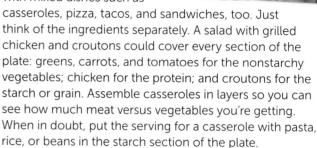

5. Apportion combinations

You can use the plate method with mixed dishes such as casseroles, pizza, tacos, and sandwiches, too. Just think of the ingredients separately. A salad with grilled chicken and croutons could cover every section of the plate: greens, carrots, and tomatoes for the nonstarchy vegetables; chicken for the protein; and croutons for the starch or grain. Assemble casseroles in layers so you can see how much meat versus vegetables you're getting. When in doubt, put the serving for a casserole with pasta, rice, or beans in the starch section of the plate.

6. Go easy on extras

When using items like salad dressings, sauces, and spreads, choose low-fat versions and keep the servings as skimpy as you can. When dining out, ask for dressing on the side and ask for substitutions.

7. Make fair trades

When you are calculating your servings (or exchanges) of fruit, milk, and starch, trade one for another to keep your carbs in check. For example, if you want two pieces of bread for a sandwich, skip the milk or fruit for that meal. The fruit, milk, or starch serving can also be traded for a cup of broth-base soup or even 1/2 cup low-fat ice cream.

8. Divide the breakfast plate

You can use the plate method for breakfast, too. Omit the nonstarchy vegetable and protein servings; just use the starch, fruit, and milk servings. Or pair a hunger-satisfying protein such as scrambled egg whites or lean pork cutlets with a small whole grain pancake.

Mix & Match

It's easy to make a healthful meal using the plate method. Create your own plates by choosing one item for each plate portion. If you wish, you can choose two nonstarchy veggies.

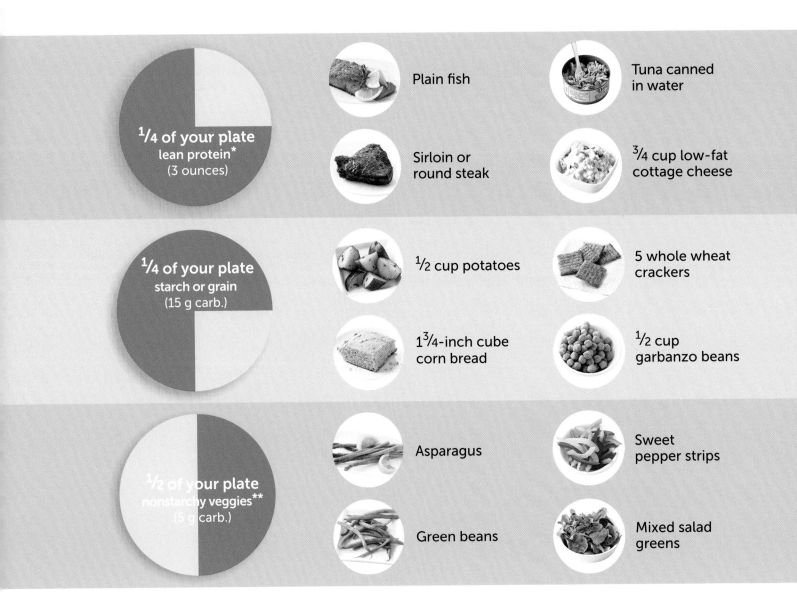

¼ of your plate
lean protein*
(3 ounces)

- Plain fish
- Sirloin or round steak
- Tuna canned in water
- ¾ cup low-fat cottage cheese

¼ of your plate
starch or grain
(15 g carb.)

- ½ cup potatoes
- 1¾-inch cube corn bread
- 5 whole wheat crackers
- ½ cup garbanzo beans

½ of your plate
nonstarchy veggies**
(5 g carb.)

- Asparagus
- Green beans
- Sweet pepper strips
- Mixed salad greens

Skinless chicken breast half

 Low-fat cheese

 ¾ cup egg product, scrambled

 Pork loin chop

 Skinless turkey breast cutlet

 95% lean ground beef patty

 ⅓ cup cooked brown rice

 4 pieces melba toast

 ½ whole wheat English muffin

 ½ cup corn

 ½ cup green peas

 2 slices reduced-calorie whole grain bread

 Sugar snap peas

 Celery sticks and radishes

 Diced green and red sweet peppers

 Cauliflower

 Brussels sprouts

 Canned wax (yellow) beans

*4 ounces of raw meat cooks to 3 ounces, which is about the size of a deck of cards.

**In general, the serving size for nonstarchy vegetables is 1 cup raw or ½ cup cooked or juiced.

9

Chicken

Chicken is an all-star option for healthful eating. It's low in calories and fat and plays well alone and in a variety of dishes.

Beautifully Balanced
Chicken Dinner

Three low-fat cooking styles—searing, steaming, and baking—keep the total fat to 9 grams for this plateful.

½ Plate

Nonstarchy Veggies: asparagus

¼ Plate

Starch or Grain: sweet potato

¼ Plate

Protein: chicken, almonds

Spicy Ginger-Marinated Chicken
Carb. per serving 7 g

SERVINGS 4 (1 chicken breast half and 2 teaspoons sauce each)
PREP 15 minutes MARINATE 4 hours COOK 5 minutes

- $\frac{1}{4}$ cup low-sugar orange marmalade
- 3 tablespoons reduced-sodium soy sauce
- 2 tablespoons rice vinegar
- 1 tablespoon canola oil
- 2 teaspoons grated fresh ginger
- $\frac{1}{8}$ to $\frac{1}{4}$ teaspoon crushed red pepper
- 4 small skinless, boneless chicken breast halves (1 to 1$\frac{1}{4}$ pounds total)
  Nonstick cooking spray

1. For marinade, in a small bowl stir together marmalade, soy sauce, vinegar, oil, ginger, and crushed red pepper. Transfer $\frac{1}{3}$ cup of the marinade to a small bowl; cover and chill until ready to serve. Set aside remaining marinade.

2. Place each chicken breast half between two pieces of plastic wrap. Using the flat side of a meat mallet, lightly pound each chicken breast half to $\frac{1}{2}$ inch thick. Remove plastic wrap. Place chicken in a large resealable plastic bag set in a deep bowl; add remaining marinade. Seal bag and turn to coat chicken. Marinate in the refrigerator for 4 to 6 hours, turning occasionally. Drain chicken, discarding marinade.

3. Coat an unheated very large nonstick skillet with cooking spray. Heat over medium-high heat. Add drained chicken breast halves. Cook for 5 to 6 minutes or until chicken is no longer pink (165°F), turning once halfway through cooking. If chicken browns too quickly, reduce heat to medium. Transfer chicken to four serving plates. Cover to keep warm.

4. For sauce, add the reserved $\frac{1}{3}$ cup marinade to the same skillet. Heat through, stirring to scrape up any browned bits. Place 1 chicken breast half on each of four serving plates. Spoon sauce over chicken.

PER SERVING: 194 cal., 6 g total fat (1 g sat. fat), 72 mg chol., 537 mg sodium, 7 g carb. (0 g fiber, 5 g sugars), 25 g pro. Exchanges: 0.5 carb., 3.5 lean meat, 0.5 fat.

Steamed Asparagus

Wash 1$\frac{1}{2}$ pounds fresh asparagus spears and break off woody bases where spears snap easily; if desired, scrape off scales. Place a steamer basket in a saucepan. Add water to just below the bottom of the basket. Bring water to boiling. Add asparagus to steamer basket. Cover pan and reduce heat; steam for 3 to 5 minutes or until crisp-tender. Divide asparagus among plates; sprinkle each serving with 1 tablespoon toasted almonds. Makes 4 servings (8 or 9 spears each).

PER SERVING: 57 cal., 3 g total fat (0 g sat. fat), 0 mg chol., 2 mg sodium, 5 g carb. (3 g fiber, 2 g sugars), 3 g pro. Exchanges: 1 vegetable, 0.5 fat.

Baked Sweet Potatoes

Preheat oven to 400°F. Scrub 4 small sweet potatoes (each weighing about 4 ounces). Pat dry. Prick potatoes with a fork. Place on a foil-lined baking sheet. Bake for 40 to 50 minutes or until tender. To serve, roll each potato gently under a towel. Using a knife, cut an X in the top of each potato. Press in and up on the ends of each potato. If desired, sprinkle with black pepper. Makes 4 servings (1 potato each).

PER SERVING: 98 cal., 0 g total fat, 0 mg chol., 62 mg sodium, 23 g carb. (3 g fiber, 5 g sugars), 2 g pro. Exchanges: 1.5 starch.

Meal Total (per plate): 349 cal., 9 g total fat (1 g sat. fat), 72 mg chol., 601 mg sodium, 35 g carb. (6 g fiber, 12 g sugars), 30 g pro. Exchanges: 1 vegetable, 1.5 starch, 3.5 lean meat, 1 fat, 0.5 carb.

Garden-Fresh Chicken

Balsamic Roasted Chicken and Vegetables
Carb. per serving 10 g

SERVINGS 4 (1 chicken breast half and ³/₄ cup vegetables each)
PREP 20 minutes ROAST 20 minutes

- 4 small skinless, boneless chicken breast halves (1 to 1¹/₄ pounds total)*
- ¹/₄ cup balsamic vinegar
- 2 tablespoons olive oil
- ¹/₄ teaspoon salt
- ¹/₄ teaspoon black pepper
- 3 cups sliced zucchini
- 3 cups sliced yellow summer squash
- 2 cloves garlic, minced
- ¹/₄ cup snipped fresh basil
- 3 tablespoons grated Parmesan cheese

1. Preheat oven to 425°F. Place chicken breast halves in a 2-quart baking dish. Drizzle with 2 tablespoons of the balsamic vinegar and 1 tablespoon of the olive oil. Sprinkle both sides of chicken evenly with the salt and pepper. Place the zucchini, summer squash, and garlic in a large shallow baking pan. Drizzle with the remaining 2 tablespoons balsamic vinegar and 1 tablespoon olive oil; toss to coat. Spread vegetables in an even layer.

2. Roast chicken and vegetables, uncovered, about 20 minutes or chicken is no longer pink (165°F) and the vegetables are tender, stirring vegetables once halfway through roasting time. To serve, place a chicken breast and vegetables on each of four serving plates. Sprinkle the vegetables with basil and Parmesan cheese.

*TEST KITCHEN TIP: Use a total of 1 to 1¹/₄ pounds of chicken. If 4 smaller chicken breasts are not available, use 2 to 3 chicken breasts. If you use chicken breast halves larger than 4 ounces each, add 5 to 10 minutes more roasting time or until chicken is no longer pink (165°F).

PER SERVING: 209 cal., 10 g total fat (2 g sat. fat), 50 mg chol., 284 mg sodium, 10 g carb. (2 g fiber, 8 g sugars), 19 g pro. Exchanges: 2 vegetable, 2 lean meat, 1.5 fat.

Garlic Toast
Rub 4 toasted 1-ounce slices Italian bread with the cut sides of a garlic clove. Makes 4 servings (1 slice each).

PER SERVING: 78 cal., 1 g total fat (0 g sat. fat), 0 mg chol., 166 mg sodium, 14 g carb. (1 g fiber, 0 g sugars), 3 g pro. Exchanges: 1 starch.

Meal Total (per plate):
287 cal., 11 g total fat (2 g sat. fat), 50 mg chol., 450 mg sodium, 24 g carb. (3 g fiber, 8 g sugars), 22 g pro. Exchanges: 2 vegetable, 1 starch, 2 lean meat, 1.5 fat.

Skinless, boneless chicken breast halves tend to be large; if so, cut them into pieces that are 4 to 5 ounces each.

Nonstarchy Veggies: zucchini, yellow summer squash

½ Plate

¼ Plate

Starch or Grain: bread

¼ Plate

Protein: chicken, cheese

Trattoria-Style
Chicken

Crisp Chicken Parmesan
Carb. per serving 38 g

SERVINGS 4 (2 to 3 chicken pieces, $^1/_2$ cup sauce, and $^1/_2$ cup pasta each) PREP 25 minutes BAKE 15 minutes

　　Olive oil nonstick cooking spray
$^1/_4$　cup refrigerated or frozen egg product, thawed, or
　　　2 egg whites, lightly beaten
　1　tablespoon water
　1　clove garlic, minced
　1　cup bran cereal flakes, crushed (about $^1/_2$ cup crushed)
$^1/_4$　cup grated Parmesan cheese
　1　teaspoon dried Italian seasoning, crushed
　1　pound chicken breast tenderloins
　4　ounces dried multigrain or whole grain spaghetti
　1　cup coarsely chopped yellow sweet pepper or 1-inch
　　　pieces cubed eggplant, peeled if desired
$1^1/_2$　cups purchased light tomato-basil pasta sauce
　1　cup torn fresh spinach leaves
$^1/_2$　cup chopped roma tomatoes

1. Preheat oven to 425°F. Line a 15x10x1-inch baking pan with foil; lightly coat foil with cooking spray. Set aside. In a shallow dish combine egg, the water, and garlic. In another shallow dish combine bran flakes, Parmesan cheese, and Italian seasoning.
2. Dip chicken pieces, one at a time, in egg mixture, turning to coat evenly and allowing excess to drip off. Dip chicken pieces in cereal mixture, turning to coat evenly. Place chicken pieces in a single layer in the prepared baking pan. Coat tops of chicken pieces with cooking spray. Bake for 15 to 20 minutes or until chicken is no longer pink (165°F).
3. Meanwhile, cook spaghetti according to package directions; drain and keep warm. Coat an unheated medium saucepan with cooking spray. Heat saucepan over medium heat. Add sweet pepper and cook about 5 minutes or until tender, stirring occasionally. Add pasta sauce; heat through. Stir in spinach and tomatoes.

4. Divide spaghetti among four serving plates. Top with sauce mixture and chicken pieces.

PER SERVING: 300 cal., 5 g total fat (1 g sat. fat), 51 mg chol., 518 mg sodium, 38 g carb. (7 g fiber, 7 g sugars), 26 g pro. Exchanges: 1 vegetable, 2 starch, 3 lean meat.

Spinach Salad
CARB. PER SERVING 13 g SERVINGS 4 (2 cups each)
START TO FINISH 15 minutes

　8　cups fresh baby spinach or torn fresh spinach
　　　(5 ounces)
$^1/_2$　cup red onion slivers
$^1/_4$　cup dried cranberries
　3　tablespoons bottled reduced-calorie Italian salad dressing

1. In a large bowl toss together spinach, onion, and dried cranberries. Drizzle dressing over the salad and toss to coat. Divide among plates.

PER SERVING: 69 cal., 1 g total fat (0 g sat. fat), 0 mg chol., 215 mg sodium, 13 g carb. (3 g fiber, 6 g sugars), 3 g pro. Exchanges: 1 vegetable, 0.5 fruit.

Meal Total (per plate):
369 cal., 6 g total fat (1 g sat. fat), 51 mg chol., 733 mg sodium, 51 g carb. (10 g fiber, 13 g sugars), 29 g pro. Exchanges: 2 vegetable, 0.5 fruit, 2 starch, 3 lean meat.

A combo of crushed bran cereal flakes and Parmesan cheese creates the crispy coating on these baked chicken planks.

¼ Plate

Protein: chicken, egg, cheese

½ Plate

Nonstarchy Veggies: spinach, onion, sweet pepper, tomatoes

¼ Plate

Starch, Grain, or Other Carb: spaghetti, cereal flakes, dried cranberries

17

Beyond the Basic BLT

Chicken BLT Wrap
Carb. per serving 17 g

SERVINGS 4 (1 wrap each) PREP 20 minutes
COOK 6 minutes

- 4 slices bacon
- Nonstick cooking spray
- 10 ounces skinless, boneless chicken breast halves, cut into thin strips
- ¼ teaspoon garlic powder
- ¼ teaspoon black pepper
- 1 medium avocado, halved, seeded, and peeled
- 4 6-inch low-carb whole wheat flour tortillas
- 2 cups shredded romaine lettuce
- ½ cup chopped tomato

1. In a large skillet cook bacon according to package directions. Drain on paper towels. Drain fat from skillet; set skillet aside to cool. Wipe out skillet with paper towels.
2. Coat the skillet with cooking spray. Heat over medium heat. Sprinkle chicken breast strips with garlic powder and pepper. Add chicken strips to skillet. Cook for 6 to 8 minutes or until chicken is no longer pink, turning once.
3. In a small bowl mash avocado with a fork. Spread each tortilla with one-fourth of the avocado. Top with 1 slice bacon, one-fourth of the chicken, ½ cup lettuce, and 2 tablespoons tomato. Roll up tortillas. Secure with a toothpick.

PER SERVING: 269 cal., 12 g total fat (3 g sat. fat), 54 mg chol., 493 mg sodium, 17 g carb. (11 g fiber, 1 g sugars), 22 g pro. Exchanges: 1 starch, 3 lean meat, 1.5 fat.

Fresh Veggies with Dip
Cut celery stalks and carrots each into 1 cup sticks to make a total of 2 cups. Break broccoli and/or cauliflower each into 1 cup florets to make a total of 2 cups. Divide the 4 cups vegetables among plates. Serve with 1 tablespoon bottled light ranch salad dressing each. Makes 4 servings (1 cup vegetabes and 1 tablespon dip each).

PER SERVING: 69 cal., 4 g total fat (0 g sat. fat), 4 mg chol., 208 mg sodium, 8 g carb. (2 g fiber, 3 g sugars), 2 g pro. Exchanges: 1 vegetable, 1 fat.

Meal Total (per plate):
338 cal., 16 g total fat (3 g sat. fat), 58 mg chol., 701 mg sodium, 25 g carb. (13 g fiber, 4 g sugars), 24 g pro. Exchanges: 1 vegetable, 1 starch, 3 lean meat, 2.5 fat.

Crunchy vegetables and bottled light ranch salad dressing are great go-tos to serve with wraps and sandwiches.

¼ Plate

Protein: bacon, chicken, avocado

¼ Plate

Starch or Grain: tortilla

½ Plate

Nonstarchy Veggies: carrots, broccoli, celery, lettuce, tomato

19

A Taste of the Tropics

For a squeeze of vitamin C and a pop of flavor, serve this spicy jerk-rubbed chicken with lime wedges.

¼ Plate

Starch, Grain, or Other Carb: sweet potato, mango

½ Plate

Nonstarchy Veggies: spinach

¼ Plate

Protein: chicken

Caribbean Chicken with Sweet Potato Cakes

Carb. per serving 34 g

SERVINGS 4 (1 chicken breast half, 2 potato patties, and scant $^1/_3$ cup salsa each) PREP 35 minutes MICROWAVE 8 minutes
COOK 4 minutes per batch GRILL 10 minutes

- 1 pound sweet potatoes, peeled and coarsely shredded*
- 2 tablespoons water
- $^1/_4$ cup refrigerated or frozen egg product, thawed, or 1 egg, lightly beaten
- 2 tablespoons water
- 1 tablespoon canola oil
- $^1/_4$ teaspoon salt
- $^1/_8$ teaspoon black pepper
- $^1/_4$ cup flour
- Nonstick cooking spray
- 1 teaspoon Jamaican jerk seasoning (salt-free)
- $^1/_4$ teaspoon salt
- $^1/_8$ teaspoon black pepper
- Dash cayenne pepper
- 4 small skinless, boneless chicken breast halves ($1^1/_4$ to $1^1/_2$ pounds total)
- 1 recipe Avocado-Mango Salsa *(right)*

1. In a large microwave-safe bowl combine sweet potatoes and 2 tablespoons water. Cover bowl loosely with plastic wrap and microwave on 50 percent power (medium) for 8 to 12 minutes or until potatoes are just tender, stirring twice. Carefully drain off any liquid if necessary. Set aside to cool slightly.

2. Preheat oven to 300°F. In another large bowl whisk together egg, 2 tablespoons water, the oil, $^1/_4$ teaspoon salt, and $^1/_8$ teaspoon black pepper. Stir in flour. Add sweet potatoes and stir until well combined. Coat an unheated large griddle or nonstick skillet with cooking spray; heat over medium heat. Working in batches, spoon a rounded $^1/_4$ cup of the potato mixture onto griddle; spread mixture to a 2- to 3-inch patty. Cook patties for 4 to 6 minutes or until golden brown, turning once halfway through cooking. Keep cooked cakes warm in oven. You should have eight cakes total.

3. Meanwhile, in a small bowl combine jerk seasoning, $^1/_4$ teaspoon salt, $^1/_8$ teaspoon black pepper, and the cayenne pepper. Sprinkle evenly over both sides of chicken breast halves. For a charcoal grill, place chicken on the grill rack directly over medium coals. Grill, uncovered, for 10 to 12 minutes or until chicken is no longer pink (165°F), turning once halfway through grilling. (For a gas grill, preheat grill; reduce heat to medium. Place chicken on grill rack over heat. Cover and grill as directed.) Remove chicken from grill. Thinly slice crosswise.

4. To serve, arrange two sweet potato patties, one sliced chicken breast half, and about $^1/_3$ cup salsa on each of four serving plates.

*TEST KITCHEN TIP: Use a food processor to shred the potatoes.
AVOCADO-MANGO SALSA: Halve, seed, peel, and chop 1 avocado and place in a medium bowl. Seed, peel, and chop 1 medium mango and add to the avocado. Add 2 tablespoons snipped fresh cilantro, $^1/_4$ teaspoon finely shredded lime peel, and 1 tablespoon lime juice. Toss to combine.

PER SERVING: 387 cal., 13 g total fat (2 g sat. fat), 91 mg chol., 534 mg sodium, 34 g carb. (6 g fiber, 11 g sugars), 35 g pro. Exchanges: 0.5 fruit, 1.5 starch, 4 lean meat, 1 fat.

Steamed Spinach

Remove large stems from two 9-ounce packages prewashed fresh spinach. Steam spinach in a large steamer basket over simmering water or in a large skillet with a small amount of water just until spinach is slightly wilted. Divide spinach among plates. Makes 4 servings (about 1 cup each).

PER SERVING: 21 cal., 0 g total fat, 0 mg chol., 69 mg sodium, 3 g carb. (2 g fiber, 0 g sugars), 3 g pro. Exchanges: 1 vegetable.

Meal Total (per plate): 408 cal., 13 g total fat (2 g sat. fat), 91 mg chol., 603 mg sodium, 37 g carb. (8 g fiber, 11 g sugars), 38 g pro. Exchanges: 1 vegetable, 0.5 fruit, 1.5 starch, 4 lean meat, 1 fat.

Flavors of Spring

Chicken with Cherry-Pepper Relish
Carb. per serving 4 g

SERVINGS 4 (1 chicken breast half and 2 tablespoons sauce each) PREP 20 minutes COOK 8 minutes

Nonstick cooking spray
4 small skinless, boneless chicken breast halves (1 to 1$^{1}/_{4}$ pounds total)
$^{2}/_{3}$ cup bottled roasted red sweet peppers, drained and finely chopped
$^{1}/_{3}$ cup frozen unsweetened pitted dark sweet cherries, thawed (undrained) and finely chopped
1 ounce semisoft goat cheese (chèvre), crumbled
1 tablespoon snipped fresh chives

1. Coat an unheated large nonstick skillet with cooking spray; heat over medium heat. Sprinkle chicken with $^{1}/_{4}$ teaspoon each *salt* and *black pepper*. Add to hot skillet. Cook for 8 to 10 minutes or until chicken is no longer pink (165°F), turning once.
2. Meanwhile, in a bowl stir together the roasted peppers, cherries, and $^{1}/_{8}$ teaspoon *salt*.
3. Transfer chicken to four serving plates. Top with pepper-cherry mixture, goat cheese, and chives.

PER SERVING: 124 cal., 4 g total fat (2 g sat. fat), 53 mg chol., 324 mg sodium, 4 g carb. (1 g fiber, 2 g sugars), 18 g pro. Exchanges: 0.5 vegetable, 2.5 lean meat.

Sautéed Swiss Chard
CARB. PER SERVING 3 g
SERVINGS 4 ($^{1}/_{3}$ cup each) START TO FINISH 20 minutes

8 cups coarsely chopped fresh Swiss chard
2 teaspoons olive oil

1. In a large skillet cook chard in hot oil until tender. Add $^{1}/_{8}$ teaspoon each *salt* and *black pepper*. Divide among plates.

PER SERVING: 34 cal., 2 g total fat (0 g sat. fat), 0 mg chol., 226 mg sodium, 3 g carb. (1 g fiber, 1 g sugars), 1 g pro. Exchanges: 0.5 vegetable, 0.5 fat.

Lemon-Almond Couscous
CARB. PER SERVING 29 g SERVINGS 4 ($^{2}/_{3}$ cup each)
START TO FINISH 15 minutes

$^{3}/_{4}$ cup whole wheat couscous
$^{1}/_{4}$ cup slivered almonds, toasted
2 tablespoons snipped fresh chives
2 teaspoons finely shredded lemon peel

1. In a medium saucepan cook couscous according to package directions, omitting salt and oil. Stir in almonds, chives, lemon peel, and $^{1}/_{8}$ teaspoon *salt*. Divide among plates.

PER SERVING: 167 cal., 4 g total fat (0 g sat. fat), 0 mg chol., 73 mg sodium, 29 g carb. (5 g fiber, 1 g sugars), 7 g pro. Exchanges: 2 starch, 1 fat.

Meal Total (per plate):
325 cal., 10 g total fat (2 g sat. fat), 53 mg chol., 623 mg sodium, 36 g carb. (7 g fiber, 4 g sugars), 26 g pro. Exchanges: 1 vegetable, 2 starch, 2.5 lean meat, 1.5 fat.

Wow! This nutrition-packed meal comes in at just 325 calories and 36 g carbs. If wilted greens is not your preference, serve with steamed broccoli, green beans, or Brussels sprouts.

¼ Plate

Starch, Grain, or Other Carb: couscous, cherries

½ Plate

Nonstarchy Veggies: Swiss chard, sweet peppers

¼ Plate

Protein: chicken, cheese, almonds

Flavor Boost Turn up the heat in this sweet cherry-and-pepper relish by stirring in ⅛ teaspoon cayenne pepper.

Mexican-Style
Chicken Rolls

Pollo Relleno
Carb. per serving 14 g

SERVINGS 4 (1 chicken breast half each)
PREP 20 minutes BAKE 40 minutes

- 1 cup finely chopped fresh poblano chile peppers (about 2) (see tip, *page 54*)
- $^2/_3$ cup finely chopped onion
- $^1/_2$ cup finely chopped celery (1 stalk)
- 1 teaspoon olive oil
- 2 tablespoons snipped fresh parsley
- $^1/_8$ teaspoon Cajun seasoning
- $^1/_8$ teaspoon dried oregano, crushed
- 4 medium skinless, boneless chicken breast halves (about $1^1/_2$ pounds total)
- $^1/_4$ cup cornmeal
- $^1/_2$ teaspoon Cajun seasoning
- 2 egg whites
- $^1/_2$ cup shredded Monterey Jack cheese (2 ounces)

1. Preheat oven to 375°F. In a saucepan cook poblano peppers, onion, and celery in hot oil over medium-high heat until tender. Stir in parsley, the $^1/_8$ teaspoon Cajun seasoning, and oregano.
2. Place each chicken breast half between two pieces of plastic wrap. Using the flat side of a meat mallet, lightly pound each chicken breast half to about $^1/_4$ inch thick. Remove plastic wrap.
3. In a shallow dish combine cornmeal and the $^1/_2$ teaspoon Cajun seasoning. Place egg whites in another shallow dish; beat lightly.
4. For each roll, spread about $^1/_4$ cup of the vegetable mixture near an edge of the chicken breast. Sprinkle with 1 tablespoon of the cheese. Fold in side edges; roll up with the vegetable mixture.
5. Dip rolls into egg whites; coat with cornmeal mixture. Place rolls, seam sides down, in a greased shallow baking pan. Coat with *nonstick cooking spray*. Bake, uncovered, for 35 to 40 minutes. Sprinkle chicken with remaining $^1/_4$ cup cheese. Bake 5 minutes more or until no longer pink (165°F). Transfer chicken to four serving plates.

PER SERVING: 328 cal., 9 g total fat (4 g sat. fat), 110 mg chol., 243 mg sodium, 14 g carb. (1 g fiber, 2 g sugars), 45 g pro. Exchanges: 1 starch, 6 lean meat.

Greens and Couscous
CARB. PER SERVING 21 g SERVINGS 4 ($^1/_2$ cup each)
START TO FINISH 15 minutes

- 2 cloves garlic, minced
- 2 teaspoons olive oil
- 3 cups coarsely chopped mustard greens or collard greens
- 1 cup reduced-sodium chicken broth
- $^1/_2$ cup whole wheat couscous

1. In a 2-quart saucepan cook garlic in hot oil over medium heat for 30 seconds. Add greens and stir; cover and cook about 5 minutes or until greens are almost tender. Add broth to the greens and bring to boiling. Stir in couscous; remove from heat. Cover and let stand for 5 minutes. Divide among plates.

PER SERVING: 122 cal., 3 g total fat (0 g sat. fat), 0 mg chol., 149 mg sodium, 21 g carb. (4 g fiber, 1 g sugars), 6 g pro. Exchanges: 1 vegetable, 1 starch, 0.5 fat.

Steamed Carrot Sticks
Peel and cut 4 large carrots into sticks. Place a steamer basket in a saucepan. Add water to just below the bottom of the basket. Bring water to boiling. Add carrots to steamer basket. Cover pan and reduce heat. Steam for 5 to 7 minutes or until crisp-tender. Divide among plates. Makes 4 servings ($^3/_4$ cup each).

PER SERVING: 33 cal., 0 g total fat, 0 mg chol., 56 mg sodium, 8 g carb. (2 g fiber, 4 g sugars), 1 g pro. Exchanges: 1 vegetable.

Meal Total (per plate): 483 cal., 12 g total fat (4 g sat. fat), 110 mg chol., 448 mg sodium, 43 g carb. (7 g fiber, 7 g sugars), 52 g pro. Exchanges: 2 vegetable, 2 starch, 6 lean meat, 0.5 fat.

When you have a choice, opt for nutrient-packed whole wheat couscous over regular couscous.

¼ Plate

Starch or Grain: couscous, cornmeal

½ Plate

Nonstarchy Veggies: carrots, mustard greens, poblano peppers

¼ Plate

Protein: chicken, cheese

Classic Comfort

Hearty Chicken Stew
Carb. per serving 24 g

SERVINGS 4 (1^{3}/4 cups each) PREP 25 minutes COOK 27 minutes

- 2 teaspoons canola oil
- 1 pound skinless, boneless chicken thighs, cut into 1½-inch pieces
- 4 medium carrots, thinly sliced (2 cups)
- 2 stalks celery, thinly sliced (1 cup)
- 2 medium leeks, thinly sliced (^{2}/3 cup)
- 3 cloves garlic, minced
- 2 cups reduced-sodium chicken broth
- 1 medium round red potato, cubed (^{3}/4 cup)
- 1 cup frozen cut green beans
- 2 teaspoons snipped fresh rosemary
- ½ cup fat-free milk
- 1 tablespoon flour

1. In a 4-quart Dutch oven heat oil over medium heat. Add chicken, carrots, celery, leeks, and garlic. Cook and stir for 5 to 8 minutes or until chicken is browned on all sides and vegetables are starting to soften. Stir in broth, potato, green beans, rosemary, and ¼ teaspoon *black pepper.* Bring to boiling; reduce heat. Simmer, covered, for 20 to 25 minutes or until vegetables are tender and chicken is no longer pink.

2. Meanwhile, in a small bowl whisk together milk and flour until smooth. Stir mixture into cooked stew mixture. Return to boiling; reduce heat. Cook and stir about 2 minutes or until stew mixture is thickened. To serve, ladle stew into four bowls.

PER SERVING: 269 cal., 7 g total fat (1 g sat. fat), 108 mg chol., 462 mg sodium, 24 g carb. (4 g fiber, 8 g sugars), 27 g pro. Exchanges: 3 vegetable, 0.5 starch, 3 lean meat, 0.5 fat.

Jack Cheese Biscuits
CARB. PER SERVING 19 g SERVINGS 8 (1 biscuit each) PREP 20 minutes BAKE 8 minutes

- 1 cup all-purpose flour
- ½ cup white whole wheat flour
- 2 teaspoons baking powder
- ½ teaspoon dried thyme, crushed
- 2 cloves garlic, minced
- ¼ teaspoon cream of tartar
- 2 ounces reduced-fat cream cheese, cut up
- 2 tablespoons butter, cut up
- ¼ cup finely shredded Monterey Jack cheese
- ½ cup fat-free milk

1. Preheat oven to 450°F. In a medium bowl combine flours, baking powder, thyme, garlic, cream of tartar, and ⅛ teaspoon *salt.* Cut in cream cheese and butter until mixture resembles coarse crumbs. Stir in 3 tablespoons Jack cheese. Make a well in center of flour mixture. Add milk; stir just until dough clings together.

2. Turn out dough onto a lightly floured surface. Knead by folding and gently pressing dough for four to six strokes or until nearly smooth. Pat or lightly roll dough into an 8×6-inch rectangle. Cut dough into eight rectangles. Sprinkle with remaining 1 tablespoon Jack cheese. Place 1 inch apart on an ungreased baking sheet.

3. Bake for 8 to 10 minutes or until golden. Serve warm. Place the remaining biscuits in a freezer bag and freeze for up to 3 months.

PER SERVING: 146 cal., 6 g total fat (3 g sat. fat), 16 mg chol., 233 mg sodium, 19 g carb. (1 g fiber, 1 g sugars), 5 g pro. Exchanges: 1 starch, 0.5 lean meat, 1 fat.

Meal Total (per plate): 415 cal., 13 g total fat (4 g sat. fat), 124 mg chol., 695 mg sodium, 43 g carb. (5 g fiber, 9 g sugars), 32 g pro. Exchanges: 3 vegetable, 1.5 starch, 3.5 lean meat, 1.5 fat.

One batch of biscuits makes eight, so stash half of them in the freezer to pull out the next time you make this hearty bowl.

¼ Plate

Protein: chicken, cheese, milk

¼ Plate

Starch or Grain: potatoes, all-purpose flour, white whole wheat flour

½ Plate

Nonstarchy Veggies: carrots, celery, leeks, green beans

Fresh Fiesta

Crunchy, chiplike jicama replaces fried tortilla chips in this light and tasty Mexican-style meal.

¼ Plate

Starch, Grain, or Other Carb: tortilla, mango

½ Plate

Nonstarchy Veggies: jicama, tomato, onion

¼ Plate

Protein: chicken

Limey Chicken Tacos with Mango Salsa
Carb. per serving 25 g

SERVINGS 4 (1 taco, 1 onion slice, and $^1/_2$ cup salsa each)
PREP 25 minutes MARINATE 30 minutes GRILL 12 minutes

- $^1/_2$ cup fresh lime juice
- 1 teaspoon ground cumin
- 1 pound skinless, boneless chicken breast halves
- 1 cup chopped mango
- 1 cup chopped tomato
- $^1/_2$ cup finely chopped red onion
- $^1/_4$ cup snipped fresh cilantro
- 1 tablespoon fresh lime juice
- 4 $^1/_2$-inch-thick onion slices
- 1 teaspoon olive oil
- 4 6-inch low-carb whole wheat flour tortillas, warmed

1. For marinade, in a shallow dish combine the $^1/_2$ cup lime juice and the cumin. Add chicken, turning to coat. Cover and marinate in the refrigerator for 30 minutes, turning once. Meanwhile, for salsa, in a medium bowl stir together mango, tomato, red onion, cilantro, and the 1 tablespoon lime juice; set salsa aside.
2. Drain and discard marinade from chicken. Brush onion slices with olive oil. For a charcoal grill, place chicken on the grill rack directly over medium coals. Grill, uncovered, for 12 to 15 minutes or until chicken is no longer pink (165°F), turning once halfway through grilling. Halfway through grilling, add onion slices and grill for 6 to 8 minutes or until onion slices are tender, turning once halfway through grilling. (For a gas grill, preheat grill. Reduce heat to medium. Place chicken on grill rack over heat. Cover; grill as directed, adding onion slices as directed.)
3. To serve, slice chicken. Serve chicken in tortillas with the mango salsa and grilled onion slices.

PER SERVING: 271 cal., 6 g total fat (2 g sat. fat), 73 mg chol., 357 mg sodium, 25 g carb. (10 g fiber, 8 g sugars), 28 g pro. Exchanges: 0.5 fruit, 1 starch, 3.5 lean meat.

Time-Saver For a fuss-free mango salsa, stir chopped refrigerated fresh mango into refrigerated pico de gallo instead of making your own.

Chili-Lime Jicama
CARB. PER SERVING 12 g SERVINGS 4 (1 cup each)
START TO FINISH 15 minutes

- 4 cups peeled jicama cut into bite-size strips or small slices
- $^1/_4$ cup fresh lime juice
- 1 teaspoon chili powder

1. In a large bowl combine jicama, lime juice, and chili powder. Toss to coat. Divide among plates.

PER SERVING: 51 cal., 0 g total fat, 0 mg chol., 16 mg sodium, 12 g carb. (6 g fiber, 0 g sugars), 1 g pro. Exchanges: 2 vegetable.

Meal Total (per plate): 322 cal., 6 g total fat (2 g sat. fat), 73 mg chol., 373 mg sodium, 37 g carb. (16 g fiber, 8 g sugars), 29 g pro. Exchanges: 2 vegetable, 0.5 fruit, 1 starch, 3.5 lean meat.

Bistro Burgers

Not your typical burger and chips, this healthful take on a classic combo features lean chicken and vitamin-packed kale.

½ Plate

Nonstarchy Veggies: kale, tomato, onion, lettuce

¼ Plate

Starch or Grain: whole wheat bun

Protein: chicken, cheese

¼ Plate

Blue Cheese Chicken Burger
Carb. per serving 30 g

SERVINGS 4 (3¹/2-ounce cooked patty, 1 bun,
3 tablespoons cooked onion, 1 tomato slice, 1 lettuce leaf,
and 1¹/2 teaspoons dressing each)
PREP 20 minutes COOK 17 minutes

- 1 medium onion
- 3 tablespoons refrigerated or frozen egg product, thawed, or 1 egg
- 3 tablespoons fine dry bread crumbs
- 2 tablespoons crumbled blue cheese
- 2 teaspoons Dijon-style mustard
- 1 clove garlic, minced
- 1/4 teaspoon black pepper
- 12 ounces uncooked ground chicken breast
- 4 teaspoons canola oil
- 1/2 teaspoon sugar (optional)
- 4 small whole wheat hamburger buns, split and toasted
- 2 tablespoons bottled low-fat blue cheese salad dressing
- 4 tomato slices
- 4 lettuce leaves

1. Thinly slice the onion. Finely chop enough slices to make 1 tablespoon chopped onion. Set aside.
2. In a bowl combine egg, bread crumbs, blue cheese, mustard, garlic, pepper, and the finely chopped onion. Add ground chicken breast; mix well. Shape into four ³/4-inch-thick patties (mixture will be slightly soft).
3. In a large skillet heat 2 teaspoons of the oil over medium heat. Carefully place patties in the skillet. Cook for 14 to 18 minutes or until done (165°F), turning once halfway through cooking.
4. Meanwhile, for caramelized onion, in a heavy large nonstick skillet heat the remaining 2 teaspoons oil over medium-low heat. Add sliced onion to skillet; cover and cook for 13 to 15 minutes or until onion is tender. Sprinkle with sugar if using. Cook, uncovered, over medium-high heat for 4 to 5 minutes more or until onion is golden brown, stirring frequently.
5. To serve, top bottom halves of buns with the patties. Spoon caramelized onion over patties. Top with salad dressing, tomato slices, lettuce leaves, and bun tops.

PER SERVING: 341 cal., 14 g total fat (3 g sat. fat), 77 mg chol., 519 mg sodium, 30 g carb. (3 g fiber, 7 g sugars), 22 g pro. Exchanges: 2 starch, 3 lean meat, 1 fat.

Homemade Kale Chips
CARB. PER SERVING 14 g SERVINGS 4 (1³/4 cups loosely packed chips each) PREP 15 minutes BAKE 20 minutes
COOL 30 minutes

- 1 bunch kale
- 1 tablespoon olive oil
- 1/4 teaspoon cracked black pepper
- 1/8 teaspoon kosher salt
- 1/8 teaspoon garlic powder

1. Preheat oven to 300°F. Arrange oven racks so one rack is in the upper third of the oven and the other rack in the middle of the oven. Line two large baking sheets with parchment paper; set aside.
2. Wash and thoroughly dry the kale leaves. Trim tough stems and tear the leaves into pieces (should have about 8 cups torn leaves). In a large bowl toss kale with olive oil, pepper, salt, and garlic powder until leaves are coated. Arrange leaves in a single layer on baking sheets.
3. Bake for 20 to 25 minutes or until crisp, rotating pans halfway through baking time. Cool 30 minutes before serving. Divide among plates.

PER SERVING: 97 cal., 4 g total fat (1 g sat. fat), 0 mg chol., 119 mg sodium, 14 g carb. (3 g fiber, 3 g sugars), 4 g pro. Exchanges: 3 vegetable, 0.5 fat.

Meal Total (per plate): 438 cal., 18 g total fat (4 g sat. fat), 77 mg chol., 638 mg sodium, 44 g carb. (6 g fiber, 10 g sugars), 26 g pro. Exchanges: 2 starch, 3 vegetable, 3 lean meat, 1.5 fat.

A Southern Sampling

Chicken Sausage and Dirty Rice
Carb. per serving 41 g

SERVINGS 4 (2 ounces cooked sausage, 1 cup vegetables, and $^1/_3$ cup rice each)
PREP 45 minutes COOK 45 minutes

2 red sweet peppers, cut into strips
2 green and/or yellow sweet peppers, cut into strips
2 cups sliced onions
2 cups sliced celery
4 teaspoons canola oil
3 cloves garlic, minced
1 cup reduced-sodium chicken broth
$^1/_2$ cup water
$^1/_2$ cup uncooked long grain brown rice
$^1/_8$ teaspoon cayenne pepper
1 small bay leaf
2 cups cherry tomatoes, halved
2 teaspoons snipped fresh thyme
4 3-ounce fully cooked Andouille chicken sausages, such as Al Fresco brand, cut into $^1/_2$-inch-thick slices

1. Finely chop about $^1/_2$ cup of the sweet peppers and $^1/_4$ cup each of the onions and celery. In a small saucepan heat 1 teaspoon of the oil over medium heat. Add the finely chopped vegetables. Cook and stir over medium heat about 5 minutes or until just tender. Stir in 1 clove of the minced garlic; cook and stir for 1 minute more. Carefully stir in chicken broth and the water. Bring to boiling. Add rice, cayenne pepper, and bay leaf. Return to boiling; reduce heat. Simmer, covered, for 45 to 50 minutes or until rice is tender.

2. Meanwhile, in a large skillet heat remaining 3 teaspoons oil over medium-high heat. Add remaining sweet pepper strips, sliced onions, and celery. Cook and stir about 5 minutes or until just tender. Add tomatoes, remaining 2 cloves garlic, and $1^1/_2$ teaspoons of the thyme. Cook and stir about 5 minutes more or until vegetables are crisp-tender. Remove vegetables from skillet; cover and keep warm.

3. Add chicken sausage to hot skillet. Cook and stir over medium-high heat for 3 to 4 minutes or until heated through and lightly browned.

4. Remove and discard bay leaf from cooked rice. Stir remaining $^1/_2$ teaspoon thyme into rice. To serve, spoon rice, vegetables, and sausage onto four serving plates.

PER SERVING: 360 cal., 13 g total fat (3 g sat. fat), 65 mg chol., 664 mg sodium, 41 g carb. (7 g fiber, 12 g sugars), 21 g pro. Exchanges: 3 vegetable, 1.5 starch, 2 medium-fat meat, 1 fat.

Meal Total (per plate):
360 cal., 13 g total fat (3 g sat. fat), 65 mg chol., 664 mg sodium, 41 g carb. (7 g fiber, 12 g sugars), 21 g pro. Exchanges: 3 vegetable, 1.5 starch, 2 medium-fat meat, 1 fat.

Seek out Andouille-style chicken sausage—ask the meat market to order it for you. It's a lean option when cooking spicy Cajun fare.

½ Plate

Nonstarchy Veggies: sweet peppers, onions, celery, tomatoes

¼ Plate

Protein: chicken sausage

¼ Plate

Starch or Grain: rice

Make It
Moroccan

Skinless chicken thighs make a healthful option. These spice-coated thighs are browned and baked to perfection.

¼ Plate

Starch or Grain: couscous, garbanzo beans

½ Plate

Nonstarchy Veggies: Broccolini, sweet pepper

¼ Plate

Protein: chicken, garbanzo beans

Moroccan Chicken Thighs
Carb. per serving 4 g

SERVINGS 4 (1 chicken thigh each)
PREP 15 minutes BAKE 35 minutes COOK 5 minutes

- 2 tablespoons flour
- 1 teaspoon chili powder
- $\frac{1}{2}$ teaspoon ground cumin
- $\frac{1}{2}$ teaspoon ground ginger
- $\frac{1}{4}$ teaspoon ground cinnamon
- 4 5-ounce bone-in chicken thighs, skinned
- 2 teaspoons canola oil

1. Preheat oven to 375°F. In a large resealable plastic bag combine flour, chili powder, cumin, ginger, and cinnamon. Add chicken thighs to bag, one at a time, shaking to coat chicken with seasoning mixture.

2. In a very large oven-going skillet heat oil over medium-high heat. Add chicken thighs. Cook for 5 to 6 minutes or until browned, turning once halfway through cooking.

3. Transfer skillet to oven. Bake, uncovered, for 35 to 40 minutes or until chicken is tender and no longer pink (at least 175°F). To serve, place chicken on four serving plates.

PER SERVING: 138 cal., 6 g total fat (1 g sat. fat), 81 mg chol., 72 mg sodium, 4 g carb. (0 g fiber, 0 g sugars), 17 g pro. Exchanges: 3 lean meat.

Meal Total (per plate):

375 cal., 9 g total fat (1 g sat. fat), 81 mg chol., 509 mg sodium, 48 g carb. (5 g fiber, 9 g sugars), 26 g pro. Exchanges: 1 vegetable, 2.5 starch, 3 lean meat, 0.5 fat.

Moroccan-Style Couscous
CARB. PER SERVING 38 g SERVINGS 4 ($\frac{3}{4}$ cup each)
PREP 15 minutes COOK 5 minutes STAND 5 minutes

- 2 teaspoons canola oil
- $\frac{1}{3}$ cup chopped onion
- $\frac{1}{4}$ cup chopped red sweet pepper
- 2 cloves garlic, minced
- 1 cup reduced-sodium chicken broth
- $\frac{1}{2}$ teaspoon chili powder
- $\frac{1}{4}$ teaspoon salt
- $\frac{1}{4}$ teaspoon ground cumin
- $\frac{1}{4}$ teaspoon ground ginger
- $\frac{1}{8}$ teaspoon ground cinnamon
- $\frac{1}{8}$ teaspoon black pepper
- $\frac{2}{3}$ cup couscous or whole wheat couscous
- $\frac{1}{4}$ cup no-salt-added canned garbanzo beans (chickpeas), rinsed and drained
- $\frac{1}{4}$ cup golden raisins
- 2 tablespoons sliced green olives

1. In a small saucepan heat oil over medium heat. Add onion, sweet pepper, and garlic. Cook and stir about 5 minutes or until just softened.

2. Carefully add broth, chili powder, salt, cumin, ginger, cinnamon, and black pepper to the saucepan; bring to boiling. Stir in couscous, garbanzo beans, raisins, and olives; remove from heat. Cover and let stand for 5 minutes. Fluff couscous with a fork. Serve immediately.

PER SERVING: 206 cal., 3 g total fat (0 g sat. fat), 0 mg chol., 370 mg sodium, 38 g carb. (3 g fiber, 7 g sugars), 6 g pro. Exchanges: 2.5 starch, 0.5 fat.

Steamed Broccolini
Trim Broccolini and measure 4 cups. Place steamer basket in a saucepan. Add water to just below the bottom of the basket. Bring water to boiling. Add Broccolini to steamer basket. Cover pan and reduce heat. Steam for 6 to 8 minutes or until tender. Sprinkle lightly with a dash of salt. Makes 4 servings (1 cup each).

PER SERVING: 31 cal., 0 g total fat, 0 mg chol., 67 mg sodium, 6 g carb. (2 g fiber, 2 g sugars), 3 g pro. Exchanges: 1 vegetable.

Weekend Brunch

This plate showcases all the components that make a healthful meal. For a sweet bonus add a bowl of fresh berries.

¼ Plate

Starch or Grain: piecrust

½ Plate

Nonstarchy Veggies: spinach, mushrooms, onion

¼ Plate

Protein: chicken, eggs, cheese

Chicken-Spinach Quiche
Carb. per serving 15 g

SERVINGS 8 (1/8 wedge of the quiche each)
PREP 30 minutes BAKE 57 minutes STAND 10 minutes

- 1/2 of a 15-ounce package rolled refrigerated unbaked piecrust (1 piecrust)
- Nonstick cooking spray
- 6 ounces skinless, boneless chicken breast, cut into 3/4-inch chunks
- 2 cups shredded fresh spinach (about 2 ounces)
- 2 cups refrigerated or frozen egg product, thawed, or 8 eggs, lightly beaten
- 3/4 cup shredded Gruyère or Swiss cheese (3 ounces)
- 1/2 cup fat-free milk
- 1/3 cup chopped bottled roasted red sweet peppers
- 2 teaspoons snipped fresh thyme or 3/4 teaspoon dried thyme, crushed
- 1/4 teaspoon salt
- 1/4 teaspoon black pepper

1. Preheat oven to 425°F. Let piecrust stand at room temperature according to package directions. Line a 9-inch pie plate with piecrust. Crimp edge as desired. Line unpricked piecrust with a double thickness of foil. Bake for 8 minutes. Remove foil. Bake for 4 to 5 minutes more or until piecrust is set and dry. Remove from oven. Reduce oven temperature to 350°F.
2. Coat an unheated medium skillet with cooking spray. Heat over medium heat. Add chicken to skillet. Cook and stir for 6 to 8 minutes or until chicken is done and no longer pink. Remove chicken from skillet. Return skillet to heat. Add spinach and cook over medium heat for 1 to 2 minutes or until wilted, turning frequently.

3. In a large bowl whisk together the eggs, chicken, spinach, cheese, milk, roasted peppers, thyme, salt, and pepper. Pour egg mixture into baked piecrust.
4. Bake for 40 minutes. If necessary to prevent overbrowning, cover edge of quiche with foil. Bake for 5 to 10 minutes more or until a knife inserted near the center comes out clean. Let stand on a wire rack for 10 minutes before serving. Cut into wedges; place one wedge of each of four serving plates.*

*TEST KITCHEN TIP: Cover leftover quiche with plastic wrap and refrigerate for up to 24 hours. To reheat, preheat oven to 350°F. Remove plastic wrap from quiche. Cover loosely with foil. Bake about 40 minutes or until heated through (165°F).

PER SERVING: 209 cal., 10 g total fat (5 g sat. fat), 28 mg chol., 396 mg sodium, 15 g carb. (1 g fiber, 1 g sugars), 15 g pro. Exchanges: 1 starch, 2 lean meat, 1 fat.

Baby Mixed Greens Salad
CARB. PER SERVING 5 g SERVINGS 4 (1 1/2 cups each)
START TO FINISH 15 minutes

- 5 cups baby mixed greens
- 1 cup sliced fresh mushrooms
- 1/2 cup thinly sliced red onion
- 1 tablespoon white wine vinegar
- 1 tablespoon lemon juice
- 1 tablespoon olive oil
- 1 teaspoon snipped fresh thyme
- 1 clove garlic, minced
- 1/4 teaspoon salt
- 1/4 teaspoon black pepper

1. In a medium bowl toss together greens, mushrooms, and red onion. For dressing, in a small bowl whisk together vinegar, lemon juice, olive oil, thyme, garlic, salt, and pepper. Pour dressing over greens; toss to coat. Divide among plates.

PER SERVING: 54 cal., 4 g total fat (1 g sat. fat), 0 mg chol., 156 mg sodium, 5 g carb. (1 g fiber, 2 g sugars), 2 g pro. Exchanges: 1 vegetable, 0.5 fat.

Meal Total (per plate): 263 cal., 14 g total fat (6 g sat. fat), 28 mg chol., 552 mg sodium, 20 g carb. (2 g fiber, 3 g sugars), 17 g pro. Exchanges: 1 vegetable, 1 starch, 2 lean meat, 1.5 fat.

37

Orange-Miso
Salad & Chicken

Vegetable Skewer Salad with Orange-Miso Vinaigrette and Chicken
Carb. per serving 16 g

SERVINGS 4 (1 chicken breast half, ³/4 cup spinach, and 2 vegetable skewers)
PREP 30 minutes MARINATE 4 hours BROIL 12 minutes

- ½ cup orange juice
- ⅓ cup rice vinegar
- 2 tablespoons white miso paste
- 1 tablespoon toasted sesame oil
- ¼ teaspoon crushed red pepper
- 4 skinless, boneless chicken breast halves (1¼ pounds)
- 2 medium red, orange, and/or yellow sweet peppers cut into 1½-inch pieces
- 8 ounces small whole fresh mushrooms,
- 1 large red onion, trimmed and cut into 1-inch wedges
- 3 cups packaged fresh baby spinach leaves
- 1 teaspoon sesame seeds, toasted

1. For marinade, in a small bowl whisk together orange juice, vinegar, miso, sesame oil, and the crushed red pepper. Transfer half of the marinade to another small bowl. Cover and refrigerate until ready to serve. Pour the remaining marinade in a large resealable plastic bag. Add chicken breast halves to the bag. Seal bag and turn to coat chicken. Place bag with chicken in a medium bowl. Marinate chicken in the refrigerator for 4 to 6 hours, turning bag occasionally.

2. Thread pepper pieces, mushrooms, and onion wedges alternately on eight 12-inch metal skewers, leaving a ¼-inch space between each piece. Lightly coat vegetables with *nonstick cooking spray*. Drain chicken, discarding any marinade.

3. Preheat broiler. Place vegetable skewers and chicken pieces on the unheated rack of a broiler pan (broil in batches if pan is not large enough). Broil 5 to 6 inches from the heat for 8 to 10 minutes for vegetables or until just tender, turning once halfway through broiling time. Broil chicken for 12 to 15 minutes or until an instant-read thermometer inserted in chicken

registers 165°F, turning once halfway through broiling time. Keep warm.

4. To serve, divide spinach among four serving plates; top with vegetable skewers. Add chicken and sprinkle with sesame seeds. Stir reserved marinade; drizzle over skewers and spinach.

PER SERVING: 282 cal., 8 g total fat (1 g sat. fat), 90 mg chol., 392 mg sodium, 16 g carb. (3 g fiber, 10 g sugars), 34 g pro. Exchanges: 1.5 vegetable, 0.5 starch, 4 lean meat, 0.5 fat.

Soba Noodles with Peanuts
CARB. PER SERVING 24 g SERVINGS 4 (½ cup noodles each)
START TO FINISH 15 minutes

- 4 ounces dried soba noodles (buckwheat noodles)
- ⅓ cup sliced green onion tops
- ¼ cup chopped lightly salted peanuts
- 1 tablespoon toasted sesame oil
- 2 teaspoons finely shredded orange peel

1. Cook noodles according to package directions. Drain and return to the pan. Add green onion tops, peanuts, sesame oil, and orange peel. Toss to combine. Divide among plates.

PER SERVING: 182 cal., 8 g total fat (1 g sat. fat), 0 mg chol., 288 mg sodium, 24 g carb. (2 g fiber, 1 g sugars), 6 g pro. Exchanges: 1.5 starch, 1.5 fat.

Meal Total (per plate): 464 cal., 16 g total fat (2 g sat. fat), 90 mg chol., 680 mg sodium, 40 g carb. (5 g fiber, 11 g sugars), 40 g pro. Exchanges: 1.5 vegetable, 2 starch, 4 lean meat, 2 fat.

If you like your foods spicy, bump the crushed red pepper to $\frac{1}{2}$ teaspoon.

½ Plate

Nonstarchy Veggies: spinach, sweet peppers, mushrooms, red onion, green onions

¼ Plate

Starch or Grain: soba noodles

¼ Plate

Protein: chicken, peanuts

39

Home-Style
Chicken Dinner

These lightened-up Sunday dinner favorites can be ready to eat in less than one hour.

¼ Plate

Protein: chicken, cheese, almonds

½ Plate

Nonstarchy Veggies: green beans, mushrooms, onion

¼ Plate

Starch or Grain: potatoes, panko

Panko-Crusted Chicken
Carb. per serving 13 g

SERVINGS 4 (1 piece chicken each)
PREP 20 minutes BAKE 40 minutes

Nonstick cooking spray
- 2/3 cup buttermilk
- 3/4 cup whole wheat or white panko bread crumbs
- 1/2 teaspoon dried oregano, crushed
- 1/2 teaspoon ground cumin
- 1/2 teaspoon smoked or regular paprika
- 1/4 teaspoon salt
- 1/8 teaspoon black pepper
- 4 small bone-in chicken breast halves, skinned (1 1/2 to 1 3/4 pounds total)

1. Preheat oven to 375°F. Line a 15x10x1-inch baking pan with foil and coat foil with cooking spray. Set aside. Pour buttermilk into a medium bowl. In another medium bowl combine panko, oregano, cumin, paprika, salt, and pepper.
2. Dip chicken pieces into buttermilk, allowing excess to drip off. Coat chicken pieces in panko mixture and place, bone sides down, in prepared pan. Coat tops of chicken pieces with cooking spray.
3. Bake for 40 to 50 minutes or until chicken is tender and no longer pink (165°F). Do not turn chicken pieces during baking. Place one chicken piece on each of four serving plates.

PER SERVING: 196 cal., 4 g total fat (1 g sat. fat), 72 mg chol., 309 mg sodium, 13 g carb. (2 g fiber, 2 g sugars), 27 g pro. Exchanges: 1 starch, 3.5 lean meat.

Meal Total (per plate): 400 cal., 15 g total fat (4 g sat. fat), 82 mg chol., 713 mg sodium, 37 g carb. (7 g fiber, 9 g sugars), 34 g pro. Exchanges: 1.5 vegetable, 2 starch, 3.5 lean meat, 2 fat.

Creamy Green Beans and Mushrooms
CARB. PER SERVING 10 g SERVINGS 4 (1/2 cup each)
PREP 15 minutes COOK 20 minutes

- 12 ounces fresh green beans, trimmed
- 1 cup sliced fresh button or cremini mushrooms
- 1/2 cup chopped onion
- 2 teaspoons olive oil
- 1/4 cup light garlic and herb spreadable cheese
- 1/4 cup fat-free milk
- 2 tablespoons sliced almonds, toasted

1. In a large nonstick skillet cook green beans, covered, in a small amount of boiling water for 10 to 15 minutes or until crisp-tender. Drain beans and set aside. Carefully wipe out skillet.
2. In the same skillet cook mushrooms and onion in hot oil over medium heat for 5 minutes or until tender, stirring occasionally. Add beans, cheese, milk, 1/4 teaspoon *salt*, and 1/8 teaspoon *black pepper* to the mushroom mixture. Cook and stir about 5 minutes more or until well combined and heated through. Spoon bean mixture onto four plates and sprinkle with almonds.

PER SERVING: 113 cal., 7 g total fat (2 g sat. fat), 10 mg chol., 243 mg sodium, 10 g carb. (3 g fiber, 5 g sugars), 5 g pro. Exchanges: 1.5 vegetable, 1.5 fat.

Lemon-Herb Roasted Potatoes
CARB. PER SERVING 14 g SERVINGS 4 (3/4 cup potatoes each)
PREP 15 minutes ROAST 40 minutes

- 12 ounces small gold potatoes, cut into 1-inch wedges
- 1 tablespoon olive oil
- 1 teaspoon finely shredded lemon peel
- 1 tablespoon lemon juice
- 2 teaspoons snipped fresh thyme or oregano

1. Preheat oven to 375°F. Place potato wedges in a 2-quart baking dish. Drizzle with oil and sprinkle with 1/4 teaspoon *salt* and 1/8 teaspoon *black pepper*. Toss to coat. Roast, uncovered, for 40 to 45 minutes or until tender and browned, stirring twice.
2. In a small bowl stir together lemon peel, lemon juice, and thyme. Just before serving, drizzle over warm potatoes.

PER SERVING: 91 cal., 4 g total fat (1 g sat. fat), 0 mg chol., 161 mg sodium, 14 g carb. (2 g fiber, 1 g sugars), 2 g pro. Exchanges: 1 starch, 0.5 fat.

Szechwan
Noodle Bowl

Control the heat by the amount of Asian chili sauce you begin with. Start mild and let each person add extra.

Nonstarchy Veggies: sweet peppers, red onion, snow peas, shredded broccoli, bamboo shoots

½ Plate

¼ Plate

Starch or Grain: rice vermicelli noodles

¼ Plate

Protein: chicken

Szechwan Chicken and Vegetable Stir-Fry
Carb. per serving 39 g

SERVINGS 4 (3 cups each) PREP 25 minutes
COOK 15 minutes

  4 ounces dry rice vermicelli noodles or bean threads
 ¼ cup water
 ¼ cup seasoned rice vinegar
  2 tablespoons reduced-sodium soy sauce
  2 tablespoons sesame oil
  4 cloves garlic, minced
  2 teaspoons finely chopped, peeled fresh ginger
  1 to 2 teaspoons Asian chili sauce (Sriracha sauce)
  1 teaspoon cornstarch
  1 pound skinless, boneless chicken breast halves, cut into bite-size strips
 1½ teaspoons five-spice powder
  4 teaspoons sesame oil
  2 medium red, orange, and/or yellow sweet peppers, cut into thin bite-size strips (2 cups)
  1 medium red onion, halved and cut into thin wedges (¾ cup)
  1 cup fresh snow peas, trimmed
  1 medium Thai chile pepper or serrano chile pepper, halved, seeded, and finely chopped (see tip, *page 54*)
  2 cups packaged shredded broccoli (broccoli slaw mix)
  1 8-ounce can sliced bamboo shoots, drained
  2 teaspoons sesame seeds, toasted

1. In a large bowl combine noodles and enough hot water to cover. Let stand for 10 to 15 minutes or until pliable but not soft. Drain well in a colander.

2. Meanwhile, in a small bowl combine the ¼ cup water, vinegar, soy sauce, 2 tablespoons sesame oil, the garlic, ginger, and chili sauce. Reserve ¼ cup of the sauce in another small bowl. Add the cornstarch to the remaining sauce. Set both sauces aside.

3. In a large bowl sprinkle chicken with five-spice powder and toss to coat. In a large wok or very large nonstick skillet heat 2 teaspoons of the sesame oil over medium-high heat. Stir-fry chicken, half at a time if necessary, in hot oil for 3 to 5 minutes or until chicken is no longer pink. Remove chicken from wok. Keep warm.

4. Add remaining 2 teaspoons sesame oil to the wok. Add sweet peppers and onion. Stir-fry for 3 minutes. Add peas and chile pepper. Stir-fry for 2 minutes more. Remove vegetables from wok.

5. Add drained noodles, shredded broccoli, and the reserved ¼ cup sauce. Stir-fry for 3 minutes or until noodles and broccoli are just tender. Divide noodle mixture among four serving plates.

6. Stir the sauce with the cornstarch. Add to the wok along with chicken, pepper mixture, and bamboo shoots. Cook and stir until thickened and bubbly. Cook and stir for 2 minutes more. Spoon chicken mixture evenly over noodles on plates. Sprinkle with sesame seeds.

PER SERVING: 419 cal., 15 g total fat (2 g sat. fat), 72 mg chol., 468 mg sodium, 39 g carb. (4 g fiber, 8 g sugars), 30 g pro. Exchanges: 2 vegetable, 1.5 starch, 0.5 carb., 3.5 lean meat, 1.5 fat.

Meal Total (per plate): 419 cal., 15 g total fat (2 g sat. fat), 72 mg chol., 468 mg sodium, 39 g carb. (4 g fiber, 8 g sugars), 30 g pro. Exchanges: 2 vegetable, 0.5 carb., 1.5 starch, 3.5 lean meat, 1.5 fat.

Romesco-Sauced
Chicken Thighs

Eggplant comes in a variety of shapes and sizes. Start with $1\frac{1}{2}$ pounds and divide the slices evenly among the plates.

½ Plate

Nonstarchy Veggies: eggplant, tomatoes, sweet peppers, spinach

¼ Plate

Protein: chicken, almonds

¼ Plate

Starch or Grain: pasta

Chicken Thighs with Romesco Sauce
Carb. per serving 6 g

SERVINGS 4 (1 chicken thigh and $1/3$ cup sauce each)
PREP 10 minutes COOK 25 minutes

  - 4 large bone-in chicken thighs, skinned (about $1 3/4$ pounds total)
  - $1/4$ teaspoon salt
  - $1/4$ teaspoon black pepper
  - 1 to 2 tablespoons olive oil
  - 2 cloves garlic, minced
  - $1 1/2$ cups chopped fresh tomatoes
  - $1/2$ cup bottled roasted red sweet peppers, chopped
  - $1/4$ cup chopped, pitted green olives
  - 2 tablespoons sherry vinegar
  - $1/8$ to $1/4$ teaspoon crushed red pepper (optional)
  - $1/4$ cup slivered almonds, toasted

1. Trim fat from chicken thighs. Sprinkle chicken with the salt and black pepper. In a large skillet cook chicken in 1 tablespoon hot oil over medium heat for 12 to 15 minutes or until chicken is no longer pink (at least 175°F). Transfer chicken to a plate; cover to keep warm.
2. If necessary, add 1 to 2 teaspoons more oil to the skillet. Add garlic; cook and stir over medium heat for 30 seconds. Add tomatoes. Cook for 3 to 4 minutes or until tomatoes are softened, stirring occasionally. Add roasted sweet peppers, the olives, vinegar, and, if desired, crushed red pepper. Cook for 3 minutes more, stirring occasionally.
3. Return chicken to the tomato sauce in the skillet. Cover and cook for 2 to 3 minutes or until chicken is heated through. Place a chicken thigh on each of four serving plates. Spoon tomato sauce over chicken and sprinkle with almonds.

PER SERVING: 241 cal., 13 g total fat (2 g sat. fat), 113 mg chol., 377 mg sodium, 6 g carb. (2 g fiber, 2 g sugars), 25 g pro. Exchanges: 1 vegetable, 3.5 lean meat, 1.5 fat.

Meal Total (per plate): 394 cal., 15 g total fat (2 g sat. fat), 113 mg chol., 678 mg sodium, 38 g carb. (11 g fiber, 9 g sugars), 31 g pro. Exchanges: 3 vegetable, 1.5 starch, 3.5 lean meat, 1.5 fat.

Herbed Eggplant
CARB. PER SERVING 10 g SERVINGS 4 (2 slices eggplant each)
START TO FINISH 15 minutes

  - $1 1/2$ pounds eggplant, cut into $1/2$-inch-thick slices
  - Olive oil nonstick cooking spray
  - $1/4$ teaspoon salt
  - $1/4$ teaspoon black pepper
  - 1 tablespoon snipped fresh oregano
  - 2 teaspoons snipped fresh thyme

1. Lightly coat both sides of eggplant slices with cooking spray. Sprinkle slices evenly with the salt and pepper. Coat an unheated indoor grill pan with cooking spray; heat pan over medium heat.
2. Add eggplant slices to the hot pan. Cook for 8 to 10 minutes or until eggplant is tender, turning once halfway through cooking. Divide eggplant slices among plates. Sprinkle with oregano and thyme.

PER SERVING: 46 cal., 1 g total fat (0 g sat. fat), 0 mg chol., 149 mg sodium, 10 g carb. (5 g fiber, 6 g sugars), 2 g pro. Exchanges: 2 vegetable.

Roasted Red Pepper-Spinach Pasta
CARB. PER SERVING 22 g SERVINGS 4 ($3/4$ cup pasta mixture each) START TO FINISH 20 minutes

  - 4 ounces dried whole grain or multigrain penne pasta
  - $1/2$ cup bottled roasted red sweet peppers, chopped
  - $1/4$ teaspoon salt
  - 1 cup coarsely chopped fresh spinach

1. Cook pasta in lightly salted water according to package directions. Before draining pasta, reserve $1/2$ cup of the pasta cooking water. Drain pasta and return to the pan.
2. Add the reserved pasta cooking water, roasted sweet peppers, and salt to the pasta. Cook and stir over medium heat for 1 to 2 minutes or until liquid is nearly absorbed. Remove from the heat. Stir in spinach. Divide pasta mixture among plates.

PER SERVING: 107 cal., 1 g total fat (0 g sat. fat), 0 mg chol., 152 mg sodium, 22 g carb. (4 g fiber, 1 g sugars), 4 g pro. Exchanges: 1.5 starch.

Turkey

Turkey need not be reserved for the holidays. Its versatile, low-in-fat cuts make it a healthful protein to serve year-round.

Sweet Barbecue
Turkey Dinner

Dip the grilled potato bites into a little light sour cream. That brings the meal total to just 261 calories and 4 grams of fat. Wow, that's light!

¼ Plate

Starch, Grain, or Other Carb: potatoes, barbecue sauce

½ Plate

Nonstarchy Veggies: green beans

¼ Plate

Protein: turkey

Sweet Barbecue Glazed Turkey
Carb. per serving 5 g

SERVINGS 4 (3 ounces cooked turkey and about
1 tablespoon sauce each)
START TO FINISH 30 minutes

- ²/₃ cup reduced-sugar ketchup
- ¼ cup orange juice
- 3 tablespoons snipped fresh cilantro
- 1 clove garlic, minced
- ¼ teaspoon ground cumin
- ¼ teaspoon black pepper
- 1 large turkey breast tenderloin (about 1 pound), split in half horizontally, or 4 skinless, boneless chicken breast halves (1 to 1¼ pounds total)

1. For sauce, in a small saucepan combine ketchup, orange juice, 2 tablespoons of the cilantro, the garlic, cumin, and pepper. Bring to boiling over medium heat, stirring constantly. Reduce heat. Simmer, uncovered, for 5 minutes. Transfer ⅓ cup of the sauce to a small bowl; keep remaining sauce warm.

2. For a charcoal grill, place turkey pieces on the grill rack directly over medium coals. Grill, uncovered, for 12 to 16 minutes (12 to 15 minutes for boneless, skinless chicken [165°F]; 25 to 35 minutes for bone-in chicken [170F]) or until no longer pink, turning once halfway through grilling and brushing with the ⅓ cup sauce for the last 2 minutes of grilling. (For a gas grill, preheat grill. Reduce heat to medium. Place poultry pieces on grill rack over heat. Cover; grill as directed.)

3. Slice turkey and divide among four serving plates. Serve with remaining sauce. Sprinkle with the remaining 1 tablespoon cilantro.

PER SERVING: 143 cal., 1 g total fat (0 g sat. fat), 70 mg chol., 511 mg sodium, 5 g carb. (0 g fiber, 4 g sugars), 28 g pro. Exchanges: 1 vegetable, 3.5 lean meat.

Grilled Potatoes
CARB. PER SERVING 14 g
SERVINGS 4 (½ cup potatoes and about 2 teaspoons sour cream each)
PREP 15 minutes **GRILL** 8 minutes

- 12 ounces tiny Yukon gold or round red potatoes
- 2 teaspoons olive oil
- ¼ teaspoon salt
- ¼ teaspoon black pepper
- 3 tablespoons light sour cream

1. Wash potatoes and cut them in half. In a medium saucepan cook the potato halves in enough boiling water to cover for 8 minutes or until nearly tender. Drain well. Brush potatoes with olive oil and sprinkle with salt and pepper.

2. For a charcoal grill, place potato halves on the grill rack directly over medium coals. Grill, uncovered, for 8 to 10 minutes or until tender and lightly browned, turning occasionally. Divide potatoes among plates. Top each serving with about 2 teaspoons sour cream.

PER SERVING: 92 cal., 3 g total fat (1 g sat. fat), 3 mg chol., 167 mg sodium, 14 g carb. (1 g fiber, 1 g sugars), 2 g pro. Exchanges: 1 starch, 0.5 fat.

Steamed Green Beans
If desired, trim ends of 3 cups fresh green beans. Place a steamer basket in a saucepan. Add water to just below the bottom of the basket. Bring water to boiling. Add beans to steamer basket; cover pan and reduce heat. Steam for 18 to 22 minutes or until crisp-tender. Spoon ¾ cup beans onto each plate. Makes 4 servings (¾ cup each).

PER SERVING: 26 cal., 0 g total fat, 0 mg chol., 5 mg sodium, 6 g carb. (2 g fiber, 3 g sugars), 2 g pro. Exchanges: 1 vegetable.

Meal Total (per plate): 261 cal., 4 g total fat (1 g sat. fat), 73 mg chol., 683 mg sodium, 25 g carb. (3 g fiber, 8 g sugars), 32 g pro. Exchanges: 2 vegetable, 1 starch, 3.5 lean meat, 0.5 fat.

Asian Burger Plates

Call on whole wheat bagel thins or sandwich thins as a low-carb substitute for burger buns.

Asian Turkey Burgers
Carb. per serving 29 g

SERVINGS 4 (1 burger patty, 1 bagel thin, 1 tablespoon mayonnaise mixture, and 2 tablespoons cabbage each)
PREP 15 minutes GRILL 10 minutes

- 1 pound uncooked ground turkey breast
- 1 cup finely chopped fresh mushrooms
- 1/4 cup chopped sweet onion
- 1/4 cup reduced-fat mayonnaise
- 1 tablespoon hoisin sauce
- 4 whole wheat bagel thins, toasted
- 1/2 cup shredded napa cabbage

1. In a medium bowl combine turkey, mushrooms, and onion. Form into four 1/2-inch-thick patties. In a small bowl stir together mayonnaise and hoisin sauce; set aside.
2. For a charcoal grill, place patties on the grill rack directly over medium coals. Grill, uncovered, for 10 to 13 minutes or until an instant-read thermometer inserted into side of each patty registers 165°F, turning once halfway through grilling. (For a gas grill, preheat grill. Reduce heat to medium. Place patties on grill rack over heat. Cover and grill as directed.)
3. For each serving, spread a bagel thin with one-fourth of the mayonnaise mixture. Top with a burger patty and one-fourth of the napa cabbage.

PER SERVING: 298 cal., 7 g total fat (1 g sat. fat), 60 mg chol., 438 mg sodium, 29 g carb. (6 g fiber, 6 g sugars), 34 g pro. Exchanges: 1 vegetable, 1.5 starch, 4 lean meat, 1 fat.

Broiled Broccolini
CARB. PER SERVING 6 g
SERVINGS 4 (6 Broccolini stalks and 1 tablespoon walnuts each)
PREP 10 minutes BROIL 5 minutes

- 24 stalks Broccolini
- 4 teaspoons olive oil
- 1/4 cup chopped walnuts, toasted

1. Preheat broiler. Place Broccolini in a shallow baking pan. Drizzle with olive oil; toss to coat. Broil 4 to 5 inches from the heat for 5 to 10 minutes or until tender, turning Broccolini once. Divide among plates and sprinkle with walnuts.

PER SERVING: 114 cal., 9 g total fat (1 g sat. fat), 0 mg chol., 19 mg sodium, 6 g carb. (1 g fiber, 2 g sugars), 3 g pro. Exchanges: 1 vegetable, 2 fat.

Meal Total (per plate):
412 cal., 16 g total fat (2 g sat. fat), 60 mg chol., 457 mg sodium, 35 g carb. (7 g fiber, 8 g sugars), 37 g pro. Exchanges: 2 vegetable, 1.5 starch, 4 lean meat, 3 fat.

½ Plate

Nonstarchy Veggies: mushrooms, onion, cabbage, broccolini

¼ Plate

Protein: turkey, walnuts

¼ Plate

Starch or Grain: bagel thin

German-Style
Greens & Sausage

Smoked turkey sausage is a tasty and lean substitute for traditional bratwurst. It saves you around 14 grams of fat per serving.

¼ Plate

Starch or Grain: potatoes

½ Plate

Nonstarchy Veggies: spinach, onion

¼ Plate

Protein: sausage

Maple-Glazed Sausage with Wilted Spinach

Carb. per serving 13 g

SERVINGS 4 (4 to 5 slices sausage and about ¹/₂ cup spinach each)
PREP 15 minutes **COOK** 7 minutes

- 10 ounces smoked turkey sausage, cut diagonally into ³/₄-inch slices
- ¹/₄ cup reduced-calorie or sugar-free maple-flavor syrup
- ¹/₄ cup reduced-sodium chicken broth
- ¹/₂ cup finely chopped sweet onion
- ¹/₄ teaspoon dried sage, crushed
- ¹/₄ teaspoon black pepper
- 2 6-ounce packages fresh baby spinach (about 10 cups)

1. In a very large nonstick skillet* cook sausage slices over medium-high heat for 3 minutes or until sausage is heated through and browned, stirring occasionally. Reduce heat to medium-low and add syrup, tossing to coat sausage. Using a slotted spoon, remove sausage from skillet. Cover and keep warm.

2. Add broth, onion, sage, and pepper to skillet. Cook for 3 to 5 minutes or until onion is just tender, stirring occasionally. Increase heat to medium. Add spinach to hot skillet; cover and cook for 1 to 2 minutes or until spinach is just wilted, tossing once.

3. Divide spinach evenly among four serving plates. Top with sausage slices.

*TEST KITCHEN TIP: Make sure your skillet is at least 12 inches in diameter. It needs to be this large to accommodate the 10 cups of fresh spinach. Use long-handled tongs to easily grab and toss the spinach in the skillet after 30 seconds of cooking.

PER SERVING: 169 cal., 7 g total fat (2 g sat. fat), 47 mg chol., 816 mg sodium, 13 g carb. (2 g fiber, 9 g sugars), 13 g pro. Exchanges: 1 vegetable, 0.5 carb., 2 lean meat, 1 fat.

Flavor Boost Add a sprinkling of freshly ground black pepper and a snip of fresh chives to season the potatoes without increasing the sodium.

Baked Potatoes

Preheat oven to 350°F. Scrub four 3-ounce Yukon gold potatoes thoroughly with a brush; pat dry. Prick potatoes with a fork. Bake about 50 minutes or until tender. To serve, roll each potato gently under a towel. Using a knife, cut an X in the top of each potato; press in and up on the ends of each potato or cut into quarters. Place potatoes on plates; top each potato with 1 teaspoon tub-style vegetable oil spread or light sour cream. Makes 4 servings (1 potato each).

PER SERVING: 94 cal., 3 g total fat (1 g sat. fat), 0 mg chol., 30 mg sodium, 15 g carb. (2 g fiber, 1 g sugars), 2 g pro. Exchanges: 1 starch, 0.5 fat.

Meal Total (per plate): 263 cal., 10 g total fat (3 g sat. fat), 47 mg chol., 846 mg sodium, 28 g carb. (4 g fiber, 10 g sugars), 15 g pro. Exchanges: 1 vegetable, 1 starch, 0.5 carb., 2 lean meat, 1.5 fat.

Mexican
Meets Comfort

Taco Meat Loaf
Carb. per serving 10 g

SERVINGS 6 (2 slices or about 6 ounces of the meat loaf each)
PREP 25 minutes **BAKE** 55 minutes **STAND** 10 minutes

- ¼ cup refrigerated or frozen egg product, thawed, or 1 egg, lightly beaten
- ¼ cup fat-free milk
- ⅓ cup yellow cornmeal
- 1 tablespoon reduced-sodium taco seasoning
- ¼ teaspoon salt
- ¾ cup finely chopped red sweet pepper
- ½ cup thinly sliced green onions (4)
- 1 fresh medium jalapeño chile pepper, seeded and finely chopped* (optional)
- 1 pound uncooked ground turkey breast
- 8 ounces uncooked ground turkey
- ½ cup taco sauce

1. Preheat oven to 350°F. In a large bowl whisk together egg and milk. Stir in cornmeal, taco seasoning, and salt. Stir in sweet pepper, onions, and jalapeño pepper (if using). Add turkey and mix well. Lightly pat turkey mixture into a 9×5×3-inch loaf pan.
2. Bake for 45 minutes. Carefully drain off any grease from the meat loaf. Spread top of meat loaf with taco sauce. Bake about 10 minutes more or until an instant-read thermometer inserted in center of meat loaf registers 165°F.
3. Let meat loaf stand for 10 minutes. Carefully drain off any grease from the meat loaf. To serve, cut loaf into 12 slices; place two slices on each of six serving plates.
*TEST KITCHEN TIP: Because chile peppers contain volatile oils that can burn your skin and eyes, avoid direct contact with them as much as possible. When working with chile peppers, wear plastic or rubber gloves. If your bare hands do touch the peppers, wash your hands and nails well with soap and warm water.

PER SERVING: 188 cal., 4 g total fat (1 g sat. fat), 63 mg chol., 505 mg sodium, 10 g carb. (1 g fiber, 3 g sugars), 28 g pro. Exchanges: 2 vegetable, 3.5 lean meat.

Avocado-Tomato Salad
CARB. PER SERVING 7 g
SERVINGS 6 (1 tomato, ⅓ avocado, ¼ cup spinach, and 4 teaspoons dressing each) **PREP** 30 minutes

- 2 small avocados
- 6 small tomatoes, cored and thinly sliced
- 1½ cups fresh baby spinach leaves
- 1 teaspoon finely shredded lime peel
- ¼ cup lime juice
- 3 tablespoons snipped fresh cilantro
- 3 tablespoons olive oil

1. Halve, seed, and peel avocados; thinly slice. Divide the tomatoes among six plates. Top evenly with the avocado slices and the spinach.
2. For dressing, in a small screw-top jar combine lime peel, lime juice, cilantro, oil, ½ teaspoon *salt,* and ½ teaspoon *black pepper.* Cover and shake well. Drizzle over salads.

PER SERVING: 130 cal., 12 g total fat (2 g sat. fat), 0 mg chol., 115 mg sodium, 7 g carb. (3 g fiber, 2 g sugars), 2 g pro. Exchanges: 1 vegetable, 2 fat.

Baked Tortilla Chips
Divide 4 ounces low-fat baked tortilla chips among plates. Makes 6 servings (⅔ ounce each).

PER SERVING: 78 cal., 1 g total fat (0 g sat. fat), 0 mg chol., 79 mg sodium, 15 g carb. (1 g fiber, 0 g sugars), 2 g pro. Exchanges: 1 starch.

Meal Total (per plate):
396 cal., 17 g total fat (3 g sat. fat), 63 mg chol., 699 mg sodium, 32 g carb. (5 g fiber, 5 g sugars), 32 g pro. Exchanges: 3 vegetable, 1 starch, 3.5 lean meat, 2 fat.

Classic American meat loaf gets a Mexican makeover with flavor accents from taco seasoning and taco sauce.

½ Plate

Nonstarchy Veggies: sweet pepper, green onions, jalapeño pepper, tomatoes, spinach

¼ Plate

Protein: turkey

¼ Plate

Starch or Grain: baked tortilla chips, cornmeal

Classic
Italian-Style Feast

Choose multigrain pasta over regular pasta whenever you get the chance. The multigrain version is lower in carbs and higher in protein and fiber, making it a health-smart option.

¼ Plate

Starch or Grain: pasta

½ Plate

Nonstarchy Veggies: lettuce, spinach, mushrooms, dried tomatoes, red onion

¼ Plate

Protein: turkey, cheese

Meatballs with Sun-Dried Tomato Sauce

Carb. per serving 25 g

SERVINGS 4 (3 meatballs, ½ cup spaghetti, and
¼ cup sauce each)
START TO FINISH 25 minutes

    Nonstick cooking spray
  1 12-ounce package refrigerated or frozen cooked
      Italian-style turkey meatballs (12)
  1 clove garlic, minced
  1 cup water
 ½ cup coarsely chopped dried tomatoes
      (not oil-packed)
  1 tablespoon balsamic vinegar
  2 tablespoons snipped fresh basil or
      2 teaspoons snipped fresh oregano
  4 ounces dried multigrain spaghetti, cooked according
      to package directions
  2 tablespoons finely shredded Parmesan cheese

1. Coat an unheated large nonstick skillet with cooking spray. Heat over medium heat. Add meatballs. Cook for 5 to 10 minutes or until meatballs are browned and heated through, turning occasionally.
2. For sauce, lightly coat an unheated small saucepan with cooking spray; heat over medium heat. Add garlic to hot pan. Cook and stir for 10 seconds. Add water and bring to boiling. Remove from heat; add dried tomatoes. Cover and let stand for 5 minutes. Transfer tomato mixture to a blender or food processor; add vinegar. Cover and blend or process until smooth. Stir in basil.
3. Add sauce to skillet with meatballs. Cook for 1 minute or until sauce is heated through, stirring to coat meatballs with sauce.

4. To serve, divide hot cooked spaghetti among four serving plates. Top with meatballs and sauce and sprinkle with Parmesan cheese.

PER SERVING: 310 cal., 13 g total fat (4 g sat. fat), 93 mg chol., 459 mg sodium, 25 g carb. (3 g fiber, 4 g sugars), 23 g pro. Exchanges: 2 vegetable, 1 starch, 3 lean meat, 1 fat.

Leafy Green Salad

CARB. PER SERVING 6 g
SERVINGS 4 (1¼ cups each)
START TO FINISH 10 minutes

  2 cups torn romaine lettuce
  2 cups fresh baby spinach
 ½ cup thinly sliced red onion
 ½ cup thinly sliced fresh mushrooms
  3 tablespoons balsamic vinegar
  1 tablespoon olive oil

1. In a large bowl toss together romaine lettuce, spinach, red onion, and mushrooms. For dressing, in a screw-top jar combine vinegar and oil; cover and shake to mix. Drizzle dressing over salad and toss to coat. Divide salad among plates.

PER SERVING: 60 cal., 3 g total fat (0 g sat. fat), 0 mg chol., 27 mg sodium, 6 g carb. (1 g fiber, 3 g sugars), 2 g pro. Exchanges: 1 vegetable, 0.5 fat.

Meal Total (per plate): 370 cal., 16 g total fat (4 g sat. fat), 93 mg chol., 486 mg sodium, 31 g carb. (4 g fiber, 7 g sugars), 25 g pro. Exchanges: 3 vegetable, 1 starch, 3 lean meat, 1.5 fat.

Thai-Style
Skewers & Salad

Coconut-Lime Turkey Skewers
Carb. per serving 13 g

SERVINGS 4 (2 skewers each) **PREP** 20 minutes
MARINATE 2 hours **GRILL** 6 minutes

- $\frac{1}{3}$ cup coconut water*
- $\frac{1}{2}$ teaspoon finely shredded lime peel
- $\frac{1}{4}$ cup lime juice
- 2 tablespoons honey
- $\frac{1}{4}$ teaspoon crushed red pepper
- 1 turkey breast tenderloin (12 to 14 ounces)
- $\frac{1}{4}$ cup flaked coconut, lightly toasted

1. For marinade, in a large resealable plastic bag combine coconut water, lime peel, lime juice, honey, and red pepper.
2. Cut turkey tenderloin lengthwise into strips, each about $\frac{1}{4}$ inch thick. Add to marinade. Seal bag; turn to coat turkey. Marinate in the refrigerator for 2 to 4 hours, turning bag occasionally.
3. Drain turkey, discarding marinade. Thread turkey accordion-style onto 10-inch skewers.** Place skewers on rack of a covered grill directly over medium heat. Grill, covered, for 6 to 8 minutes or until turkey is no longer pink, turning once halfway through. To serve, divide among four serving plates and sprinkle with coconut.
*TEST KITCHEN TIP: Coconut water is a clear liquid that is tapped from the centers of young, green coconuts. It is low in calories and is naturally free of fat and cholesterol. Look for it in the beverage or health food section of the supermarket.
**TEST KITCHEN TIP: If using wooden skewers, soak in enough water to cover for 30 minutes before using.

PER SERVING: 151 cal., 2 g total fat (1 g sat. fat), 53 mg chol., 76 mg sodium, 13 g carb. (1 g fiber, 11 g sugars), 21 g pro. Exchanges: 1 carb., 3 lean meat.

Rice Noodle Vegetable Salad
CARB. PER SERVING 27 g **SERVINGS** 4 ($1\frac{1}{4}$ cups each)
START TO FINISH 25 minutes

- 4 ounces dried brown or white wide rice noodles
- 3 cups coarsely shredded romaine lettuce
- 1 cup chopped fresh cucumber
- 1 cup purchased coarsely shredded carrots
- 3 green onions, thinly sliced
- $\frac{1}{3}$ cup coconut water (see tip, *left*)
- $\frac{1}{4}$ cup rice vinegar
- 2 tablespoons toasted sesame oil
- 2 teaspoons grated fresh ginger

1. Cook noodles according to package directions. Drain and rinse with cold water; drain again. In a bowl toss together noodles, lettuce, cucumber, carrots, and green onions.
2. In a screw-top jar combine coconut water, vinegar, oil, ginger, $\frac{1}{2}$ teaspoon *salt*, and $\frac{1}{4}$ teaspoon *black pepper*. Cover; shake well. Drizzle over salad; toss to coat. Divide among plates.

PER SERVING: 196 cal., 8 g total fat (1 g sat. fat), 0 mg chol., 335 mg sodium, 27 g carb. (3 g fiber, 3 g sugars), 3 g pro. Exchanges: 1 vegetable, 1.5 starch, 1.5 fat.

Grilled Stone Fruit

Cut 4 plums or 2 nectarines in half; remove pits. Add halves, cut sides down, to rack of the covered grill the last 4 to 5 minutes with skewers. Divide among plates. Makes 4 servings.

PER SERVING: 30 cal., 0 g total fat, 0 mg chol., 0 mg sodium, 8 g carb. (1 g fiber, 7 g sugars), 0 g pro. Exchanges: 0.5 fruit.

Meal Total (per plate): 377 cal., 10 g total fat (2 g sat. fat), 53 mg chol., 411 mg sodium, 48 g carb. (5 g fiber, 21 g sugars), 24 g pro. Exchanges: 1 vegetable, 0.5 fruit, 1.5 starch, 1 carb., 3 lean meat, 1.5 fat.

A couple of minutes on the grill gives fresh plum halves roasty flavor and sweet juiciness, complementing the hints of ginger and lime in the rest of the meal.

Starch, Grain, or Other Carb: rice noodles, plums

¼ Plate

¼ Plate

Protein: turkey

½ Plate

Nonstarchy Veggies: lettuce, cucumber, carrots, green onions

59

Autumn
Harvest Dinner

When the air cools, warm up your meals with nutritious fall foods, such as mushrooms, squash, and turkey.

Turkey with Mushroom-Wine Sauce
Carb. per serving 10 g

SERVINGS 4 ($3^1/_2$ ounces cooked turkey and $^1/_3$ cup mushroom sauce each)
PREP 15 minutes **COOK** 21 minutes

1	pound turkey tenderloin
$^1/_4$	teaspoon salt
$^1/_8$	teaspoon black pepper
	Nonstick cooking spray
1	tablespoon butter
$1^1/_2$	cups sliced fresh mushrooms (such as cremini, button, and/or stemmed shiitake)
$^1/_2$	cup chopped sweet onion
$^1/_4$	cup dry white wine or reduced-sodium chicken broth
$^3/_4$	cup fat-free evaporated milk
1	teaspoon cornstarch
1	tablespoon snipped fresh chives

1. Sprinkle turkey with salt and pepper. Coat an unheated large nonstick skillet with cooking spray. Heat over medium heat. Cook turkey in hot skillet for 14 to 20 minutes or until turkey is no longer pink (170°F), turning once. Remove turkey from skillet; cover and keep warm.

2. Add butter to the same skillet. Add mushrooms and onion. Cook for 3 to 4 minutes or until tender, stirring occasionally. Remove from heat and add wine. Return to heat and cook about 2 minutes or until wine is reduced by about half, stirring to scrape up any browned bits from the bottom of the skillet. In a small bowl whisk together evaporated milk and cornstarch until smooth. Add to skillet. Cook and stir until thickened and bubbly; cook and stir for 2 minutes more.

3. Slice turkey and divide among four serving plates. Spoon mushroom sauce over turkey and sprinkle with chives.

PER SERVING: 214 cal., 4 g total fat (2 g sat. fat), 78 mg chol., 289 mg sodium, 10 g carb. (1 g fiber, 8 g sugars), 32 g pro. Exchanges: 0.5 starch, 4 lean meat.

Tossed Salad Greens

Toss 4 cups mixed salad greens with 3 tablespoons bottled reduced-fat balsamic vinaigrette dressing. Divide among plates. Makes 4 servings (1 cup each).

PER SERVING: 17 cal., 0 g total fat, 0 mg chol., 87 mg sodium, 3 g carb. (0 g fiber, 2 g sugars), 0 g pro. Exchanges: 0.5 vegetable.

Roasted Acorn Squash

Preheat oven to 350°F. Cut 1 medium acorn squash in half through the stem end. Discard seeds. Place squash halves, cut sides down, in a baking dish. Roast for 45 to 50 minutes or until tender. Cut each half into six slices. Arrange three squash slices on each plate. Makes 4 servings (3 slices each).

PER SERVING: 43 cal., 0 g total fat, 0 mg chol., 3 mg sodium, 11 g carb. (2 g fiber, 0 g sugars), 1 g pro. Exchanges: 0.5 starch.

Meal Total (per plate):
274 cal., 4 g total fat (2 g sat. fat), 78 mg chol., 379 mg sodium, 24 g carb. (3 g fiber, 10 g sugars), 33 g pro. Exchanges: 0,5 vegetable, 1 starch, 4 lean meat.

Time-Saver Prepare squash as directed, except add 2 tablespoons water to the baking dish. Microwave, covered, on high for 7 to 10 minutes or until tender.

½ Plate

Nonstarchy Veggies: mixed greens, mushrooms, onion

¼ Plate

Protein: turkey

Starch, Grain, or Other Carb: acorn squash, white wine, evaporated milk

¼ Plate

61

Holiday-Special
Turkey Dinner

Bacon-Wrapped Stuffed Turkey
Carb. per serving 1 g

SERVINGS 6 (2 or 3 slices turkey and 1 tablespoon juices each)
PREP 20 minutes **COOK** 6 minutes **ROAST** 15 minutes

- 2 tablespoons snipped fresh parsley
- 2 tablespoons snipped fresh thyme
- 2 tablespoons snipped fresh oregano or sage or
  2 teaspoons snipped fresh rosemary
- 5 cloves garlic, minced
- 2 teaspoons olive oil
- 2 12- to 14-ounce turkey breast tenderloins
- 4 slices turkey bacon

1. Preheat oven to 400°F. Combine herbs, garlic, and $1/4$ teaspoon *black pepper;* stir in olive oil. Cut a long pocket in the side of each turkey tenderloin by cutting horizontally to, but not through, the opposite side. Spoon herb mixture evenly into pockets. Wrap bacon around stuffed tenderloins.

2. Coat an unheated large oven-going nonstick skillet with *nonstick cooking spray.* Heat skillet over medium heat. Add tenderloins. Cook for 6 to 8 minutes or until browned on all sides. Remove from heat. Carefully pour in $3/4$ cup *water.*

3. Roast, uncovered, for 15 to 20 minutes or until turkey is no longer pink (170°F). To serve, slice turkey crosswise and divide among six serving plates. Drizzle with some of the pan juices.

PER SERVING: 163 cal., 4 g total fat (1 g sat. fat), 80 mg chol., 177 mg sodium, 1 g carb. (0 g fiber, 0 g sugars), 30 g pro. Exchanges: 4 lean meat.

Parmesan Mashed Potatoes
CARB. PER SERVING 23 g **SERVINGS** 6 ($2/3$ cup each)
PREP 15 minutes **COOK** 20 minutes

- 1 pound medium round red potatoes
- 2 medium parsnips (about 12 ounces total)
- 2 tablespoons light butter

- 3 to 4 tablespoons fat-free milk
- $3/4$ cup shredded Parmesan cheese (3 ounces)

1. Scrub potatoes; cut in half. Peel parsnips; cut into 2-inch pieces. In a large saucepan cook potatoes and parsnips, covered, in boiling water about 20 minutes or until vegetables are tender; drain.

2. Using a potato masher, mash potatoes and parsnips. Add butter and $1/8$ teaspoon *black pepper.* Mash in enough of the milk to make mixture light and fluffy. Stir in cheese. Divide among plates.

PER SERVING: 172 cal., 7 g total fat (4 g sat. fat), 12 mg chol., 212 mg sodium, 23 g carb. (3 g fiber, 4 g sugars), 8 g pro. Exchanges: 1.5 starch, 1 fat.

Roasted Zucchini
Preheat oven to 400°F. Trim ends of 3 medium zucchini. Cut in half crosswise, then cut lengthwise. Brush pieces with 1 tablespoon olive oil; sprinkle with $1/4$ teaspoon kosher salt and $1/8$ teaspoon black pepper. Arrange in a shallow baking pan. Roast, uncovered, for 20 to 25 minutes or until zucchini is just tender, turning once. Cut into bite-size pieces to serve. Makes 6 servings ($1/2$ zucchini each).

PER SERVING: 37 cal., 3 g total fat (0 g sat. fat), 0 mg chol., 90 mg sodium, 3 g carb. (1 g fiber, 2 g sugars), 1 g pro. Exchanges: 0.5 vegetable, 0.5 fat.

Meal Total (per plate):
372 cal., 14 g total fat (5 g sat. fat), 92 mg chol., 479 mg sodium, 27 g carb. (4 g fiber, 6 g sugars), 39 g pro. Exchanges: 0.5 vegetable, 1.5 starch, 4 lean meat, 1.5 fat.

Turkey bacon makes a colorful wrap around the herb-stuffed turkey. If needed, secure the bacon with wooden toothpicks and remove them before slicing.

¼ Plate

Protein: turkey, bacon, cheese

¼ Plate

Starch or Grain: potatoes, parsnips

Nonstarchy Veggies: zucchini

½ Plate

63

Unpasta and
Meatballs

Naturally low in calories, carbohydrate, and fat, spaghetti squash is a wonderful substitute for pasta. Its mild flavor lets the sauce and meatballs be the stars.

½ Plate

Nonstarchy Veggies: mushrooms, onion, eggplant, pasta sauce

¼ Plate

Protein: turkey, cheese

¼ Plate

Starch, Grain, or Other Carb: Spaghetti squash, apple

Turkey-Apple Meatballs with Spaghetti Squash

Carb. per serving 39 g

SERVINGS 4 (1¼ cups squash mixture and 3 meatballs each)
PREP 25 minutes **MICROWAVE** 12 minutes **COOK** 20 minutes

- 1 3-pound spaghetti squash
- Nonstick cooking spray
- 1 cup chopped fresh mushrooms
- 1 small onion, chopped
- 1 medium apple, cored and coarsely shredded (about 1 cup)
- 1 teaspoon dried thyme, crushed
- ¼ teaspoon black pepper
- ⅛ teaspoon salt
- 1 pound uncooked ground turkey breast
- 4 teaspoons canola oil
- 3 cups coarsely chopped, peeled eggplant
- 2 cups bottled light chunky-style pasta sauce
- 2 tablespoons finely shredded Parmesan cheese

1. Cut squash in half lengthwise; remove seeds and strings. Place one half, cut side down, in a microwave-safe baking dish. Using a fork, prick the skin all over. Microwave on 100 percent power (high) for 6 to 7 minutes or until tender when pierced with a fork; carefully remove from baking dish. Repeat with the other squash half. Cool squash slightly. Using a fork, shred and separate the squash pulp into strands. You should have about 4 cups.

2. Coat an unheated large nonstick skillet with cooking spray; heat over medium heat. Add mushrooms and half of the onion; cook for 5 minutes, stirring occasionally. Transfer mushroom mixture to a large bowl. Stir in apple, thyme, pepper, and salt. Add turkey and mix well. Shape mixture into 12 meatballs, each about 2 inches in diameter.

3. In the same skillet heat 2 teaspoons of the oil over medium heat. Add meatballs. Cook for 10 to 12 minutes or until no longer pink (165°F), turning occasionally so meatballs brown evenly. Reduce heat if meatballs start to get too brown.

4. Meanwhile, in a large nonstick saucepan cook the eggplant and remaining onion in the remaining 2 teaspoons oil over medium heat for 5 to 10 minutes or until tender, stirring occasionally. Stir in the pasta sauce.

5. To serve, divide squash among four serving plates. Top with meatballs and sauce mixture. Sprinkle with Parmesan cheese.

PER SERVING: 343 cal., 8 g total fat (2 g sat. fat), 57 mg chol., 580 mg sodium, 39 g carb. (11 g fiber, 21 g sugars), 33 g pro. Exchanges: 1 vegetable, 2 starch, 4 lean meat, 0.5 fat.

Flavor Boost Top each serving with snipped fresh herbs such as Italian parsley, basil, and/or oregano for a burst of freshness.

__Meal Total (per plate):__ 343 cal., 8 g total fat (2 g sat. fat), 57 mg chol., 580 mg sodium, 39 g carb. (11 g fiber, 21 g sugars), 33 g pro. Exchanges: 1 vegetable, 2 starch, 4 lean meat, 0.5 fat.

Light Carbonara-Style
Pasta Bowls

Fat-free half-and-half and refrigerated or frozen egg product step in for the high-fat equivalents to create a light and creamy sauce. Maple-flavor syrup is the secret to its subtle sweetness.

¼ Plate

Starch or Grain: linguine, parsnip

½ Plate

Nonstarchy Veggies: mushrooms, leeks, sugar snap peas

¼ Plate

Protein: turkey, turkey bacon, walnuts

Turkey-Mushroom Pasta with Maple-Cream Sauce

Carb. per serving 39 g

SERVINGS 6 (1 cup each)
PREP 35 minutes COOK 25 minutes

- 2 cups fresh cremini or button mushrooms, thinly sliced
- 2 medium leeks, trimmed and thinly sliced
- 2 cloves garlic, minced
- 1 tablespoon olive oil
- 6 ounces dried whole grain linguine or dried multigrain spaghetti
- 2 medium parsnips, peeled and cut into julienne strips (2 cups)
- $3/4$ cup fat-free half-and-half
- $1/4$ cup reduced-calorie maple-flavor syrup
- $1/2$ teaspoon salt
- 2 cups coarsely shredded cooked turkey
- 2 tablespoons snipped fresh sage or $1 1/2$ teaspoons dried sage, crushed
- $1/2$ cup refrigerated or frozen egg product, thawed
- 3 slices turkey bacon, cooked according to package directions and crumbled
  Freshly ground black pepper

Meal Total (per plate):
392 cal., 14 g total fat (3 g sat. fat), 55 mg chol., 575 mg sodium, 44 g carb. (8 g fiber, 12 g sugars), 25 g pro. Exchanges: 2 vegetable, 2 starch, 2 lean meat, 2 fat.

1. In a very large nonstick skillet cook mushrooms, leeks, and garlic in hot oil over medium heat about 6 minutes or until mushrooms are tender and leeks are starting to brown, stirring occasionally.

2. Meanwhile, cook linguine according to package directions, adding parsnips for the last 4 minutes of cooking time. Drain and keep warm.

3. Add half-and-half, syrup, and salt to the mushroom mixture in skillet. Cook and stir just until boiling. Add turkey, sage, and drained pasta mixture. Cook and toss for 2 to 3 minutes to heat through. Remove from the heat. Add egg and quickly toss to coat (mixture may appear curdled).

4. Divide pasta mixture among six serving plates. Top with bacon and sprinkle with pepper.

PER SERVING: 309 cal., 7 g total fat (2 g sat. fat), 55 mg chol., 476 mg sodium, 39 g carb. (6 g fiber, 10 g sugars), 23 g pro. Exchanges: 1 vegetable, 2 starch, 2 lean meat, 0.5 fat.

Lemon-Walnut Snap Peas

CARB. PER SERVING 5 g
SERVINGS 6 ($2/3$ cup each) START TO FINISH 15 minutes

- 4 cups fresh sugar snap peas, trimmed
- $1/3$ cup coarsely chopped walnuts
- 2 cloves garlic, very thinly sliced
- 1 tablespoon olive oil
- 2 tablespoons lemon juice
- $1/4$ teaspoon salt

1. In a large nonstick skillet cook peas, walnuts, and garlic in hot oil over medium-high heat for 3 to 4 minutes or until peas are crsip tender and walnuts are lightly toasted, stirring frequently.

2. Remove from the heat. Add lemon juice and salt just before serving and toss to coat. Divide among plates.

PER SERVING: 83 cal., 7 g total fat (1 g sat. fat), 0 mg chol., 99 mg sodium, 5 g carb. (2 g fiber, 2 g sugars), 2 g pro. Exchanges: 1 vegetable, 1.5 fat.

Bistro-Style
Breakfast

Enjoy an upscale breakfast without leaving your kitchen. These homemade breakfast sausages coupled with roasted tomatoes are easy-to-make restaurant-style fare.

Honey-Sage Breakfast Sausage with Roasted Tomatoes
Carb. per serving 21 g

SERVINGS 6 (3 sausages and 2 slices tomato each)
PREP 35 minutes **BAKE** 15 minutes

- 1 egg, lightly beaten
- ½ cup quick-cooking rolled oats
- ¼ cup honey
- 1 tablespoon snipped fresh sage or 1 teaspoon dried sage, crushed
- 1 teaspoon fennel seeds, finely crushed
- 1 pound uncooked ground turkey breast
- 8 ounces uncooked lean ground turkey
- 1¼ to 1½ pounds fresh tomatoes (about 3 medium), cored and cut into ½-inch-thick slices
- 1 medium shallot, peeled and cut into ¼-inch-thick slices
- 2 tablespoons olive oil
- 2 cups lightly packed fresh arugula or packaged fresh baby spinach

1. Preheat oven to 425°F. Line a large baking sheet with parchment paper; set aside. For turkey sausages, in a large bowl combine egg, oats, honey, sage, fennel, ³⁄₄ teaspoon *salt,* and ½ teaspoon *black pepper.* Add ground turkey and mix well. Divide turkey mixture into 18 equal portions. Using damp hands, shape each portion into 4-inch-long sausages. Place sausages on prepared baking sheet, leaving ½ inch between sausages.
2. Line a 15×10×1-inch baking pan with parchment paper. Add tomato and shallot slices to the pan. Drizzle with oil and sprinkle with ¼ teaspoon *salt* and ⅛ teaspoon *black pepper.* Roast, uncovered, for 5 minutes.

3. Add pan of sausages to the oven with the tomatoes. Bake for 10 minutes or until tomatoes and shallots are softened and lightly browned and sausages are cooked through (165°F).
4. Divide arugula among six serving plates. Top arugula with the sausages. Add tomato slices to the plates with sausages. Finely chop the shallot slices and sprinkle over the tomato slices.

PER SERVING: 277 cal., 10 g total fat (2 g sat. fat), 96 mg chol., 487 mg sodium, 21 g carb. (2 g fiber, 14 g sugars), 28 g pro. Exchanges: 1 vegetable, 1 starch, 3.5 lean meat, 0.5 fat.

Whole Grain Toast
Toast 12 thin slices whole grain baguette. Spread toast slices with 3 tablespoon light tub-style vegetable oil spread. Place two slices on each plate. Makes 6 servings (2 slices each).

PER SERVING: 93 cal., 4 g total fat (1 g sat. fat), 0 mg chol., 140 mg sodium, 11 g carb. (2 g fiber, 2 g sugars), 3 g pro. Exchanges: 1 starch, 0.5 fat.

Meal Total (per plate):
370 cal., 14 g total fat (3 g sat. fat), 96 mg chol., 627 mg sodium, 32 g carb. (4 g fiber, 16 g sugars), 31 g pro. Exchanges: 1 vegetable, 2 starch, 3.5 lean meat, 1 fat.

¼ Plate

Starch, Grain, or Other Carb: rolled oats, honey, whole grain bread

Nonstarchy Veggies: tomatoes, shallot, arugula

½ Plate

¼ Plate

Protein: turkey

Beef

Beef boasts big flavors and provides a bundle of essential nutritents. Add variety to your weekly menus with lean beef.

Indian-Style
Beef & Rice

A blend of eight spices creates a tasty crust on the steak. When thinly sliced, the beef delivers a pop of flavor with each bite.

Nonstarchy Veggies: cauliflower, zucchini, green onions

½ Plate

Starch, Grain, or Other Carb: rice, peach, grapes

¼ Plate

¼ Plate

Protein: beef

Indian-Spiced Beef with Peach-Grape Salsa
Carb. per serving 8 g

SERVINGS 4 (3 ounces cooked meat and $^1/_3$ cup salsa each)
PREP 10 minutes BROIL 17 minutes STAND 5 minutes

       1 teaspoon ground coriander
  $^1/_2$ teaspoon garlic powder
  $^1/_2$ teaspoon ground cumin
  $^1/_4$ teaspoon salt
  $^1/_4$ teaspoon ground ginger
  $^1/_4$ teaspoon ground turmeric
  $^1/_4$ teaspoon black pepper
  $^1/_8$ teaspoon crushed red pepper
       1 pound beef flank steak
       1 recipe Peach-Grape Salsa *(below)*

1. Preheat broiler. In a small bowl combine coriander, garlic powder, cumin, salt, ginger, turmeric, black pepper, and crushed red pepper. Trim fat from steak. Score both sides of steak in a diamond pattern by making shallow diagonal cuts at 1-inch intervals. Sprinkle steak evenly with spice mixture, rubbing in with your fingers.

2. Place steak on the unheated rack of a broiler pan. Broil 3 to 4 inches from the heat for 17 to 21 minutes or until medium (160°F), turning once. Cover steak with foil; let steak stand for 5 minutes before thinly slicing. Divide steak among four serving plates; top steak slices with the Peach-Grape Salsa.

PEACH-GRAPE SALSA: Remove the pit and coarsely chop 1 medium peach. In a small bowl stir together peach; $^1/_2$ cup red grapes, quartered; 1 tablespoon snipped fresh mint; and 1 tablespoon lemon juice.

PER SERVING: 209 cal., 8 g total fat (3 g sat. fat), 74 mg chol., 208 mg sodium, 8 g carb. (1 g fiber, 6 g sugars), 25 g pro. Exchanges: 0.5 fruit, 3.5 lean meat, 0.5 fat.

Meal Total (per plate): 367 cal., 13 g total fat (4 g sat. fat), 74 mg chol., 490 mg sodium, 36 g carb. (6 g fiber, 10 g sugars), 30 g pro. Exchanges: 1 vegetable, 0.5 fruit, 1.5 starch, 3.5 lean meat, 1 fat.

Herbed Basmati Rice
CARB. PER SERVING 21 g

SERVINGS 4 ($^1/_3$ cup each) START TO FINISH 50 minutes

  $1^1/_4$ cups lower-sodium vegetable broth
   $^1/_2$ cup uncooked brown basmati rice
        1 clove garlic, minced
   $^1/_4$ cup thinly sliced green onion tops
        2 tablespoons snipped fresh cilantro and/or parsley
        1 tablespoon snipped fresh mint
  $1^1/_2$ teaspoons finely shredded lemon peel
   $^1/_8$ teaspoon black pepper

1. In a medium saucepan combine broth, rice, and garlic. Bring to boiling; reduce heat. Simmer, covered, for 40 to 45 minutes or until rice is tender and liquid is absorbed. Remove from heat and let stand, covered, for 5 minutes. Stir in green onion tops, cilantro, mint, lemon peel, and pepper. Divide among plates.

PER SERVING: 95 cal., 1 g total fat (0 g sat. fat), 0 mg chol., 175 mg sodium, 21 g carb. (2 g fiber, 1 g sugars), 2 g pro. Exchanges: 1.5 starch.

Skillet-Roasted Cauliflower and Squash
CARB. PER SERVING 7 g

SERVINGS 4 (1 cup each)
PREP 15 minutes COOK 20 minutes

   4 cups cauliflower florets
   1 tablespoon olive oil
   1 medium zucchini and/or yellow summer squash, halved lengthwise and cut crosswise into $^1/_2$-inch-thick slices (about $1^1/_2$ cups)
  $^1/_8$ teaspoon salt

1. In a large nonstick skillet cook cauliflower, covered, in hot oil over medium heat for 15 minutes, stirring occasionally. Turn heat to medium-low if cauliflower browns too quickly. Add zucchini, salt, and $^1/_8$ teaspoon *black pepper*; toss to coat. Cover and cook for 5 to 10 minutes more or until vegetables are just tender and lightly browned, stirring occasionally. Divide among plates.

PER SERVING: 63 cal., 4 g total fat (1 g sat. fat), 0 mg chol., 107 mg sodium, 7 g carb. (3 g fiber, 3 g sugars), 3 g pro. Exchanges: 1 vegetable, 0.5 fat.

Sizzlin' Steak & Veggie
Skewers

Three loaded kabobs make a filling meal that's portioned right and perfect for when you're craving iron-packed red meat.

Peppery Balsamic Beef Kabobs
Carb. per serving 35 g

SERVINGS 4 (3 skewers and $^1/_2$ cup couscous each)
PREP 25 minutes MARINATE 30 minutes
GRILL 8 minutes

- 1 pound beef sirloin steak, cut into 1-inch cubes
- 2 large red sweet peppers, cut into 1-inch pieces
- 1 large onion, cut into 1-inch pieces
- $^1/_2$ cup bottled reduced-fat balsamic vinaigrette
- $^2/_3$ cup whole wheat couscous

1. Place steak, sweet peppers, and onion in a large resealable plastic bag set in a shallow dish. Pour vinaigrette over meat and vegetables. Seal bag; marinate at room temperature 30 minutes or in the refrigerator up to 4 hours, turning bag occasionally.

2. Drain steak and vegetables, discarding marinade. Thread steak, sweet peppers, and onion onto twelve 10-inch skewers (see tip, *page 58*), leaving $^1/_4$-inch spaces between pieces. For a charcoal grill, place kabobs on the grill rack directly over medium coals. Grill, uncovered, 8 to 12 minutes or until steak is desired doneness, turning occasionally. (For a gas grill, preheat grill. Reduce heat to medium. Place kabobs on grill rack over heat. Cover and grill as directed.) Prepare couscous according to package directions. Divide couscous and kabobs among four serving plates.

PER SERVING: 325 cal., 6 g total fat (2 g sat. fat), 69 mg chol., 201 mg sodium, 35 g carb. (6 g fiber, 8 g sugars), 31 g pro. Exchanges: 1 vegetable, 2 starch, 3.5 lean meat.

Arugula Salad
CARB. PER SERVING 5 g
SERVINGS 4 (2 cups each)
START TO FINISH 15 minutes

- 6 cups fresh arugula
- 2 cups coarsely chopped radicchio
- $^1/_4$ cup bottled reduced-fat balsamic vinaigrette
- $^1/_4$ cup toasted pine nuts

1. In a large bowl toss together arugula and radicchio. Drizzle vinaigrette over the salad and toss to coat. Divide among plates. Sprinkle with pine nuts.

PER SERVING: 85 cal., 7 g total fat (0 g sat. fat), 0 mg chol., 118 mg sodium, 5 g carb. (1 g fiber, 3 g sugars), 2 g pro. Exchanges: 1 vegetable, 1.5 fat.

Meal Total (per plate):
410 cal., 13 g total fat (2 g sat. fat), 69 mg chol., 319 mg sodium, 40 g carb. (7 g fiber, 11 g sugars), 33 g pro. Exchanges: 2 vegetable, 2 starch, 3.5 lean meat, 1.5 fat.

½ Plate

Nonstarchy Veggies: arugula, radicchio, onion, sweet peppers

¼ Plate

Starch or Grain: couscous

¼ Plate

Protein: beef, pine nuts

Make It Mine Vary the salad by using mixed baby lettuces, mesclun, baby spinach, or torn romaine lettuce instead of the arugula and radicchio combo.

All-American
Steak Dinner

A flavorful red wine sauce gives basic pan-seared steak a lift in this satisfying take on meat and potatoes that has only 30 grams of carb per plateful.

½ Plate

Nonstarchy Veggies: broccoli, carrots, mushrooms

¼ Plate

Starch, Grain, or Other Carb: potatoes, wine, balsamic vinegar

¼ Plate

Protein: beef

Wine-Glazed Steak
Carb. per serving 10 g

SERVINGS 4 (3 ounces steak and 2 tablespoons mushroom-wine sauce mixture each)
START TO FINISH 30 minutes

- 1 pound boneless beef top sirloin steak, cut ½ to ¾ inch thick
- 1 tablespoon olive oil
- 2 cups sliced fresh mushrooms
- 4 cloves garlic, minced
- ¼ teaspoon crushed red pepper
- ½ cup dry red wine or low-calorie cranberry juice*
- ¼ cup balsamic vinegar
- 2 tablespoons reduced-sodium soy sauce
- 2 teaspoons honey*

1. Trim fat from steak; cut steak into four equal portions. In a large skillet heat oil over medium-high heat. Add steaks. Reduce heat to medium; cook 10 to 13 minutes or until desired doneness (145°F for medium rare or 160°F for medium), turning steaks occasionally. If steaks brown too quickly, reduce heat to medium-low. Transfer steaks to four serving plates; cover to keep warm.
2. Add mushrooms to skillet; cook and stir for 2 minutes. Remove mushrooms and set aside. Add garlic and red pepper to the skillet; cook and stir for 30 seconds. Remove skillet from heat and carefully add wine. Return to heat. Boil gently, uncovered, for 3 to 5 minutes or until most of the liquid is evaporated. Add balsamic vinegar, soy sauce, and honey; return to simmering. Cook and stir for 2 minutes or until slightly thickened. Spoon mushrooms and sauce over steaks on plates.

*TEST KITCHEN TIP: If using the cranberry juice option, omit the honey.

PER SERVING: 229 cal., 7 g total fat (2 g sat. fat), 57 mg chol., 335 mg sodium, 10 g carb. (1 g fiber, 7 g sugars), 23 g pro. Exchanges: 2 vegetable, 3 lean meat, 1 fat.

Steak Fries
CARB. PER SERVING 14 g
SERVINGS 4 (6 wedges each)
PREP 15 minutes BAKE 30 minutes

- 3 large red and/or yellow potatoes (about 12 ounces total)
- 2 teaspoons olive oil
- ¼ teaspoon dried rosemary, crushed
- ¼ teaspoon dried thyme, crushed
- ¼ teaspoon salt
- ¼ teaspoon black pepper

1. Preheat oven to 450°F. Cut each potato into eight wedges. In a large bowl stir together olive oil, rosemary, thyme, salt, and pepper. Add potato wedges; toss to coat. Spread wedges in a single layer in a shallow roasting pan. Bake for 30 to 35 minutes or until crisp, turning once. Divide among plates.

PER SERVING: 80 cal., 2 g total fat (0 g sat. fat), 0 mg chol., 161 mg sodium, 14 g carb. (2 g fiber, 1 g sugars), 2 g pro. Exchanges: 1 starch.

Steamed Broccoli and Carrots
Wash and remove outer leaves and tough parts of broccoli stalks. Break into 3 cups florets. Peel and cut 2 carrots into ½- to 1-inch pieces. Place steamer basket in a saucepan. Add water to just below bottom of basket. Bring water to boiling. Add vegetables to steamer basket. Cover pan; reduce heat. Steam vegetables for 8 to 10 minutes or until crisp-tender. Divide vegetables among plates. Makes 4 servings (1 cup each).

PER SERVING: 27 cal., 0 g total fat , 0 mg chol., 35 mg sodium, 6 g carb. (1 g fiber, 3 g sugars), 2 g pro. Exchanges: 1 vegetable.

Meal Total (per plate): 336 cal., 9 g total fat (2 g sat. fat), 57 mg chol., 531 mg sodium, 30 g carb. (4 g fiber, 11 g sugars), 27 g pro. Exchanges: 3 vegetable, 1 starch, 3 lean meat, 1 fat.

Tried-&-True
Meat Loaves

Horseradish BBQ-Topped Mini Meat Loaves
Carb. per serving 13 g

SERVINGS 6 (2 meat loaves each)
PREP 30 minutes COOK 5 minutes
BAKE 25 minutes COOL 5 minutes

- 1½ cups finely chopped fresh mushrooms
- 1 medium onion, chopped (½ cup)
- 1 stalk celery, finely chopped (½ cup)
- ½ cup fat-free milk
- ⅓ cup refrigerated or frozen egg product, thawed, or 2 egg whites, lightly beaten
- ¾ cup quick-cooking rolled oats
- ¼ teaspoon salt
- ¼ teaspoon black pepper
- 1½ pounds 90 percent lean ground beef
- ⅓ cup low-calorie barbecue sauce
- 1 tablespoon prepared horseradish

1. Preheat oven to 350°F. Coat a large nonstick skillet with *nonstick cooking spray.* Heat over medium heat. Add mushrooms, onion, and celery. Cook 5 minutes, stirring often. Remove from heat.

2. In a bowl combine milk and egg. Stir in mushroom mixture, oats, salt, and pepper. Add beef; gently mix until combined. Divide evenly among twelve 2½-inch muffin cups; pat mixture into cups.

3. Bake about 20 minutes or until centers of meat loaves register 145°F to 150°F on an instant-read thermometer. Meanwhile, in a small bowl combine barbecue sauce and horseradish. Spoon sauce mixture evenly over meat loaves. Bake for 5 to 10 minutes more or until centers register 160°F on an instant-read thermometer.

4. Cool meat loaves in pan on a wire rack for 5 minutes. Carefully remove meat loaves from cups and place two loaves on each of six serving plates.

PER SERVING: 274 cal., 12 g total fat (5 g sat. fat), 74 mg chol., 374 mg sodium, 13 g carb. (2 g fiber, 4 g sugars), 27 g pro. Exchanges: 1 vegetable, 0.5 starch, 3.5 lean meat, 1 fat.

Chopped Romaine Salad
CARB. PER SERVING 8 g
SERVINGS 6 (1½ cups each)
PREP 20 minutes

- 8 cups chopped romaine lettuce
- ½ cup coarsely chopped fresh basil
- 1 cup cherry or grape tomatoes, halved
- ½ cup coarsely shredded carrot
- 3 tablespoons slivered almonds, chopped walnuts, or pine nuts, lightly toasted
- ⅔ cup desired low-calorie vinaigrette or salad dressing

1. In a large bowl toss together lettuce and basil. Divide among plates. Top with tomatoes, carrot, and almonds. Drizzle with vinaigrette.

PER SERVING: 65 cal., 3 g total fat (0 g sat. fat), 0 mg chol., 197 mg sodium, 8 g carb. (2 g fiber, 5 g sugars), 2 g pro. Exchanges: 1 vegetable, 1 fat.

Meal Total (per plate):
339 cal., 15 g total fat (5 g sat. fat), 74 mg chol., 571 mg sodium, 21 g carb. (4 g fiber, 9g sugars), 29 g pro. Exchanges: 2 vegetable, 0.5 starch, 3.5 lean meat, 2 fat.

Add variety to this salad by substituting your favorite leafy green or combination for the romaine. Think kale, spinach, cabbage!

¼ Plate

Protein: beef, nuts

½ Plate

Nonstarchy Veggies: lettuce, tomatoes, carrot, onion, celery

¼ Plate

Starch, Grain or Other Carb: rolled oats, barbecue sauce

Time-Saver Quick-start the meat loaf prep by making the meat mixture and patting it into cups as directed. Cover and refrigerate overnight. Bake as directed, adding time as needed until the meat loaves reach an internal temp of 160°F.

79

Ginger-Sesame
Beef Skewers

Cool and creamy yogurt-dressed cucumbers tame the heat of the grilled ginger-marinated beef.

1/4 Plate

Starch, Grain, or Other Carb: soba noodles, yogurt

1/4 Plate

Protein: beef, yogurt

1/2 Plate

Nonstarchy Veggies: cucumber, radishes, onions

Ginger-Sesame Beef Skewers
Carb. per serving 24 g

SERVINGS 4 (2 skewers and $^1/_2$ cup noodles each)
PREP 25 minutes MARINATE 1 hour GRILL 3 minutes

> 3   green onions
> $^1/_3$ cup rice vinegar
> 3   tablespoons reduced-sodium soy sauce
> 1   tablespoon toasted sesame oil
> 1   tablespoon finely chopped fresh ginger
> 1   teaspoon toasted sesame seeds
> $^1/_2$ teaspoon crushed red pepper
> 1   pound beef sirloin steak, cut 1 inch thick
> 4   ounces soba (buckwheat) noodles, cooked
>   according to package directions
>   Sliced green onion tops (optional)

1. Thinly slice the 3 green onions, keeping green tops separate from the white parts. Set aside green tops. For marinade, in a medium bowl combine white parts of green onions, the rice vinegar, soy sauce, sesame oil, ginger, sesame seeds, and crushed red pepper. Transfer half of the marinade to a small bowl; set aside.
2. Cut beef into $^1/_8$- to $^1/_4$-inch-thick slices.* Add beef to the remaining marinade in the medium bowl. Toss to coat beef. Cover and marinate in the refrigerator for 1 to 4 hours. Remove beef from marinade; discard any remaining marinade in the medium bowl. Thread beef strips onto eight 8-inch skewers.**
3. For a charcoal grill, place skewers on the grill rack directly over medium coals. Grill, uncovered, for 3 to 5 minutes or until meat is slightly pink in centers, turning once. (For a gas grill, preheat grill; reduce heat to medium. Place beef skewers on grill rack over heat. Cover and grill as directed.)
4. Meanwhile, toss cooked soba noodles with the reserved marinade and green tops of the 3 green onions. Divide soba

noodles evenly among four serving plates and top with beef skewers. If desired, garnish with a few additional green onion tops.

*TEST KITCHEN TIP: Freeze beef about 30 minutes for easier slicing.
**TEST KITCHEN TIP: If using wooden skewers, soak skewers in enough water to cover for 30 minutes before using.

PER SERVING: 300 cal., 9 g total fat (2 g sat. fat), 68 mg chol., 610 mg sodium, 24 g carb. (2 g fiber, 1 g sugars), 30 g pro. Exchanges: 1.5 starch, 4 lean meat.

Cucumber-Radish Salad
CARB. PER SERVING 8 g
SERVINGS 4 (1 cup each)
PREP 15 minutes CHILL 4 hours

> $^1/_2$ cup plain low-fat yogurt
> 1   clove garlic, minced
> $^1/_8$ teaspoon salt
>   Dash black pepper
> 1   large cucumber, thinly sliced
>   (about 3 cups)
> $^1/_2$ cup thinly sliced red onion
> $^1/_2$ cup thinly sliced radishes

1. In a medium bowl stir together yogurt, garlic, salt, and pepper. Add cucumber, red onion, and radishes. Toss to coat. Cover and chill for 4 to 24 hours, stirring often. Stir before dividing among plates.

PER SERVING: 44 cal., 1 g total fat (0 g sat. fat), 2 mg chol., 102 mg sodium, 8 g carb. (1 g fiber, 5 g sugars), 3 g pro. Exchanges: 1.5 vegetable.

Meal Total (per plate): 344 cal., 10 g total fat (2 g sat. fat), 70 mg chol., 712 mg sodium, 32 g carb. (3 g fiber, 6 g sugars), 33 g pro. Exchanges: 1.5 vegetable, 1.5 starch, 4 lean meat.

Taco Burger Plate

With all the fixings on the side, this bunless burger makes an easy and healthful taco salad-style meal.

Taco Salad Plate
Carb. per serving 21 g

SERVINGS 4 (1 beef patty, 1 cup lettuce, 3 tablespoons beans, 2 tablespoons tomato, 2 tablespoons sweet pepper, $^{1}/_{4}$ cup avocado mixture, and $^{1}/_{2}$ cup chips each)
PREP 25 minutes GRILL 14 minutes

- 1 pound 90 percent lean ground beef
- $^{1}/_{3}$ cup bottled salsa
- 4 cups shredded romaine lettuce
- $^{1}/_{2}$ of a 15-ounce can lower-sodium black beans, rinsed and drained ($^{2}/_{3}$ cup)
- 1 medium tomato, chopped
- $^{1}/_{2}$ cup chopped yellow or orange sweet pepper
- 1 ripe avocado, halved, seeded, peeled, and cut up
- 3 tablespoons water
- 1 tablespoon lime juice
- $^{1}/_{8}$ teaspoon crushed red pepper (optional)
- $^{1}/_{8}$ teaspoon ground cumin
- 2 cups baked tortilla chips (1 ounce)

1. In a medium bowl combine beef and salsa. Shape beef mixture into four $^{3}/_{4}$-inch-thick patties.
2. For a charcoal grill, place burgers on the grill rack directly over medium coals. Grill, uncovered, for 14 to 18 minutes or until done (160°F), turning once halfway through grilling. (For a gas grill, preheat grill. Reduce heat to medium. Place burgers on grill rack over heat. Cover; grill as directed.)
3. Meanwhile, divide lettuce among four serving plates. Top each evenly with beans, tomato, and sweet pepper. In a small resealable plastic bag place the avocado, water, lime juice, crushed red pepper (if using), and cumin. Seal bag and knead the bag until avocado is mashed and mixture is combined.
4. Place a grilled burger on each plate. Snip a hole in one corner of the bag containing the avocado mixture; squeeze the mixture over burgers and arrange tortilla chips on plates.

PER SERVING: 337 cal., 17 g total fat (5 g sat. fat), 72 mg chol., 308 mg sodium, 21 g carb. (7 g fiber, 3 g sugars), 28 g pro. Exchanges: 1 vegetable, 1 starch, 3.5 lean meat, 2 fat.

Meal Total (per plate): 337 cal., 17 g total fat (5 g sat. fat), 72 mg chol., 308 mg sodium, 21 g carb. (7 g fiber, 3 g sugars), 28 g pro. Exchanges: 1 vegetable, 1 starch, 3.5 lean meat, 2 fat.

Flavor Boost Add a minced garlic clove to the avocado in the plastic bag. If desired, add some crunch by folding in a tablespoon or two of chopped, seeded cucumber or jicama.

½ Plate

Nonstarchy Veggies: salsa, lettuce, tomato, sweet pepper

¼ Plate

Starch or Grain: chips, black beans

¼ Plate

Protein: beef, black beans

83

Sit-Down
Simple Sunday Fare

Beef Medallions with Horseradish Sauce
Carb. per serving 2 g

SERVINGS 4 ($3^1/2$ ounces cooked meat and 2 tablespoons sauce each)
PREP 10 minutes COOK 4 minutes

- 20 ounces boneless beef shoulder tenders
- $1/2$ teaspoon lemon-pepper seasoning or freshly ground black pepper
- 2 teaspoons olive oil
- $1/2$ cup plain fat-free Greek yogurt
- 2 tablespoons prepared horseradish
- $1/8$ teaspoon salt
- $1/2$ to 2 teaspoons fat-free milk

1. Cut beef crosswise into 1-inch slices. Place each slice between two pieces of plastic wrap. Using the flat side of a meat mallet, lightly pound beef to $1/4$ inch thick. Discard plastic wrap. Sprinkle beef with lemon-pepper seasoning.
2. In a very large skillet heat oil over medium-high heat. Cook beef in hot oil for 4 to 6 minutes or until medium, turning once halfway through cooking.
3. For horseradish sauce, stir together yogurt, horseradish, and salt. Add the milk, $1/2$ teaspoon at a time, until desired consistency. Divide beef evenly among four serving plates and serve with the horseradish sauce.

PER SERVING: 243 cal., 11 g total fat (3 g sat. fat), 81 mg chol., 190 mg sodium, 2 g carb. (0 g fiber, 2 g sugars), 32 g pro. Exchanges: 4.5 lean meat, 1 fat.

Mashed Vegetables
CARB. PER SERVING 27 g
SERVINGS 4 (1 cup each)
PREP 15 minutes **COOK** 25 minutes

- 3 cups peeled and cut-up turnips
- 2 cups peeled and cut-up carrots
- 2 cups peeled and cut-up parsnips
- 1 medium onion, cut into wedges
- 2 tablespoons butter
- 2 tablespoons fat-free milk
- $1/2$ teaspoon salt
- $1/8$ teaspoon black pepper

1. In a Dutch oven combine turnips, carrots, parsnips, and onion. Add enough water to cover. Bring to boiling; reduce heat. Cover and simmer for 25 to 30 minutes or until vegetables are tender. Drain well. Return vegetables to the hot pan. Mash vegetables with a potato masher while adding the butter, milk, salt, and pepper. Vegetables should still have plenty of texture and not be completely smooth. Divide among plates.

PER SERVING: 167 cal., 6 g total fat (4 g sat. fat), 15 mg chol., 460 mg sodium, 27 g carb. (7 g fiber, 11 g sugars), 3 g pro. Exchanges: 2 vegetable, 1 starch, 1 fat.

Steamed Green Beans
If desired, trim ends of 2 cups fresh green beans. Place a steamer basket in a saucepan. Add water to just below the bottom of the basket. Bring water to boiling. Add beans to steamer basket. Cover pan and reduce heat. Steam beans for 18 to 22 minutes or until crisp-tender. Divide beans among plates. Makes 4 servings ($1/2$ cup each).

PER SERVING: 17 cal., 0 g total fat, 0 mg chol., 3 mg sodium, 4 g carb. (1 g fiber, 2 g sugars), 1 g pro. Exchanges: 0.

Meal Total (per plate): 427 cal., 17 g total fat (7 g sat. fat), 96 mg chol., 653 mg sodium, 33 g carb. (8 g fiber, 15 g sugars), 36 g pro. Exchanges: 2 vegetable, 1 starch, 4.5 lean meat, 2 fat.

The carrots and onion in the Mashed Vegetables add to the nonstarchy vegetable section of the plate.

¹/₂ Plate

Nonstarchy Veggies: green beans, carrots, onion

¹/₄ Plate

Starch, Grain, or Other Carb: turnips, parsnips, Greek yogurt

¹/₄ Plate

Protein: beef, Greek yogurt

Beef Cookout

Watercress is a peppery, herblike leafy vegetable. If you have trouble finding it, use baby spinach or arugula in both the pesto and the slaw.

Protein: beef, almonds

¼ Plate

¼ Plate

Starch, Grain, or Other Carb: corn, beets, apple

½ Plate

Nonstarchy Veggies: beets, celeriac, watercress

Steak with Watercress Pesto
Carb. per serving 3 g

SERVINGS 4 (1 steak and 1 tablespoon pesto each)
PREP 20 minutes GRILL 7 minutes

- 1 cup lightly packed fresh watercress, tough stems removed
- ½ cup lightly packed fresh mint
- 3 tablespoons slivered almonds, toasted
- 2 cloves garlic, minced
- 2 tablespoons water
- 1 tablespoon olive oil
- 4 4-ounce beef chuck top blade (flat iron) steaks, cut ¾ inch thick

1. For pesto, in a food processor or blender combine watercress, mint, almonds, garlic, and ¼ teaspoon *kosher salt*. Cover and pulse with several on-off turns to chop the watercress and mint. With the processor or blender running, gradually add water and oil through the feed tube until mixture is well combined, scraping sides of bowl as needed.
2. Sprinkle steaks evenly with ⅛ teaspoon *kosher salt* and ⅛ teaspoon *black pepper*. For a gas or charcoal grill, place steaks on the greased grill rack of a covered grill directly over medium heat. Grill, covered, to desired doneness, turning once halfway through grilling. Allow 7 to 9 minutes for medium rare (145°F) or 10 to 12 minutes for medium (160°F). Divide steaks among four serving plates and top with the pesto.

PER SERVING: 200 cal., 12 g total fat (3 g sat. fat), 56 mg chol., 248 mg sodium, 3 g carb. (1 g fiber, 0 g sugars), 20 g pro. Exchanges: 3 lean meat, 1.5 fat.

Meal Total (per plate): 412 cal.,
20 g total fat (4 g sat. fat), 63 mg chol., 669 mg sodium, 37 g carb. (7 g fiber, 17 g sugars), 24 g pro. Exchanges: 2 vegetable, 1.5 starch, 3 lean meat, 2.5 fat.

Fresh Beet Slaw
CARB. PER SERVING 26 g
SERVINGS 4 (¾ cup each)
PREP 20 minutes

- 12 ounces fresh beets (without greens), trimmed, peeled, and coarsely shredded*
- 12 ounces celeriac, trimmed, peeled, and coarsely shredded, or 2 medium parsnips, peeled and coarsely shredded*
- 1 cup fresh watercress, tough stems removed
- 1 large apple, cored and chopped
- ⅓ cup light mayonnaise
- ¼ cup cider vinegar
- 2 tablespoons snipped fresh basil
- ¼ teaspoon kosher salt
- ⅛ teaspoon black pepper

1. In a large bowl combine beets, celeriac, watercress, and apple. Set aside.
2. In a small bowl combine mayonnaise, vinegar, basil, salt, and pepper until well combined. Add to beet mixture; toss to coat. Serve immediately or cover and chill for up to 8 hours. Divide among plates.
*TEST KITCHEN TIP: Use a food processor fitted with a coarse shredder to easily shred the beets and celeriac or parsnips.

PER SERVING: 173 cal., 7 g total fat (1 g sat. fat), 7 mg chol., 414 mg sodium, 26 g carb. (5 g fiber, 14 g sugars), 3 g pro. Exchanges: 2 vegetable, 1 starch, 1 fat.

Sweet Corn
Remove husks and silks from 2 fresh ears of corn. Break each ear in half. Cook, covered, in enough boiling lightly salted water to cover for 5 to 7 minutes or until kernels are tender. (To grill the corn, soak corn in the husks for 1 hour; drain. Grill over medium heat about 25 minutes or until kernels are tender.) Remove husks and silks; cut cobs in half for serving. Makes 4 servings (½ ear each).

PER SERVING: 39 cal., 1 g total fat (0 g sat. fat), 0 mg chol., 7 mg sodium, 8 g carb. (1 g fiber, 3 g sugars), 1 g pro. Exchanges: 0.5 starch.

Italian Pasta Bowls

Italian Beef and Broccoli
Carb. per serving 48 g

SERVINGS 4 (2 cups each)
START TO FINISH 50 minutes

6 ounces dried multigrain or whole grain penne pasta (2 cups)
3 cups small broccoli florets
Olive oil nonstick cooking spray
1 medium onion, halved and thinly sliced
12 ounces boneless beef sirloin steak, cut into thin bite-size strips
2 teaspoons dried Italian seasoning, crushed
4 teaspoons olive oil
4 cloves garlic, very thinly sliced
2 cups cherry tomatoes, halved, or 2 cups chopped, cored fresh tomatoes
2 cups coarsely chopped fresh spinach
$\frac{1}{2}$ cup fat-free half-and-half
2 ounces Parmesan cheese, shaved or coarsely shredded
$\frac{1}{2}$ cup coarsely chopped fresh basil or 2 tablespoons snipped fresh oregano

1. In a large pot cook penne in a large amount of boiling salted water according to package directions, adding the broccoli florets for the last 3 minutes of cooking. Before draining the pasta, remove and set aside $\frac{1}{2}$ cup of the pasta cooking water. Drain pasta and broccoli; set aside.
2. Meanwhile, coat a very large nonstick skillet with cooking spray; heat over medium heat. Add onion. Cook for 5 minutes or until tender, stirring occasionally. Transfer onion to a medium bowl and set aside.

3. Place steak strips in a large bowl. Sprinkle with Italian seasoning, $\frac{1}{4}$ teaspoon *salt,* and $\frac{1}{4}$ teaspoon *black pepper.* Toss to coat. Add 2 teaspoons of the olive oil to the skillet used for cooking the onion. Heat over medium-high heat. Add steak strips. Cook for 3 to 5 minutes or until steak strips are slightly pink in centers, stirring frequently. Add cooked beef to bowl with onion.
4. Add remaining 2 teaspoons olive oil to the same skillet and heat over medium heat. Add garlic; cook and stir for 10 to 20 seconds or until garlic is just starting to brown. Add tomatoes. Cook for 2 to 3 minutes or until tomatoes are softened. Using the back of a wooden spoon, mash tomatoes slightly.
5. Add pasta and broccoli and the reserved pasta cooking water to the skillet with tomatoes. Cook, uncovered, for 2 to 3 minutes or until heated through. Add the beef and onion mixture, spinach, and half-and-half. Cook and stir for 1 to 2 minutes or until heated through and sauce clings to pasta. Divide pasta mixture among four shallow bowls. Sprinkle with Parmesan cheese and fresh basil.

PER SERVING: 426 cal., 14 g total fat (5 g sat. fat), 57 mg chol., 577 mg sodium, 48 g carb. (9 g fiber, 8 g sugars), 30 g pro. Exchanges: 3 vegetable, 2 starch, 3 lean meat, 1.5 fat.

Meal Total (per plate):
426 cal., 14 g total fat (5 g sat. fat), 57 mg chol., 577 mg sodium, 48 g carb. (9 g fiber, 8 g sugars), 30 g pro. Exchanges: 3 vegetable, 2 starch, 3 lean meat, 1.5 fat.

Creamy, rich, and flavorful—this skillet meal seems indulgent, but fresh vegetables and fat-free half-and-half lighten it up and boost the nutrition.

½ Plate

Nonstarchy Veggies: broccoli, onion, tomatoes, spinach

¼ Plate

Starch or Grain: pasta

¼ Plate

Protein: beef, cheese

Slow-Cooked
Indies-Inspired Supper

Slow-cooking the meat and vegetables all day lets preparing the side of fruit compote and polenta be your focus just before serving.

½ Plate

Nonstarchy Veggies: onion, carrots, tomatoes, Brussels sprouts

¼ Plate

Protein: beef, almonds

¼ Plate

Starch, Grain, or Other Carb: polenta, raisins

Spiced Beef with Vegetables
Carb. per serving 13 g

SERVINGS 6 (3 ounces meat and $^2/_3$ cup vegetables each)
PREP 15 minutes COOK 8 to 10 hours (low) or 4 to 5 hours (high)

- 3 medium carrots, peeled and cut into 2- to 3-inch pieces
- 1 medium onion, cut into wedges
- 1 14.5-ounce can no-salt-added stewed tomatoes, snipped and undrained
- 1 teaspoon ground coriander
- 1 teaspoon ground cardamom
- 1 teaspoon ground ginger
- 1 teaspoon ground turmeric
- $^1/_4$ teaspoon cayenne pepper
- $^1/_4$ teaspoon salt
- $^1/_4$ teaspoon black pepper
- 1 2-pound boneless beef chuck arm pot roast or beef chuck cross rib roast, trimmed of fat
- 2 cups large fresh Brussels sprouts

1. Place carrots and onion in a 4- to 5-quart slow cooker. In a bowl combine tomatoes, cardamom, coriander, ginger, turmeric, cayenne pepper, salt, and black pepper. Place beef over vegetables in slow cooker. Pour tomato mixture over beef. Top with Brussels sprouts.

2. Cover and cook on low-heat setting for 8 to 10 hours or on high-heat setting for 4 to 5 hours. Remove vegetables and beef. Cut beef into pieces and serve with vegetables, dividing among six plates. If desired, drizzle with some of the cooking juices.

PER SERVING: 268 cal., 8 g total fat (3 g sat. fat), 76 mg chol., 242 mg sodium, 13 g carb. (4 g fiber, 6 g sugars), 35 g pro. Exchanges: 2 vegetable, 4 lean meat, 0.5 fat.

Meal Total (per plate):
401 cal., 13 g total fat (3 g sat. fat), 76 mg chol., 472 mg sodium, 34 g carb. (6 g fiber, 12 g sugars), 38 g pro. Exchanges: 2 vegetable, 1.5 starch, 4 lean meat, 1 fat.

Polenta with Olive-Raisin Compote
CARB. PER SERVING 21 g

SERVINGS 6 (2 slices polenta and $2^1/_2$ tablespoons compote each)
START TO FINISH 25 minutes

- 1 medium onion, chopped ($^1/_2$ cup)
- $^1/_8$ teaspoon ground coriander
- $^1/_8$ teaspoon ground ginger
- $^1/_3$ cup golden raisins
- $^1/_4$ cup sliced almonds
- 2 tablespoons coarsely chopped pitted Kalamata olives
- $^1/_2$ teaspoon finely shredded orange peel
- 1 tablespoon olive oil
- 1 16-ounce tube refrigerated cooked polenta, cut crosswise into 12 slices

1. Preheat oven to 300°F. For compote, lightly coat a small saucepan with *nonstick cooking spray;* heat over medium heat. Add onion; cook for 3 to 5 minutes or just until tender, stirring occasionally. Stir in coriander and ginger. Add $^1/_2$ cup *water* and the raisins. Bring to boiling; reduce heat. Simmer, uncovered, for 3 to 5 minutes or until water is almost evaporated. Stir in almonds, olives, and orange peel.

2. Meanwhile, heat oil in a very large nonstick skillet over medium heat. Add half of the polenta slices. Cook for 4 to 6 minutes or until warm and lightly browned (oil will spatter slightly), turning once. Transfer to a baking sheet and keep warm in oven while cooking remaining polenta slices. Serve two polenta slices on each plate and top with compote.

PER SERVING: 133 cal., 5 g total fat (0 g sat. fat), 0 mg chol., 230 mg sodium, 21 g carb. (2 g fiber, 6 g sugars), 3 g pro. Exchanges: 1.5 starch, 0.5 fat.

Backyard
Burger BBQ

Grilled Chili Burgers
Carb. per serving 21 g

SERVINGS 6 (1 burger, 2 pita quarters, and 2 tablespoons topping each)
PREP 20 minutes GRILL 10 minutes

  1 recipe Chimichurri Topping *(below)*
  1 pound 95% lean ground beef
  8 ounces lean ground pork
  1 tablespoon chili powder
  1/2 teaspoon onion powder
  1/4 teaspoon ground cumin
  1/8 teaspoon salt
  3 whole wheat pita bread rounds, quartered and toasted
  3/4 cup bottled roasted red sweet peppers, drained and cut into strips

1. Prepare Chimichurri Topping; set aside. In a large bowl combine beef, pork, chili powder, onion powder, cumin, and salt. Mix well. Shape into six 1/2-inch-thick patties.
2. For a charcoal grill, place patties on the grill rack directly over medium coals. Grill, uncovered, for 10 to 13 minutes or until an instant-read thermometer inserted into side of each patty registers 160°F, turning once halfway through grilling. (For a gas grill, preheat grill. Reduce heat to medium. Place patties on grill rack over heat. Cover and grill as directed.)
3. Place a grilled patty on top of two of the pita quarters on each of six serving plates. Top with roasted pepper strips and Chimichurri Topping.
CHIMICHURRI TOPPING: In a small bowl combine 1/2 cup finely snipped fresh Italian (flat-leaf) parsley; 1/2 cup finely snipped fresh cilantro; 2 tablespoons red wine vinegar; 1 tablespoon olive oil; 2 cloves garlic, minced; 1/4 teaspoon salt; 1/4 teaspoon black pepper; and 1/8 teaspoon cayenne pepper.

PER SERVING: 306 cal., 13 g total fat (4 g sat. fat), 73 mg chol., 390 mg sodium, 21 g carb. (4 g fiber, 0 g sugars), 27 g pro. Exchanges: 1.5 starch, 3 lean meat, 1.5 fat.

Apple Spinach Salad
CARB. PER SERVING 14 g
SERVINGS 6 (1 cup each) START TO FINISH 25 minutes

  6 cups fresh baby spinach
  1 large green-skin apple, such as Granny Smith, cored and sliced
  1/2 cup thin wedges red onion
  3 tablespoons snipped dried tart red cherries
  2 tablespoons olive oil
  2 tablespoons white or regular balsamic vinegar
  1 teaspoon snipped fresh thyme or 1/4 teaspoon dried thyme, crushed
  1/2 teaspoon Dijon-style mustard
  1/2 cup crumbled feta cheese or blue cheese (2 ounces)

1. In a large bowl toss together spinach, apple, onion, and cherries. In a screw-top jar combine olive oil, vinegar, thyme, mustard, and 1/8 teaspoon *salt*. Cover and shake well. Drizzle over salad and toss gently to coat. Divide salad among plates and top individual servings with about 1 tablespoon cheese each.

PER SERVING: 130 cal., 7 g total fat (3 g sat. fat), 11 mg chol., 244 mg sodium, 14 g carb. (3 g fiber, 9 g sugars), 4 g pro. Exchanges: 0.5 vegetable, 0.5 fruit, 1.5 fat.

Meal Total (per plate): 435 cal., 20 g total fat (7 g sat. fat), 84 mg chol., 633 mg sodium, 35 g carb. (6 g fiber, 9 g sugars), 30 g pro. Exchanges: 0.5 vegetable, 0.5 fruit, 1.5 starch, 3 lean meat, 3 fat.

Bring freshness to grilled burgers with a blend of spices, a zesty topping, and roasted red pepper strips.

¼ Plate

Protein: beef, pork, cheese

¼ Plate

Starch, Grain, or Other Carb: pita bread, apple, dried cherries

½ Plate

Nonstarchy Veggies: spinach, onion, sweet peppers

93

Beef & Beans

Espresso powder adds depth to the flavor of the stove-top "baked" beans.

¼ Plate

Starch, Grain, or Other Carb: pinto beans, molasses

¼ Plate

Protein: beef

½ Plate

Nonstarchy Veggies: tomatoes, cucumbers, onion

Coffee-Rubbed Beef with Red-Eye Beans
Carb. per serving 24 g or 23 g

SERVINGS 4 (1 steak and $^1/_3$ cup beans each)
PREP 20 minutes GRILL 8 minutes STAND 5 minutes

2	teaspoons ground ancho chile pepper
2	teaspoons instant espresso coffee powder
1	teaspoon paprika
1	teaspoon dry mustard
1	teaspoon packed brown sugar*
1	teaspoon dried oregano, crushed
$^1/_2$	teaspoon black pepper
$^1/_4$	teaspoon ground cumin
$^1/_4$	teaspoon salt
1	pound beef shoulder petite tenders
	Nonstick cooking spray
1	recipe Red-Eye Beans (below)
$^1/_4$	cup finely chopped red onion

1. In a small bowl stir together the ancho chile pepper, espresso powder, paprika, mustard, brown sugar, oregano, black pepper, cumin, and salt. Trim fat from meat. Lightly coat meat with cooking spray. Sprinkle meat evenly with spice mixture, rubbing it in with your fingers.

2. For a gas or charcoal grill, place beef tenders on the grill rack directly over medium heat. Grill, covered, to desired doneness, turning once halfway through grilling. Allow 8 to 12 minutes for medium rare (145°F) or 10 to 15 minutes for medium (160°F). Let tenders stand for 5 minutes. Slice tenders. To serve, spoon Red-Eye Beans into four shallow dishes. Place beef slices on top of beans and sprinkle with red onion.

RED-EYE BEANS: In a small saucepan cook $^1/_4$ cup chopped onion and 1 clove garlic, minced, in 1 teaspoon hot canola oil over medium heat for 4 to 6 minutes or until tender. Stir in one

15-ounce can no-salt-added pinto beans, rinsed and drained; $^1/_2$ cup water; 1 tablespoon molasses; 2 teaspoons reduced-sodium Worcestershire sauce; 1 teaspoon instant espresso coffee powder; 1 teaspoon ground ancho chile pepper; $^1/_2$ teaspoon ground cumin; $^1/_4$ teaspoon black pepper; and $^1/_8$ teaspoon salt. Bring to boiling; reduce heat. Simmer, covered, for 15 minutes to blend flavors, stirring occasionally.

*SUGAR SUBSTITUTES: Choose from Splenda Brown Sugar Blend or Sugar Twin Granulated Brown. Follow package directions to use product amount equivalent to 1 teaspoon brown sugar.

PER SERVING: 303 cal., 10 g total fat (3 g sat. fat), 65 mg chol., 323 mg sodium, 24 g carb. (6 g fiber, 6 g sugars), 29 g pro. Exchanges: 1.5 starch, 3.5 lean meat, 0.5 fat.

PER SERVING WITH SUBSTITUTE: Same as above, except 301 cal., 322 mg sodium, 23 g carb.

Tomato-Cucumber Salad with Garlic Buttermilk Dressing
CARB. PER SERVING 8 g
SERVINGS 4 ($^3/_4$ cup each) START TO FINISH 25 minutes

2	cloves garlic
$^1/_4$	teaspoon coarse kosher or sea salt
2	tablespoons light mayonnaise
1	tablespoon cider vinegar
$^1/_3$	cup buttermilk
2	tablespoons snipped fresh basil
3	medium tomatoes (about 1 pound), cored and thinly sliced
$^1/_2$	of a medium cucumber, thinly sliced (about 1 cup)
	Freshly ground black pepper

1. For dressing, mince the garlic on a cutting board. Sprinkle the garlic with the salt and use the side of a chef's knife to mash and rub the garlic and salt together into a paste. Transfer garlic mixture to a small bowl. Whisk in mayonnaise and vinegar until smooth. Slowly whisk in buttermilk until smooth. Stir in basil.

2. Layer tomato slices and cucumber slices in dishes, sprinkling pepper lightly between the layers. Drizzle salads with the dressing.

PER SERVING: 56 cal., 2 g total fat (0 g sat. fat), 2 mg chol., 207 mg sodium, 8 g carb. (2 g fiber, 5 g sugars), 2 g pro. Exchanges: 1 vegetable, 0.5 fat.

Meal Total (per plate): 359 cal., 12 g total fat (3 g sat. fat), 67 mg chol., 530 mg sodium, 32 g carb. (8 g fiber, 11 g sugars), 31 g pro. Exchanges: 1 vegetable, 1.5 starch, 3.5 lean meat, 1 fat.

Pan-Seared
Steak Supper

Preheat the skillet before adding the steaks. This step ensures a sizzling sear on the steaks and locks in the juices.

¼ Plate

Starch, Grain, or Other Carb: potatoes

½ Plate

Nonstarchy Veggies: Brussels sprouts, mushrooms, onion

¼ Plate

Protein: beef, cheese

Strip Steak with Mushroom-Mustard Sauce
Carb. per serving 8 g

SERVINGS 4 (3$\frac{1}{2}$ ounces beef and $\frac{1}{2}$ cup sauce each)
PREP 15 minutes COOK 17 minutes

 2 8- to 10-ounce boneless beef top loin steaks,
     cut about $\frac{3}{4}$ inch thick
 $\frac{1}{4}$ teaspoon black pepper
 1 tablespoon canola oil
 $\frac{1}{4}$ cup dry white wine or reduced-sodium chicken broth
 8 ounces sliced fresh mushrooms
 $\frac{1}{2}$ cup chopped onion
 2 tablespoons Dijon-style mustard
 1 clove garlic, minced
 1$\frac{1}{4}$ cups reduced-sodium chicken broth
 2 tablespoons flour

1. Sprinkle steaks with the pepper and dash *salt*. In a large skillet heat oil over medium-high heat. Add steaks. Cook for 10 to 12 minutes or until medium rare (145°F), turning once.
2. Remove from heat. Remove beef from skillet; cover and keep warm. Carefully add wine to the skillet. Return to medium-high heat. Cook and stir, scraping up any browned bits from the bottom of the pan. Add mushrooms, onion, mustard, and garlic to pan. Cook and stir for 5 minutes or until mushrooms are tender. Add 1 cup of the broth; bring to boiling.
3. Meanwhile, in a small bowl combine the remaining $\frac{1}{4}$ cup broth and flour. Stir into mushroom mixture. Return to boiling. Cook and stir for 2 minutes or until thickened and bubbly.
4. To serve, cut steaks in half crosswise, making four servings. Place one steak piece on each of four serving plates. Spoon mushroom sauce over the meat and potatoes.

PER SERVING: 235 cal., 10 g total fat (2 g sat. fat), 76 mg chol., 449 mg sodium, 8 g carb. (1 g fiber, 2 g sugars), 28 g pro. Exchanges: 0.5 vegetable, 0.5 starch, 3.5 lean meat, 1 fat.

Meal Total (per plate): 444 cal., 19 g total fat (5 g sat. fat), 89 mg chol., 756 mg sodium, 34 g carb. (6 g fiber, 6 g sugars), 37 g pro. Exchanges: 2.5 vegetable, 1.5 starch, 4 lean meat, 2 fat.

Parmesan-Crusted Brussels Sprouts
CARB. PER SERVING 10 g
SERVINGS 4 ($\frac{3}{4}$ cup each) START TO FINISH 20 minutes

 1 pound fresh Brussels sprouts, trimmed and
     halved (about 4 cups)
 1 tablespoon olive oil
 1$\frac{1}{2}$ ounces Parmesan cheese, finely shredded ($\frac{1}{3}$ cup)
 $\frac{1}{4}$ teaspoon black pepper

1. In a large broilerproof skillet combine Brussels sprouts and just enough water to cover. Bring to boiling; boil for 4 to 6 minutes or until sprouts are just tender. Drain well. Carefully wipe skillet dry.
2. Add oil to the same skillet. Heat over medium heat. Add sprouts, cut sides down. Cook, uncovered, for 4 to 5 minutes or until golden brown. Remove from the heat. Sprinkle with cheese and pepper. Divide sprouts among plates.

PER SERVING: 118 cal., 7 g total fat (2 g sat. fat), 8 mg chol., 206 mg sodium, 10 g carb. (4 g fiber, 2 g sugars), 7 g pro. Exchanges: 2 vegetable, 0.5 lean meat, 1 fat.

Garlic Mashed Potatoes
CARB. PER SERVING 16 g
SERVINGS 4 ($\frac{1}{2}$ cup each) PREP 15 minutes COOK 20 minutes

 1 pound russet potatoes, peeled , cut into 2-inch pieces
 2 teaspoons butter
 2 cloves garlic, minced
 $\frac{1}{4}$ teaspoon ground white pepper
 $\frac{1}{8}$ teaspoon salt
 $\frac{1}{4}$ to $\frac{1}{3}$ cup fat-free milk
 1 tablespoon snipped fresh chives

1. In a medium saucepan cook potatoes in boiling water, covered, for 20 to 25 minutes or until tender; drain. Mash with a potato masher or an electric mixer on low speed. Beat in butter, garlic, white pepper, and salt. Gradually beat in enough milk to make potatoes light and fluffy. Sprinkle with chives.

PER SERVING: 91 cal., 2 g total fat (1 g sat. fat), 5 mg chol., 101 mg sodium, 16 g carb. (1 g fiber, 1 g sugars), 2 g pro. Exchanges: 1 starch.

Southern-Style
Beef Bowls

Garlic-Pepper Beef with Lima Bean and Barley Ragout
Carb. per serving 23 g

SERVINGS 8 (5 to 6 ounces beef and $^3/_4$ cup ragout each)
PREP 25 minutes **SLOW COOK** 8 to 9 hours (low) or
4 to 4$^1/_2$ hours (high) **STAND** 5 minutes

- 1 2- to 2$^1/_2$-pound boneless beef chuck arm pot roast
- 1 teaspoon ground ancho chile pepper or paprika
- $^1/_2$ teaspoon salt
- $^1/_2$ teaspoon garlic powder
- $^1/_2$ teaspoon black pepper
- 1 tablespoon canola oil
- 1$^1/_2$ cups frozen lima beans, thawed
- $^2/_3$ cup regular pearled barley
- 2 stalks celery, thinly sliced (1 cup)
- 2 medium carrots, thinly sliced (1 cup)
- 2 medium leeks, trimmed, halved lengthwise, and cut crosswise into $^1/_2$-inch slices ($^2/_3$ cup)
- 1 14.5-ounce can reduced-sodium chicken broth
- $^1/_4$ teaspoon salt
- 1 cup frozen cut okra, thawed

1. Trim fat from roast. Cut roast into four equal pieces. In a small bowl combine ancho pepper, $^1/_2$ teaspoon salt, garlic powder, and pepper. Sprinkle over beef pieces and rub in with your fingers. In a large skillet cook beef, half at a time if needed, in hot oil over medium heat until browned; remove from skillet.
2. Meanwhile, in a 3$^1/_2$- to 4-quart slow cooker combine lima beans, barley, celery, carrots, leeks, broth, and the $^1/_4$ teaspoon salt. Top with browned beef pieces.
3. Cover and cook on low-heat setting for 8 to 9 hours or on high-heat setting for 4 to 4$^1/_2$ hours. Remove the beef pieces from the cooker; cover to keep warm. Add okra to barley mixture in cooker; stir to combine. Cover and let stand for 5 minutes. Divide barley mixture and beef among eight serving bowls. Top with greens and reserved bacon.

PER SERVING: 290 cal., 8 g total fat (2 g sat. fat), 74 mg chol., 462 mg sodium, 23 g carb. (6 g fiber, 2 g sugars), 30 g pro. Exchanges: 1 vegetable, 1 starch, 3.5 lean meat, 0.5 fat.

Honey-Bacon Greens
CARB. PER SERVING 13 g
SERVINGS 8 (1$^1/_2$ tablespoons each)
START TO FINISH 15 minutes

- 4 slices lower-sodium less-fat bacon, chopped
- 12 cups coarsely chopped kale, Swiss chard, and/or collard greens
- $^1/_3$ cup water
- $^1/_4$ teaspoon salt
- $^1/_4$ teaspoon black pepper
- 2 tablespoons honey

1. In a very large skillet cook bacon until crisp; remove bacon from the skillet using a slotted spoon. Drain bacon on paper towels and reserve drippings in the skillet.
2. Add greens, water, salt, and pepper to bacon drippings in the skillet. Cook, uncovered, over medium heat for 4 to 6 minutes or until greens are tender, stirring occasionally. Drizzle with honey and toss to coat. Divide greens among bowls, spooning it onto ragout mixture. Sprinkle with reserved bacon.

PER SERVING: 77 cal., 2 g total fat (0 g sat. fat), 2 mg chol., 146 mg sodium, 13 g carb. (2 g fiber, 7 g sugars), 5 g pro. Exchanges: 1.5 vegetable, 0.5 starch.

Meal Total (per plate): 367 cal., 10 g total fat (2 g sat. fat), 76 mg chol., 608 mg sodium, 36 g carb. (8 g fiber, 9 g sugars), 36 g pro. Exchanges: 2.5 vegetable, 1.5 starch, 3.5 lean meat, 0.5 fat.

Who knew 12 cups of chopped kale wilts down to less than 1 cup? Combined with salty bacon and sweet honey, it perks up the plate of this slow-cooked meal.

¼ Plate

Starch, Grain, or Other Carb: lima beans, barley, honey

¼ Plate

Protein: beef, bacon

½ Plate

Nonstarchy Veggies: kale, celery, carrots, leeks, okra

From-the-Oven
Meatball Meal

Meatballs and vegetables cook side by side in the oven. If they don't fit on the same rack, bake them on separate racks.

¼ Plate

Starch, Grain, or Other Carb: quinoa, cherries, plums, potatoes, parsnips

¼ Plate

Protein: beef, pork

½ Plate

Nonstarchy Veggies: shallots, beets, cauliflower

Cherry-Plum Balsamic Meatballs
Carb. per serving 15 g

SERVINGS 6 (3 meatballs and $^1/_4$ cup sauce each)
PREP 20 minutes BAKE 15 minutes

     Nonstick cooking spray
  1 egg
 $^1/_2$ cup cooked quinoa
 $^1/_4$ cup finely chopped shallot
 $^1/_2$ teaspoon salt
 $^1/_2$ teaspoon ground coriander
 $^1/_4$ teaspoon black pepper
 $^1/_4$ teaspoon ground allspice
 12 ounces 95% lean ground beef
  6 ounces ground pork
  1 recipe Cherry-Plum Balsamic Sauce *(below)*

1. Preheat oven to 425°F. Line a 15×10×1-inch baking pan with foil; lightly coat foil with cooking spray. Set aside. In a large bowl beat egg lightly with a fork. Stir in quinoa, shallot, salt, coriander, pepper, and allspice. Add beef and pork; mix well. Shape meat mixture into 18 meatballs. Place meatballs in prepared pan.
2. Bake meatballs for 15 to 18 minutes or until cooked through (165°F). Meanwhile, prepare Cherry-Plum Balsamic Sauce. To serve, divide meatballs among six serving plates. Spoon sauce over meatballs.

CHERRY-PLUM BALSAMIC SAUCE: In a small saucepan combine $^3/_4$ cup water and $^1/_2$ cup pitted dried plums. Bring to boiling. Remove from the heat and let stand for 5 minutes. Transfer mixture to a blender or food processor. Cover and blend or process until smooth. Return mixture to the saucepan. Add 1 cup frozen unsweetened dark sweet cherries, coarsely chopped, to the plum mixture. Bring just to boiling. In a small bowl stir together 2 tablespoons balsamic vinegar and 1 teaspoon cornstarch until smooth. Add all at once to cherry sauce. Cook and stir until slightly thickened and bubbly. Cook and stir for 2 minutes more. Spoon sauce over meatballs.

PER SERVING: 232 cal., 10 g total fat (4 g sat. fat), 87 mg chol., 263 mg sodium, 15 g carb. (2 g fiber, 10 g sugars), 19 g pro. Exchanges: 0.5 fruit, 0.5 starch, 2 lean meat, 0.5 medium-fat meat, 1 fat.

Roasted Vegetables
SERVINGS 6 (1 cup each)
CARB. PER SERVING 22 g
PREP 15 minutes ROAST 40 minutes

  3 medium parsnips
  1 pound small beets, such as gold or Chioggia,* trimmed, peeled, and cut into 1-inch wedges
 10 ounces small red or gold potatoes, cut into 1-inch wedges
  2 tablespoons olive oil
  1 teaspoon salt
 $^1/_4$ to $^1/_2$ teaspoon black pepper
  3 cups cauliflower florets
  2 tablespoons snipped fresh tarragon or fresh Italian (flat-leaf) parsley

1. Preheat oven to 425°F. Peel parsnips and cut in half crosswise. Cut the thin halves in half lengthwise. Cut the thick halves into lengthwise quarters. In a 3-quart rectangular baking dish combine parsnip pieces, beet wedges,* and potato wedges. Drizzle with oil and sprinkle with the salt and pepper. Toss to coat.
2. Cover and roast for 20 minutes, stirring once. Stir in the cauliflower. Roast, uncovered, for 20 to 25 minutes more or until vegetables are just tender, stirring once. Divide vegetables among plates. Sprinkle vegetables with tarragon.

*TEST KITCHEN TIP: If you are using red beets, put the beets in a small baking dish separate from the potatoes, parsnips, and cauliflower so that the red color doesn't bleed into the other vegetables.

PER SERVING: 136 cal., 5 g total fat (1 g sat. fat), 0 mg chol., 453 mg sodium, 22 g carb. (5 g fiber, 7 g sugars), 3 g pro. Exchanges: 1 vegetable, 1 starch, 1 fat.

Meal Total (per plate): 368 cal., 15 g total fat (5 g sat. fat), 87 mg chol., 716 mg sodium, 37 g carb. (7 g fiber, 17 g sugars), 23 g pro. Exchanges: 1 vegetable, 0.5 fruit, 1.5 starch, 2 lean meat, 0.5 medium-fat meat, 2 fat.

Lamb

When cooked to perfection, lean lamb is succulently divine. Braising, grilling, and roasting bring out its best.

Spiced Lamb Bowls

Tender lamb pieces are encrusted in spices common to the cuisine of India—fennel seeds, coriander, cumin, cinnamon, and black pepper.

¼ Plate

Starch or Grain: garbanzo beans

½ Plate

Nonstarchy Veggies: carrots, celery, onion, zucchini, spinach

¼ Plate

Protein: lamb

Spiced Lamb with Chickpeas
Carb. per serving 30 g

SERVINGS 4 (3 to 4 pieces lamb and 1 cup bean mixture each)
PREP 25 minutes COOK 1 hour

- 1 teaspoon fennel seeds, crushed
- 1 teaspoon ground coriander
- 1 teaspoon ground cumin
- $\frac{1}{2}$ teaspoon salt
- $\frac{1}{4}$ teaspoon black pepper
- $\frac{1}{4}$ teaspoon ground cinnamon
- 1 pound boneless leg of lamb, trimmed of fat and cut into $1\frac{1}{2}$-inch pieces
- 2 tablespoons canola oil
- $\frac{3}{4}$ cup water
- 3 medium carrots, thinly sliced ($1\frac{1}{2}$ cups)
- 2 stalks celery, thinly sliced (1 cup)
- 1 medium onion, chopped ($\frac{1}{2}$ cup)
- 1 medium zucchini, chopped ($1\frac{1}{4}$ cups)
- 3 cloves garlic, minced
- 1 15-ounce can no-salt-added garbanzo beans (chickpeas), rinsed and drained
- 1 cup reduced-sodium chicken broth
- 1 tablespoon flour
- 4 cups packaged fresh baby spinach
- 1 teaspoon garam masala
- 2 tablespoons snipped fresh cilantro and/or mint

Time-Saver Plan ahead by preparing this stewlike mixture through stirring in the beans the day before. Cool, place it in an airtight container, and chill. To serve, reheat, stir in the broth-flour mixture, and continue.

1. In a large bowl combine fennel, coriander, cumin, salt, pepper, and cinnamon. Add lamb pieces; toss to coat. In a large saucepan cook lamb in 1 tablespoon of the oil over medium heat until browned, stirring occasionally. Remove from heat and carefully add the water to lamb in saucepan. Bring to boiling; reduce heat. Simmer, covered, about 1 hour or until lamb is tender.

2. Meanwhile, in a large skillet cook carrots, celery, and onion in remaining 1 tablespoon oil over medium heat for 5 minutes, stirring occasionally. Add zucchini and garlic. Cook about 5 minutes more or until vegetables are just tender. Stir in garbanzo beans. In a small bowl whisk together chicken broth and flour. Add to bean mixture. Cook and stir until slightly thickened and bubbly; cook and stir for 1 minute more. Remove from heat; stir in spinach and garam masala.

3. To serve, divide bean mixture among four serving plates. Top with lamb; if desired, use a fork to pull the lamb into smaller pieces. Sprinkle with cilantro and/or mint.

PER SERVING: 367 cal., 13 g total fat (2 g sat. fat), 71 mg chol., 587 mg sodium, 30 g carb. (8 g fiber, 5 g sugars), 33 g pro. Exchanges: 2 vegetable, 1 starch, 4 lean meat, 1.5 fat.

Meal Total (per plate):
367 cal., 13 g total fat (2 g sat. fat),
71 mg chol., 587 mg sodium,
30 g carb. (8 g fiber, 5 g sugars),
33 g pro. Exchanges: 2 vegetable,
1 starch, 4 lean meat, 1.5 fat.

Fire Up the Grill

Once you get the grill going, the entire meal
will cook in less than 15 minutes.

Grilled Lamb Chops with Thyme
Carb. per serving 0 g

SERVINGS 4 (2 chops each)
PREP 15 minutes GRILL 12 minutes

  8 lamb loin or rib chops, cut 1 inch thick
     (about 2$\frac{1}{2}$ pounds total)
  2 teaspoons snipped fresh thyme
  $\frac{1}{8}$ to $\frac{1}{4}$ teaspoon crushed red pepper

1. Trim fat from chops. Sprinkle both sides of chops evenly with
thyme and crushed red pepper, rubbing in with your fingers.
2. For a gas or charcoal grill, place chops on the greased rack of
a covered grill directly over medium heat. Grill, covered, to
desired doneness, turning once halfway through grilling. Allow
12 to 14 minutes for medium rare (145°F) or 15 to 17 minutes
for medium (160°F). Place 2 lamb chops on each of four
serving plates.

PER SERVING: 203 cal., 8 g total fat (3 g sat. fat), 96 mg chol.,
85 mg sodium, 0 g carb. (0 g fiber, 0 g sugars), 31 g pro.
Exchanges: 4.5 lean meat.

Grilled Romaine with Feta
CARB. PER SERVING 4 g
SERVINGS 4 ($\frac{1}{2}$ heart of romaine, 2 tablespoons vinaigrette,
and 2 tablespoons cheese each)
PREP 20 minutes GRILL 1 minute

  $\frac{1}{3}$ cup lemon juice
  3 tablespoons olive oil
  2 cloves garlic, minced
  $\frac{1}{4}$ teaspoon kosher salt
  $\frac{1}{8}$ teaspoon black pepper
  2 hearts of romaine lettuce, halved lengthwise
     Nonstick olive oil cooking spray
  $\frac{1}{4}$ cup crumbled reduced-fat feta cheese

1. In a screw-top jar combine lemon juice, olive oil, garlic, salt, and
pepper. Cover and set aside. Lightly coat cut sides of hearts of
romaine with cooking spray.
2. For a gas or charcoal grill, place romaine, cut sides down, on
the rack of a covered grill directly over medium heat. Grill,
covered, for 1 to 3 minutes or until grill marks develop and the
romaine is slightly wilted.
3. Place each romaine half on a plate. Shake lemon juice mixture
well to combine and drizzle evenly over grilled romaine. Sprinkle
with feta.

PER SERVING: 124 cal., 11 g total fat (2 g sat. fat), 3 mg chol.,
246 mg sodium, 4 g carb. (1 g fiber, 1 g sugars), 3 g pro.
Exchanges: 1 vegetable, 2 fat.

Pita Wedges
Place 2 whole wheat pita bread rounds on the grill rack while
grilling the romaine just until heated. Remove from heat; cut
each into eight wedges. Divide pita wedges among plates. Makes
4 servings (4 wedges each).

PER SERVING: 85 cal., 1 g total fat (0 g sat. fat), 0 mg chol., 170 mg
sodium, 18 g carb. (2 g fiber, 0 g sugars), 3 g pro. Exchanges: 1 starch.

Meal Total (per plate):
412 cal., 20 g total fat (5 g sat. fat),
99 mg chol., 501 mg sodium,
22 g carb. (3 g fiber, 1 g sugars),
37 g pro. Exchanges: 1 vegetable,
1 starch, 4.5 lean meat, 2 fat.

Make It Mine If you have other herbs growing in your garden, try these chops made with rosemary, oregano, or sage instead of the thyme.

½ **Plate**
Nonstarchy Veggies: romaine

Protein: lamb, cheese
¼ **Plate**

¼ **Plate**
Starch or Grain: pita bread

107

Southwestern
Lamb Skewers

Ground ancho chile pepper fires up the pureed
tomato sauce with subtle heat.

½ Plate

Nonstarchy Veggies: sweet pepper, celery, onion, squash, spinach, tomato sauce

¼ Plate

Protein: lamb

¼ Plate

Starch or Grain: brown rice

Grilled Lamb Skewers
Carb. per serving 34 g

SERVINGS 4 (3$\frac{1}{2}$ ounces cooked lamb, $\frac{1}{2}$ cup rice, and $\frac{1}{3}$ cup sauce each)
PREP 30 minutes COOK 8 minutes GRILL 10 minutes

1 tablespoon ground ancho chile pepper or chili powder
1$\frac{1}{2}$ teaspoons ground cumin
1 teaspoon olive oil
$\frac{1}{2}$ teaspoon garlic powder
$\frac{1}{2}$ teaspoon onion powder
$\frac{1}{4}$ teaspoon salt
$\frac{1}{4}$ teaspoon black pepper
1$\frac{1}{4}$ pounds boneless lamb sirloin roast
2 cups hot cooked brown rice
1 recipe Southwest Tomato Sauce *(below)*
Snipped fresh cilantro (optional)

1. In a medium bowl stir together the ancho chile pepper, cumin, olive oil, garlic powder, onion powder, salt, and black pepper; set aside. Trim fat from meat. Cut meat into 1 to 1$\frac{1}{4}$-inch pieces. Place meat in bowl with spice mixture; stir to coat. Thread meat onto eight 6-inch skewers,* leaving a $\frac{1}{4}$-inch space between pieces. Set aside.
2. For gas or charcoal grill, place kabobs on the grill rack directly over medium heat. Grill, covered, for 10 to 12 minutes or until meat reaches desired doneness, turning once halfway through grilling. Divide rice among four serving plates. Top with skewers and tomato sauce. If desired, sprinkle with cilantro.
SOUTHWEST TOMATO SAUCE: In a large saucepan cook $\frac{1}{2}$ cup chopped onion and 1 clove garlic, minced, in 1 teaspoon hot olive oil over medium heat for 4 to 6 minutes or until tender, stirring occasionally. Stir in one 14.5- to 15-ounce can crushed tomatoes, undrained; $\frac{1}{2}$ teaspoon ground ancho chile pepper;

$\frac{1}{2}$ teaspoon dried oregano, crushed; $\frac{1}{4}$ teaspoon ground cumin; $\frac{1}{4}$ teaspoon dried thyme, crushed; and $\frac{1}{4}$ teaspoon black pepper. Bring to boiling; reduce heat. Simmer, uncovered, for 8 to 10 minutes or until slightly thickened. Process sauce with an immersion blender or cool slightly and process in a blender until smooth. Keep warm.
*TEST KITCHEN TIP: If using wooden skewers, soak skewers in enough water to cover for 30 minutes before using.

PER SERVING: 327 cal., 10 g total fat (3 g sat. fat), 67 mg chol., 354 mg sodium, 34 g carb. (5 g fiber, 6 g sugars), 27 g pro. Exchanges: 1 vegetable, 2 starch, 3 lean meat, 0.5 fat.

Squash Skillet Toss
CARB. PER SERVING 6 g
SERVINGS 4 ($\frac{3}{4}$ cup each)
START TO FINISH 25 minutes

1 medium red sweet pepper, chopped
1 medium stalk celery, thinly sliced
1 small red onion, chopped
1 tablespoon olive oil
1 medium yellow summer squash or 2 cups small pattypan squash
3 cloves garlic, minced
$\frac{1}{4}$ teaspoon salt
$\frac{1}{8}$ to $\frac{1}{4}$ teaspoon crushed red pepper (optional)
2 cups coarsely chopped fresh spinach
2 tablespoons snipped fresh chives or green onion tops

1. In a large skillet cook sweet pepper, celery, and onion in hot oil over medium heat for 5 minutes, stirring occasionally.
2. Meanwhile, trim squash. If using yellow summer squash, cut in half lengthwise and then cut crosswise into $\frac{1}{2}$-inch-thick slices. If using pattypan squash, cut in half.
3. Add squash and garlic to vegetables in skillet. Cook for 5 minutes more or until squash is just tender, stirring occasionally. Sprinkle with the salt and, if desired, crushed red pepper. Remove from the heat. Add spinach and toss to combine. Immediately divide mixture among plates and sprinkle with chives.

PER SERVING: 58 cal., 4 g total fat (1 g sat. fat), 0 mg chol., 168 mg sodium, 6 g carb. (2 g fiber, 3 g sugars), 1 g pro. Exchanges: 1 vegetable, 0.5 fat.

Meal Total (per plate): 385 cal., 14 g total fat (4 g sat. fat), 67 mg chol., 522 mg sodium, 40 g carb. (7 g fiber, 9 g sugars), 28 g pro. Exchanges: 2 vegetable, 2 starch, 3 lean meat, 1 fat.

Mediterranean
Holiday Dinner

Fennel-Coriander Roasted Leg of Lamb
Carb. per serving 1 g

SERVINGS 8 (4 ounces cooked lamb each)
PREP 20 minutes **ROAST** 1 hour **STAND** 15 minutes

   1   3- to 4-pound portion leg of lamb (with bone)
   1   tablespoon fennel seeds, crushed
   1   teaspoon ground coriander

1. Preheat oven to 325°F. Trim fat from meat. Cut several 1-inch-deep slits in meat. Combine fennel seeds, coriander, 1 teaspoon *salt,* and $^1/_2$ teaspoon *black pepper.* Rub over roast, pressing some of the spice mixture into the slits.
2. Place meat, fat side up, on a rack in a shallow roasting pan. Insert an oven-going meat thermometer into center of roast. The thermometer should not touch bone. Roast, uncovered, for 1 to $1^1/_2$ hours or until thermometer registers 135°F for medium rare. Remove from oven. Cover with foil; let stand for 15 minutes. The temperature of the meat after standing should be 145°F. (For medium doneness, roast for $1^1/_2$ to 2 hours or until meat thermometer registers 150°F.) Slice meat. Divide among plates.

PER SERVING: 235 cal., 9 g total fat (4 g sat. fat), 106 mg chol., 380 mg sodium, 1 g carb. (0 g fiber, 0 g sugars), 35 g pro. Exchanges: 5 lean meat.

Garlic-Green Onion Couscous
CARB. PER SERVING 19 g
SERVINGS 8 ($^1/_3$ cup each) **START TO FINISH** 20 minutes

   2   green onions, thinly sliced, green and
       white parts kept separate
$1^1/_2$ cups reduced-sodium chicken broth
   3   cloves garlic, minced
   1   cup dry whole wheat couscous
$^1/_4$ teaspoon freshly ground black pepper

1. In a medium saucepan combine white parts of green onions, broth, and garlic. Bring just to boiling. Stir in couscous; cover and remove from heat. Let stand for 5 minutes.

2. Fluff couscous with a fork. Stir in green parts of onions and the pepper. Divide couscous among plates.

PER SERVING: 91 cal., 0 g total fat, 0 mg chol., 105 mg sodium, 19 g carb. (3 g fiber, 1 g sugars), 4 g pro. Exchanges: 1.5 starch.

Lemon and Pine Nut Beans and Broccoli
CARB. PER SERVING 9 g
SERVINGS 8 ($^3/_4$ cup each) **PREP** 25 minutes **COOK** 8 minutes

   5   cups fresh green beans, trimmed (about 12 ounces)
   5   cups fresh broccoli florets
   2   tablespoons olive oil
   1   teaspoon finely shredded lemon peel
$^1/_4$ cup pine nuts, toasted

1. Fill a 4- to 5-quart Dutch oven half full of water; bring to boiling. Add beans; return to boiling. Cook, uncovered, for 4 minutes. Add broccoli; return to boiling. Cook, uncovered, about 4 minutes more or until vegetables are just tender; drain.
2. Combine oil, lemon peel, and $^1/_4$ teaspoon *salt.* Drizzle over vegetables; toss to coat. Divide vegetables among plates. Sprinkle with pine nuts. Squeeze *lemon wedges* over vegetables.

PER SERVING: 100 cal., 7 g total fat (1 g sat. fat), 0 mg chol., 96 mg sodium, 9 g carb. (4 g fiber, 3 g sugars), 3 g pro. Exchanges: 1.5 vegetable, 1 fat.

Meal Total (per plate): 426 cal., 16 g total fat (5 g sat. fat), 106 mg chol., 581 mg sodium, 29 g carb. (7 g fiber, 4 g sugars), 42 g pro. Exchanges: 1.5 vegetable, 1.5 starch, 5 lean meat, 1 fat.

The green combo of beans and broccoli provides a nutrient boost. If you'd rather, use 10 cups of only one vegetable.

½ Plate

Nonstarchy Veggies: green beans, broccoli, green onions

¼ Plate

Starch or Grain: couscous

¼ Plate

Protein: lamb, pine nuts

Pork

Lean pork is prime when it comes to versatility. Its mild flavor is perfect for pairing with dishes of many cuisines.

Curried
Pork & Pasta

The portions of this plate that represent nonstarchy vegetables and starch or grain are combined in one nutrient-packed side dish.

½ Plate

Nonstarchy Veggies: cauliflower, carrots, green onions

¼ Plate

Protein: pork, peanuts

¼ Plate

Starch, Grain, or Other Carb: fettuccine, orange juice

Curry-Glazed Pork Tenderloin Kabobs
Carb. per serving 2 g

SERVINGS 4 (1 kabob each)
PREP 15 minutes MARINATE 4 hours
BAKE 12 minutes

- 1 pound pork tenderloin, cut into 1½-inch pieces
- 3 tablespoons orange juice
- 2 tablespoons yellow curry paste

1. Place pork pieces in a large resealable plastic bag. In a small bowl stir together orange juice and curry paste until smooth. Add to pork in bag. Seal bag and turn to coat pork evenly. Marinate in the refrigerator for 4 to 24 hours, turning bag occasionally.
2. Preheat oven to 425°F. Drain pork, discarding marinade. Thread pork pieces onto four 8- to 10-inch skewers,* leaving ¼-inch spaces between pieces. Place kabobs on a lightly greased baking sheet.
3. Bake pork kabobs for 12 to 15 minutes or until pork pieces are slightly pink in the centers, turning once halfway through baking. Place one kabob on each of four serving plates.
*TEST KITCHEN TIP: If using wooden skewers, soak skewers in enough water to cover for 30 minutes before using.

PER SERVING: 128 cal., 2 g total fat (1 g sat. fat), 72 mg chol., 368 mg sodium, 2 g carb. (0 g fiber, 1 g sugars), 23 g pro. Exchanges: 3.5 lean meat.

Meal Total (per plate): 372 cal., 11 g total fat (2 g sat. fat), 72 mg chol., 511 mg sodium, 40 g carb. (5 g fiber, 14 g sugars), 31 g pro. Exchanges: 1 vegetable, 1.5 starch, 0.5 carb., 3.5 lean meat, 1.5 fat.

Peanut Fettuccine with Roasted Cauliflower
CARB. PER SERVING 38 g
SERVINGS 4 (1½ cups each)
PREP 20 minutes ROAST 20 minutes

- 6 cups bite-size cauliflower florets
- 1 tablespoon olive oil
- ⅛ teaspoon black pepper
- 4 ounces whole grain fettuccine
- 1 cup packaged fresh jullienned carrots
- ½ cup thinly sliced green onions (4)
- 2 tablespoons coarse-ground mustard
- 2 tablespoons honey
- ¼ cup snipped fresh cilantro
- ¼ cup chopped unsalted peanuts

1. Preheat oven to 425°F. Place cauliflower in a shallow baking pan; drizzle with olive oil and sprinkle with pepper. Toss to coat. Roast, uncovered, for 20 to 30 minutes or until cauliflower is just tender and lightly browned, stirring twice.
2. Meanwhile, cook fettuccine according to package directions, adding carrots for the last 2 minutes of cooking. Before draining, remove ½ cup of the pasta cooking liquid and set aside. Drain pasta mixture and transfer to a large bowl. Add green onions and cauliflower; toss to combine.
3. In a small bowl combine reserved pasta water, the mustard, and honey. Add to pasta mixture and toss to coat. Divide among plates and sprinkle with cilantro and peanuts.

PER SERVING: 244 cal., 9 g total fat (1 g sat. fat), 0 mg chol., 143 mg sodium, 38 g carb. (5 g fiber, 13 g sugars), 8 g pro. Exchanges: 1 vegetable, 1.5 starch, 0.5 carb., 1.5 fat.

Asian-Style
Noodle Bowls

Five-Spice Pork and Soba Bowls
Carb. per serving 37 g

SERVINGS 4 (2 cups each)
PREP 30 minutes COOK 15 minutes

12 ounces pork tenderloin,
     cut into very thin bite-size strips
1½ teaspoons five-spice powder
¼ teaspoon ground ginger
     Nonstick cooking spray
4 medium carrots, thinly sliced
2 cups thinly sliced, stemmed shiitake or
     button mushrooms
1 stalk celery, thinly sliced
1 tablespoon canola oil
3 cups water
1 cup no-salt-added chicken broth
4 ounces dry soba (buckwheat noodles)
1 tablespoon flour
1 tablespoon reduced-sodium soy sauce
3 cups thickly sliced, trimmed bok choy
2 cups snow peas, trimmed
½ cup thinly sliced green onions (4)
¼ cup orange juice

1. In a medium bowl toss pork strips with five-spice powder and ginger. Coat an unheated 4- to 6-quart nonstick Dutch oven with cooking spray. Heat over medium-high heat. Add pork strips. Cook for 4 to 6 minutes or until pork is browned, stirring occasionally. Remove pork from Dutch oven and set aside.
2. In the same Dutch oven cook carrots, mushrooms, and celery in hot oil over medium heat for 5 minutes, stirring occasionally. Add the water and broth. Bring to boiling. Add soba; return to boiling and cook, uncovered, for 3 to 4 minutes or until noodles are just tender.

Flavor Boost Serve this meal with a bottle of hot pepper sauce on the table so those who like can add a drop or two for some fiery heat.

3. Meanwhile, in a small bowl combine flour and soy sauce until smooth. Add to noodle mixture along with bok choy, snow peas, green onions, and cooked pork. Cook and stir until just boiling; cook and stir for 1 minute more. Remove from heat. Stir in orange juice just before serving. Ladle mixture into four serving bowls.

PER SERVING: 302 cal., 6 g total fat (1 g sat. fat), 55 mg chol., 541 mg sodium, 37 g carb. (5 g fiber, 7 g sugars), 27 g pro. Exchanges: 1 vegetable, 2 starch, 3 lean meat.

Meal Total (per plate):
302 cal., 6 g total fat (1 g sat. fat),
55 mg chol., 541 mg sodium,
37 g carb. (5 g fiber, 7 g sugars),
27 g pro. Exchanges: 1 vegetable,
2 starch, 3 lean meat.

An assortment of vitamin-packed vegetables pairs with pork and buckwheat noodles in this one-bowl meal that fits the healthful formula: half nonstarchy vegetables, a quarter protein, and a quarter grains.

¼ Plate

Protein: pork

½ Plate

Nonstarchy Veggies: carrots, mushrooms, celery, pea pods, bok choy

¼ Plate

Starch or Grain: soba noodles

Greek-Style
Pork Burgers

A lightly dressed salad complements the flavors of these mushroom-infused burgers that are topped with a creamy, herby spread.

½ Plate

Nonstarchy Veggies: red onion, arugula, asparagus, mushrooms, green onions, sweet peppers

¼ Plate

Starch or Grain: pita bread

¼ Plate

Protein: pork, yogurt, cheese

Pork Burgers with Feta-Rosemary Spread
Carb. per serving 14 g

SERVINGS 4 (1 sandwich each)
PREP 20 minutes GRILL 14 minutes

- 10 ounces lean ground pork
- 1 cup finely chopped fresh mushrooms
- ½ cup thinly sliced green onions (4)
- ¼ teaspoon salt
- ⅛ teaspoon black pepper
- ⅓ cup plain fat-free yogurt
- 3 tablespoons crumbled reduced-fat feta cheese
- 1 clove garlic, minced
- 1 teaspoon snipped fresh rosemary
- 1 whole wheat pita bread round, quartered
- ¾ cup bottled roasted red sweet peppers, drained and thinly sliced

1. In a large bowl combine pork, mushrooms, green onions, salt, and black pepper. Mix well. Divide pork mixture into four equal portions; form each portion into a ¾-inch-thick patty.

2. For a charcoal or gas grill, place patties on the grill rack directly over medium heat. Grill, covered, for 14 to 18 minutes or until done (160°F), turning once halfway through grilling.

3. Meanwhile, in a small bowl combine yogurt, feta cheese, garlic, and rosemary. Spread yogurt mixture evenly inside pita quarters. Add grilled pork patties and sweet peppers to make four sandwiches. Place one on each of four serving plates.

PER SERVING: 240 cal., 12 g total fat (5 g sat. fat), 48 mg chol., 383 mg sodium, 14 g carb. (3 g fiber, 2 g sugars), 18 g pro. Exchanges: 1 starch, 2.5 lean meat, 1 fat.

Arugula-Asparagus Salad
CARB. PER SERVING 5 g
SERVINGS 4 (1¼ cups each) PREP 15 minutes
STAND 30 minutes COOK 2 minutes

- ½ of a medium red onion, very thinly sliced
- ⅓ cup white wine vinegar
- 1 pound fresh asparagus spears, trimmed*
- 3 cups fresh arugula
- 2 tablespoons snipped fresh mint
- 2 tablespoons olive oil
- ¼ teaspoon salt
- ⅛ teaspoon black pepper

1. In a small bowl combine onion and vinegar. Press down on the onion so as much of it is covered by the vinegar as possible. Cover and let stand at room temperature for at least 30 minutes or in the refrigerator for up to 24 hours, stirring occasionally.

2. Cook asparagus, covered, in enough boiling water to cover for 2 to 3 minutes or until crisp-tender. Drain and rinse asparagus with cold water to cool quickly. Drain well. In a large bowl combine drained asparagus, arugula, and mint.

3. Using a slotted spoon, transfer onions to the asparagus mixture. Pour 3 tablespoons of the vinegar from the onion bowl into a small screw-top jar. Add oil, salt, and pepper. Cover and shake well. Drizzle over asparagus mixture; toss gently to coat. Serve immediately.

*TEST KITCHEN TIP: If you have pencil-thin asparagus spears, leave them whole, but if the spears are thicker, cut them into 2- to 3-inch lengths.

PER SERVING: 90 cal., 7 g total fat (1 g sat. fat), 0 mg chol., 153 mg sodium, 5 g carb. (2 g fiber, 2 g sugars), 2 g pro. Exchanges: 1 vegetable, 1.5 fat.

Meal Total (per plate): 330 cal., 19 g total fat (6 g sat. fat), 48 mg chol., 536 mg sodium, 19 g carb. (5 g fiber, 4 g sugars), 20 g pro. Exchanges: 1 vegetable, 1 starch, 2.5 lean meat, 2.5 fat.

Southern Pork Plate

Baked Honey-Dijon Pork Chops
Carb. per serving 2 g

SERVINGS 4 (1 pork chop each)
PREP 5 minutes BAKE 30 minutes

- 4 4-ounce boneless pork loin chops
- 2 tablespoons honey-Dijon mustard
- Black pepper

1. Preheat oven to 400°F. Place pork chops in a baking dish. Brush pork chops evenly with mustard and sprinkle with pepper. Bake, covered, about 30 minutes or until done (145°F). Cover with foil and let stand for 3 minutes. Place one chop on each of four serving plates.

PER SERVING: 167 cal., 5 g total fat (2 g sat. fat), 63 mg chol., 114 mg sodium, 2 g carb. (0 g fiber, 1 g sugars), 25 g pro. Exchanges: 3.5 lean meat.

Baked Sweet Potato Fries
CARB. PER SERVING 16 g
SERVINGS 4 ($1/2$ cup each)
PREP 15 minutes BAKE 25 minutes

- Nonstick cooking spray
- 1 pound sweet potatoes
- 2 teaspoons olive oil

1. Preheat oven to 400°F. Line a baking sheet with foil. Lightly coat foil with cooking spray; set aside. Peel sweet potatoes and cut lengthwise into $1/2$-inch-thick strips. Spread sweet potatoes on prepared baking sheet. Drizzle with the olive oil and toss to coat. Arrange in a single layer.

2. Bake for 25 to 30 minutes or until golden brown, stirring once halfway through baking. Divide sweet potatoes among plates.

PER SERVING: 90 cal., 2 g total fat (0 g sat. fat), 0 mg chol., 45 mg sodium, 16 g carb. (2 g fiber, 3 g sugars), 1 g pro. Exchanges: 1 starch, 0.5 fat.

Sautéed Kale

In two batches, in a large skillet cook 12 cups chopped kale and 2 cloves garlic, minced, in 2 teaspoons hot oil over medium heat for 8 to 10 minutes or until kale is tender, stirring frequently. Divide among plates. Makes 4 servings (1 cup each).

PER SERVING: 121 cal., 4 g total fat (0 g sat. fat), 0 mg chol., 77 mg sodium, 18 g carb. (4 g fiber, 4 g sugars), 9 g pro. Exchanges: 3.5 vegetable, 1 fat.

Meal Total (per plate): 377 cal., 11 g total fat (2 g sat. fat), 63 mg chol., 236 mg sodium, 36 g carb. (7 g fiber, 9 g sugars), 35 g pro. Exchanges: 3.5 vegetable, 1 starch, 3.5 lean meat, 1.5 fat.

Sautéed greens and sweet potato fries are two classic sides served in the South. Both are rich in vitamin C and potassium.

½ Plate
Nonstarchy Veggies: kale

¼ Plate
Starch or Grain: sweet potatoes

¼ Plate
Protein: pork

121

Light & Lean
Cajun Cuisine

Massaging kale with your hands may seem odd, but it turns this mildly bitter and dense green sweet and silky.

½ Plate

Nonstarchy Veggies: kale, shallot, celery, onion, tomatoes, okra, parsley

¼ Plate

Starch or Grain: barley

¼ Plate

Protein: ham, walnuts

It doesn't take much cheese to top this crisp, thin-crust pizza when you use a flavor-rich combo of mozzarella and goat cheeses.

Protein: pork, pancetta, mozzarella cheese, goat cheese
¼ Plate

¼ Plate
Starch or Grain: pizza crust

½ Plate
Nonstarchy Veggies: spinach, fennel, onion, sweet peppers

127

Lightly Spiced
Pork & Rice

The cooking time for regular brown rice is about 45 minutes, so start cooking it before you begin preparing the pork and spinach.

½ Plate

Nonstarchy Veggies: tomatoes, spinach, green onions

¼ Plate

Starch or Grain: brown rice

¼ Plate

Protein: pork, pecans

Pork Medallions with Lemon-Pecan Spinach
Carb. per serving 5 g

SERVINGS 4 (3 ounces pork and $^{1}/_{2}$ cup spinach each)
START TO FINISH 20 minutes

- 1 pound pork tenderloin,* cut crosswise into 8 slices
- $^{1}/_{4}$ teaspoon salt
- $^{1}/_{4}$ teaspoon coarsely ground black pepper
- 1 tablespoon canola oil or margarine
- 2 tablespoons lemon juice
- $^{1}/_{8}$ teaspoon bottled hot pepper sauce
- 1 10-ounce package frozen chopped spinach, thawed and well drained
- 2 green onions, sliced
- 2 tablespoons chopped pecans
- 1 tablespoon snipped fresh parsley
- $^{1}/_{8}$ teaspoon salt
- Lemon slices, halved (optional)

1. If necessary, press each pork tenderloin slice to 1-inch thickness. Sprinkle pork slices lightly with the $^{1}/_{4}$ teaspoon salt and the black pepper. In a large skillet heat oil over medium-high heat. Add pork slices; cook for 6 to 8 minutes or until pork is slightly pink in the center (145°F), turning once halfway through cooking. Remove pork slices from skillet, reserving drippings in the skillet. Cover pork and keep warm.

2. Stir lemon juice and hot pepper sauce into reserved drippings in skillet. Stir in spinach, green onions, pecans, parsley, and the $^{1}/_{8}$ teaspoon salt; cook over low heat until spinach mixture is heated through. Divide spinach mixture among four serving plates; arrange pork slices on top. If desired, garnish with lemon slices.

*TEST KITCHEN TIP: To keep the sodium in this dish in check, choose natural pork rather than enhanced pork.

PER SERVING: 200 cal., 8 g total fat (1 g sat. fat), 73 mg chol., 320 mg sodium, 5 g carb. (3 g fiber, 1 g sugars), 27 g pro. Exchanges: 1 vegetable, 3.5 lean meat, 0.5 fat.

Brown Rice
In a small saucepan bring 1 cup water to boiling. Slowly add $^{1}/_{2}$ cup regular brown rice and return to boiling; reduce heat. Simmer, covered, about 45 minutes or until most of the water is absorbed and the rice is tender. Let stand, covered, for 5 minutes. Divide the rice evenly among plates. Makes 4 servings (about $^{1}/_{3}$ cup each).

PER SERVING: 86 cal., 1 g total fat (0 g sat. fat), 0 mg chol., 3 mg sodium, 18 g carb. (1 g fiber, 0 g sugars), 2 g pro. Exchanges: 1 starch.

Sliced Tomatoes
Cut 2 medium ripe tomatoes into 4 slices each. Arrange 2 slices on each plate. Makes 4 servings (2 slices each).

PER SERVING: 11 cal., 0 g total fat, 0 mg chol., 3 mg sodium, 2 g carb. (1 g fiber, 2 g sugars), 1 g pro. Exchanges: 0.5 vegetable.

Meal Total (per plate: 297 cal., 9 g total fat (1 g sat. fat), 73 mg chol., 326 mg sodium, 25 g carb. (5 g fiber, 3 g sugars), 30 g pro. Exchanges: 1.5 vegetable, 1 starch, 3.5 lean meat, 0.5 fat.

Pork Dinner

With little prep and few ingredients, you can have this dinner on the table in less than 30 minutes.

Apricot-Glazed Pork Chops
Carb. per serving 6 g

SERVINGS 4 (1 pork chop each)
PREP 5 minutes GRILL 8 minutes

    1/4 cup low-sugar apricot preserves
    1/8 teaspoon ground cinnamon
    4   6-ounce bone-in pork loin rib chops,*
         cut 1/2 to 3/4 inch thick
    Snipped fresh thyme

1. For glaze, in a small bowl stir together apricot preserves and cinnamon.
2. For a charcoal grill, place chops on the grill rack directly over medium coals. Grill, uncovered, for 8 to 10 minutes or until done (145°F), turning once and brushing with glaze halfway through grilling. (For a gas grill, preheat grill. Reduce heat to medium. Place chops on grill rack over heat. Cover and grill as directed.) Remove from grill; let stand, covered, for 3 minutes. Place 1 chop on each of four serving plates and sprinkle chops with thyme.
*TEST KITCHEN TIP: To keep the sodium in this dish in check, choose natural pork rather than enhanced pork.

PER SERVING: 225 cal., 11 g total fat (2 g sat. fat), 64 mg chol., 57 mg sodium, 6 g carb. (0 g fiber, 5 g sugars), 23 g pro. Exchanges: 0.5 fruit, 3.5 lean meat.

Mashed Sweet Potatoes

Heat 2 cups refrigerated mashed sweet potatoes according to package directions. Divide potatoes among plates. Makes 4 servings (1/2 cup each).

PER SERVING: 90 cal., 1 g total fat (0 g sat. fat), 2 mg chol., 100 mg sodium, 18 g carb. (2 g fiber, 10 g sugars), 2 g pro. Exchanges: 1 starch.

Roasted Asparagus Spears

Preheat oven to 425°F. Arrange 1 pound fresh asparagus, trimmed, in a shallow roasting pan. Drizzle with 1 tablespoon olive oil and sprinkle with 1/8 teaspoon salt and 1/8 teaspoon black pepper. Toss to coat; arrange asparagus in an even layer. Roast, uncovered, for 8 to 10 minutes or until crisp-tender, tossing once. Divide among plates. Makes 4 servings (about 9 spears each).

PER SERVING: 42 cal., 3 g total fat (0 g sat. fat), 0 mg chol., 74 mg sodium, 2 g carb. (1 g fiber, 1 g sugars), 1 g pro. Exchanges: 1 vegetable, 0.5 fat.

Meal Total (per plate): 357 cal., 15 g total fat (2 g sat. fat), 66 mg chol., 231 mg sodium, 26 g carb. (3 g fiber, 16 g sugars), 26 g pro. Exchanges: 1 vegetable, 0.5 fruit, 1 starch, 3.5 lean meat, 0.5 fat.

¼ Plate

Starch, Grain,
or Other Carb:
sweet potatoes,
apricot preserves

Make It Mine
If asparagus is not a veggie
you enjoy, serve the Spinach
Salad from *page 16* or the
Steamed Broccolini from
page 35 instead.

½ Plate

Nonstarchy
Veggies:
asparagus

¼ Plate

Protein: pork

131

Mexican Pork
Hand Pies

You don't have to be a bread baker to make these cheesy meat-and-veggie pies—frozen bread dough is an easy fix.

¼ Plate

Starch or Grain: whole wheat bread, corn

½ Plate

Nonstarchy Veggies: jicama, onion, sweet peppers, green onions, tomatoes

¼ Plate

Protein: pork, cheese

132

Chipotle Pork Empanadas
Carb. per serving 46 g

SERVINGS 6 (2 empanadas each)
PREP 40 minutes BAKE 20 minutes

- ¼ cup cornmeal
- 1 16-ounce loaf frozen whole wheat bread dough, thawed
- 12 ounces lean ground pork
- 1 medium onion, chopped
- 1 medium red, yellow, or green sweet pepper, chopped
- 2 cloves garlic, minced
- 1 14.5-ounce can no-salt-added diced tomatoes, drained
- ¼ cup frozen whole kernel corn
- 1 teaspoon finely chopped chipotle pepper in adobo sauce (see tip, *page 155*)
- ½ teaspoon ground cumin
- ½ cup shredded Monterey Jack cheese (2 ounces)

1. Preheat oven to 375°F. Lightly grease a baking sheet. Sprinkle baking sheet with cornmeal; set aside. On a lightly floured surface, let thawed bread dough stand, covered, while preparing the filling.

2. For filling, in a large skillet cook pork, onion, sweet pepper, and garlic over medium heat until meat is browned, stirring to break up meat as it cooks. Drain off fat. Stir in tomatoes, corn, chipotle pepper, cumin, and ⅛ teaspoon *salt* until well combined. Remove from heat. Stir in cheese. Set aside.

3. Divide bread dough into 12 equal portions. On the lightly floured surface, roll each dough portion into a 5-inch circle. Divide filling evenly among dough rounds, spooning filling onto center of each dough round. Brush edge of each dough round lightly with water; fold dough round in half, pinching edge to seal. If desired, press edges with tines of a fork. Place filled empanadas on the prepared baking sheet. Prick tops with tines of a fork.

4. Bake for 20 to 25 minutes or until empanadas are golden brown and heated through. Place two empanadas on each of six serving plates.

PER SERVING: 402 cal., 15 g total fat (5 g sat. fat), 45 mg chol., 590 mg sodium, 46 g carb. (5 g fiber, 4 g sugars), 23 g pro. Exchanges: 3 starch, 2 medium-fat meat.

Jicama Slaw
CARB. PER SERVING 9 g
SERVINGS 6 (⅔ cup each)
PREP 25 minutes CHILL 6 hours

- 2 cups very thin jicama strips
- 2 large red and/or green sweet peppers, chopped
- ½ cup thinly sliced green onions (4)
- ¼ cup chopped fresh cilantro
- ½ cup light sour cream
- ½ teaspoon finely shredded lime peel
- 2 tablespoons lime juice
- 1 teaspoon sugar*
- ½ teaspoon ground cumin
- ¼ teaspoon salt
- ⅛ teaspoon cayenne pepper

1. In a large bowl toss together jicama, sweet peppers, green onions, and cilantro. In a small bowl combine sour cream, lime peel, lime juice, sugar, cumin, salt, and cayenne pepper. Add sour cream mixture to jicama mixture; stir until well combined. Serve immediately or cover and chill up to 6 hours before serving. Divide among plates.

*SUGAR SUBSTITUTES: Choose from Splenda Granular, Equal Spoonful or packets, Sweet'N Low bulk or packets, or Truvia Spoonable or packets. Follow package directions to use product amount equivalent to 1 teaspoon sugar.

PER SERVING: 58 cal., 2 g total fat (1 g sat. fat), 6 mg chol., 114 mg sodium, 9 g carb. (3 g fiber, 3 g sugars), 2 g pro. Exchanges: 2 vegetable.

PER SERVING WITH SUBSTITUTE: Same as above, except 56 cal., 2 g sugars.

Meal Total (per plate):
460 cal., 17 g total fat (6 g sat. fat), 51 mg chol., 704 mg sodium, 55 g carb. (8 g fiber, 7 g sugars), 25 g pro. Exchanges: 2 vegetable, 3 starch, 2 medium-fat meat.

Mediterranean
Tapas Plate

Greek Pork Tenderloin
Carb. per serving 4 g

SERVINGS 4 (3^1/2 ounces pork and about 3 tablespoons sauce each)
PREP 20 minutes ROAST 25 minutes STAND 3 minutes

- 1 pound pork tenderloin
- 1 tablespoon finely shredded lemon peel
- ^{1}/2 teaspoon dried oregano, crushed
- ^{1}/4 teaspoon salt
- ^{1}/4 teaspoon dried rosemary, crushed
- ^{1}/8 teaspoon black pepper
- 2 teaspoons olive oil
- 1 6-ounce carton plain low-fat yogurt
- 2 tablespoons snipped fresh mint
- 1 clove garlic, minced

1. Preheat oven to 425°F. Trim fat from pork. In a small bowl combine lemon peel, oregano, salt, rosemary, and pepper. Sprinkle over all sides of the pork and rub in with your fingers.
2. In a large oven-going skillet heat oil over medium-high heat. Add roast to hot skillet; cook for 4 minutes or until browned, turning to brown all sides evenly. Transfer skillet to oven. Roast about 20 minutes or until an instant-read thermometer inserted into thickest portion of meat registers 145°F. Remove from oven and let stand, covered, for 3 minutes.
3. Meanwhile, for sauce, in a small bowl combine yogurt, mint, and garlic. To serve, thinly slice pork and divide among four serving plates. Top with yogurt mixture.

PER SERVING: 174 cal., 5 g total fat (2 g sat. fat), 76 mg chol., 236 mg sodium, 4 g carb. (1 g fiber, 3 g sugars), 26 g pro. Exchanges: 4 lean meat.

Pita Bread Wedges
Preheat oven to 350°F. Wrap 2 whole wheat pita bread rounds in foil. Bake about 10 minutes or until warm. To serve, cut each round into six wedges. Place three wedges on each plate. Makes 4 servings (3 wedges each).

PER SERVING: 83 cal., 0 g total fat , 0 mg chol., 161 mg sodium, 17 g carb. (1 g fiber, 0 g sugars), 3 g pro. Exchanges: 1 starch.

Crisp Vegetables
Cut 2 medium red sweet peppers into strips to make 2 cups. Cut 1 large cucumber into sticks to make 2 cups. Place ^{1}/2 cup sweet pepper strips and ^{1}/2 cup cucumber sticks on each plate. Makes 4 servings (1 cup each)

PER SERVING: 27 cal., 0 g total fat, 0 mg chol., 3 mg sodium, 6 g carb. (2 g fiber, 3 g sugars), 1 g pro. Exchanges: 1 vegetable.

Hummus
Using one 7-ounce container roasted red pepper hummus, spoon 3 tablespoons hummus onto each plate. Makes 4 servings (3 tablespoons each).

PER SERVING: 92 cal., 6 g total fat (0 g sat. fat), 0 mg chol., 276 mg sodium, 9 g carb. (1 g fiber, 1 g sugars), 2 g pro. Exchanges: 0.5 starch, 1 fat.

Meal Total (per plate): 376 cal., 11 g total fat (2 g sat. fat), 76 mg chol., 676 mg sodium, 36 g carb. (5 g fiber, 7 g sugars), 32 g pro. Exchanges: 1 vegetable, 1.5 starch, 4 lean meat, 1 fat.

This appetizer-style plateful of fresh and flavorful foods is a fun way to serve a well-balanced meal.

Make It Mine
Feel free to mix it up for the nonstarchy veggie dippers: Try celery, zucchini sticks, jicama sticks, carrots, broccoli—even sugar snap peas.

¼ Plate

Starch, Grain, or Other Carb: pita bread, hummus, yogurt

¼ Plate

Protein: pork, hummus, yogurt

½ Plate

Nonstarchy Veggies: sweet peppers, cucumber

135

Maple-Pecan
Pork Dinner

For succulent pork chops, test doneness with an instant-read thermometer—they are done at 145°F.

¼ Plate

Starch, Grain, or Other Carb: maple syrup, sweet potato, apples

½ Plate

Nonstarchy Veggies: shallot, lettuce, red onion

Protein: pork, pecans

¼ Plate

Maple-Pecan Pork Chops
Carb. per serving 3 g

SERVINGS 4 (1 pork chop each)
START TO FINISH 15 minutes

4 pork loin rib chops, about ¾ inch thick (1½ pounds total)
¼ teaspoon salt
¼ teaspoon black pepper
1 tablespoon canola oil
2 tablespoons finely chopped shallot
2 tablespoons chopped pecans, toasted
2 tablespoons sugar-free maple-flavor syrup
2 teaspoons butter, melted
1 tablespoon snipped fresh thyme

1. Sprinkle pork chops with the salt and pepper. In a very large skillet heat oil over medium-high heat. Add shallot; cook and stir for 1 minute. Add chops; cook for 8 to 10 minutes or until pork juices run clear (145°F), turning once halfway through cooking time. Cover with foil and allow chops to rest for 3 minutes after removing from heat.
2. Meanwhile, in a bowl combine pecans, syrup, butter, and thyme. Place one pork chop on each of four serving plates and top with the pecan mixture.

PER SERVING: 216 cal., 12 g total fat (3 g sat. fat), 62 mg chol., 224 mg sodium, 3 g carb. (1 g fiber, 1 g sugars), 23 g pro. Exchanges: 3.5 lean meat, 1.5 fat.

Meal Total (per plate): 365cal., 15 g total fat (3 g sat. fat), 62 mg chol., 354 mg sodium, 32 g carb. (6 g fiber, 13 g sugars), 25 g pro. Exchanges: 0.5 vegetable, 0.5 fruit, 1 starch, 3.5 lean meat, 2 fat.

Romaine-Apple Salad
CARB. PER SERVING 13 g
SERVINGS 4 (1½ cups each)
START TO FINISH 10 minutes

6 cups torn romaine or mixed greens
2 small apples, cored and sliced
½ of a small red onion, halved and thinly sliced
3 tablespoons reduced-fat balsamic vinaigrette

1. In a salad bowl combine romaine, apples, and red onion. Drizzle balsamic vinaigrette over salad; toss to coat. Divide salad among plates.

PER SERVING: 59 cal., 1 g total fat (0 g sat. fat), 0 mg chol., 85 mg sodium, 13 g carb. (3 g fiber, 9 g sugars), 1 g pro. Exchanges: 0.5 vegetable, 0.5 fruit.

Baked Sweet Potato Fries
CARB. PER SERVING 16 g
SERVINGS 4 (½ cup each)
PREP 15 minutes BAKE 25 minutes

Nonstick cooking spray
1 pound sweet potatoes
2 teaspoons olive oil

1. Preheat oven to 400°F. Line a baking sheet with foil. Lightly coat foil with cooking spray; set aside. Peel sweet potatoes and cut lengthwise into ½-inch-thick strips. Spread sweet potatoes on prepared baking sheet. Drizzle with the olive oil and toss to coat. Arrange in a single layer.
2. Bake for 25 to 30 minutes or until golden brown, stirring once halfway through baking. Divide sweet potatoes among plates.

PER SERVING: 90 cal., 2 g total fat (0 g sat. fat), 0 mg chol., 45 mg sodium, 16 g carb. (2 g fiber, 3 g sugars), 1 g pro. Exchanges: 1 starch, 0.5 fat.

European-Style
Roasted Pork

Roasted Pork with Zucchini
Carb. per serving 4 g

SERVINGS 4 (4 ounces pork and 2 pieces zucchini each)
PREP 10 minutes ROAST 20 minutes

- 1 teaspoon caraway seeds, crushed
- 1/4 teaspoon celery seeds
- 1 to 1 1/4 pounds pork tenderloin, trimmed of fat
- 2 medium zucchini, trimmed and halved lengthwise

1. Preheat oven to 425°F. Combine caraway seeds, celery seeds, 1/4 teaspoon *salt,* and 1/4 teaspoon *black pepper.* Sprinkle evenly over pork, rub in. Place pork on a rack in a shallow roasting pan.
2. Lightly coat zucchini halves with *nonstick cooking spray* and sprinkle with 1/8 teaspoon *salt* and 1/8 teaspoon *black pepper.* Arrange zucchini halves in a single layer around pork in pan.
3. Roast pork and zucchini for 20 to 25 minutes or until an instant-read thermometer inserted into center of roast registers 145°F and zucchini is just tender, turning zucchini once.
4. Place pork roast on a cutting board; cover with foil and let rest for 3 minutes. Thinly slice pork. Divide among four serving plates. Slice zucchini pieces and divide among plates.

PER SERVING: 135 cal., 2 g total fat (1 g sat. fat), 70 mg chol., 272 mg sodium, 4 g carb. (1 g fiber, 2 g sugars), 24 g pro. Exchanges: 0.5 vegetable, 3 lean meat.

Garlic Polenta
CARB. PER SERVING 15 g
SERVINGS 4 (1/2 cup each) START TO FINISH 30 minutes

- 2 cups reduced-sodium chicken broth
- 1/2 cup polenta-style cornmeal
- 2 cloves garlic, minced
- 1/4 cup fat-free milk

1. In a large saucepan combine broth, polenta, and garlic. Bring to boiling, stirring constantly. Reduce heat. Simmer, uncovered, for 20 minutes, stirring frequently. Add milk to the polenta. Cook for 5 to 10 minutes more or until polenta is tender and thick, stirring frequently. Divide polenta among plates.

PER SERVING: 81 cal., 0 g total fat, 0 mg chol., 284 mg sodium, 15 g carb. (1 g fiber, 1 g sugars), 4 g pro. Exchanges: 1 starch.

Pickled Cabbage
CARB. PER SERVING 4 g
SERVINGS 4 (1/2 cup cabbage each)
START TO FINISH 15 minutes

- 6 slices lower-sodium, less-fat bacon, chopped
- 1/4 cup cider vinegar
- 2 tablespoons canola oil
- 4 cups finely shredded green cabbage

1. In a large skillet cook bacon just until crisp, stirring occasionally. Add vinegar and oil. Heat just to boiling. Add cabbage; cook and stir for 3 minutes. Divide cabbage among plates.

PER SERVING: 116 cal., 9 g total fat (1 g sat. fat), 5 mg chol., 118 mg sodium, 4 g carb. (2 g fiber, 2 g sugars), 4 g pro. Exchanges: 1 vegetable, 2 fat.

> **Meal Total (per plate):** 332 cal., 11 g total fat (2 g sat. fat), 75 mg chol., 674 mg sodium, 23 g carb. (4 g fiber, 5 g sugars), 32 g pro. Exchanges: 1.5 vegetable, 1 starch, 3 lean meat, 2 fat.

Pickling vegetables is a vintage cooking techique popular on restaurant menus. The spunky veggies are often served as a salad or condiment.

½ Plate

Nonstarchy Veggies: zucchini, cabbage

¼ Plate

Protein: pork, bacon

¼ Plate

Starch, Grain, or Other Carb: polenta, apples

Bacon-Wrapped
Pork & Vegetables

Prepare the flavorful pesto while the pork and veggies roast in the oven. Voilà! Dinner is done.

¼ Plate

Protein: pork, turkey bacon, cheese, almonds

¼ Plate

Starch or Grain: potatoes

½ Plate

Nonstarchy Veggies: cauliflower, arugula

Bacon-Wrapped Pork Tenderloin and Roasted Vegetables with Arugula Pesto
Carb. per serving 32 g

SERVINGS 4 (4 ounces cooked pork, 1 1/2 cups vegetables, and 1 1/2 tablespoons pesto each)
PREP 25 minutes ROAST 25 minutes STAND 3 minutes

- 2 tablespoons Dijon-style mustard
- 2 tablespoons honey
- 1 1-pound pork tenderloin
- 3 slices turkey bacon
- 12 ounces small red potatoes, scrubbed and quartered
- 6 cups cauliflower florets
- 1/4 teaspoon salt
- 1/4 teaspoon black pepper
- 3/4 cup packed fresh arugula, spinach, or sorrel (about 1 1/2 ounces)
- 1/4 cup packed fresh Italian (flat-leaf) parsley
- 1 ounce Parmesan cheese, grated
- 2 tablespoons slivered almonds
- 1 clove garlic, minced
- 2 tablespoons olive oil
- 2 teaspoons lemon juice
- 1 to 2 tablespoons water

1. Preheat oven to 425°F. In a small bowl combine mustard and honey. Spread half of the mixture evenly over outside of pork. Wrap bacon around pork, leaving ends of bacon slices under the pork. Place pork on a rack in a large shallow roasting pan. Arrange potatoes and cauliflower around pork in pan. Drizzle with remaining mustard mixture. Toss vegetables to coat. Sprinkle potato mixture with the salt and pepper.

2. Roast for 25 to 30 minutes or until an instant-read thermometer inserted in thickest part of the pork tenderloin registers 145°F and potatoes and cauliflower are just tender. Cover pork with foil and let stand for 3 minutes.

3. Meanwhile, for pesto, in a food processor place arugula, parsley, cheese, almonds, and garlic. Cover and process until finely chopped. With the processor running, add oil, lemon juice, and water through the feed tube until mixture is well combined.

4. To serve, divide pesto among four serving plates. Cut pork crosswise into eight slices and arrange on plates. Divide vegetables among the plates.

PER SERVING: 404 cal., 17 g total fat (4 g sat. fat), 84 mg chol., 726 mg sodium, 32 g carb. (5 g fiber, 13 g sugars), 33 g pro. Exchanges: 2 vegetable, 1 starch, 0.5 carb., 4 lean meat, 1.5 fat.

Meal Total (per plate): 404 cal., 17 g total fat (4 g sat. fat), 84 mg chol., 726 mg sodium, 32 g carb. (5 g fiber, 13 g sugars), 33 g pro. Exchanges: 2 vegetable, 1 starch, 0.5 carb., 4 lean meat, 1.5 fat.

Juicy Pork
& Bean Duo

Roast Pork and Crispy Green Beans
Carb. per serving 16 g

SERVINGS 6 (2$^1/_2$ ounces pork and 1 cup green beans each)
PREP 25 minutes ROAST 30 minutes BAKE 5 minutes

- 1$^1/_4$ pounds pork top loin roast (single loin)
- $^1/_4$ teaspoon salt
- $^1/_8$ teaspoon black pepper
- 6 cups fresh green beans, trimmed (about 1 pound)
- $^1/_2$ cup refrigerated or frozen egg product, thawed
- $^1/_4$ teaspoon black pepper
- $^3/_4$ cup whole wheat or regular panko bread crumbs
- 3 tablespoons flaxseed meal
- Butter-flavor nonstick cooking spray
- Snipped fresh oregano (optional)

1. Preheat oven to 425°F. Trim fat from roast. Sprinkle pork evenly with salt and $^1/_8$ teaspoon pepper. Place pork on a rack in a shallow roasting pan. Roast, uncovered, for 30 to 35 minutes or until an instant-read thermometer inserted into the center of the pork roast registers 145°F. Transfer roast to a cutting board; cover with foil to keep warm and let stand while green beans bake.
2. Meanwhile, in a 4-quart Dutch oven cook green beans, covered, in enough lightly salted water to cover for 8 to 10 minutes or until beans are just tender. Drain and rinse with cold water water to cool beans quickly. Spread beans onto paper towels and let dry completely.
3. In a shallow dish combine egg and $^1/_4$ teaspoon pepper. In a separate shallow dish combine panko and flaxseed meal. Dip green beans in batches in egg mixture. Allow excess to drip off. Dip beans in panko mixture, tossing to coat evenly. Arrange beans in a single layer in a 15×10×1-inch baking pan. Lightly coat beans with cooking spray. While the roast stands, bake coated beans for 5 to 8 minutes or until crumbs are lightly browned.
4. To serve, slice pork crosswise. Divide pork and green beans among six serving plates. If desired, sprinkle with fresh oregano.

PER SERVING: 220 cal., 5 g total fat (1 g sat. fat), 59 mg chol., 191 mg sodium, 16 g carb. (5 g fiber, 4 g sugars), 27 g pro. Exchanges: 1 vegetable, 1 starch, 3 lean meat.

Tomato-Pesto Cannellini Beans
CARB. PER SERVING 15 g
SERVINGS 6 ($^2/_3$ cup each) START TO FINISH 25 minutes

- $^1/_2$ cup chopped onion
- 2 teaspoons olive oil
- 2 cloves garlic, minced
- 2 15-ounce cans no-salt-added cannellini beans, rinsed and drained
- 1 14.5-ounce can no-salt-added diced tomatoes
- $^1/_3$ cup purchased dried tomato pesto

1. In a large saucepan cook onion in hot oil over medium heat for 8 minutes or until onion is very tender, stirring occasionally. Add garlic; cook and stir for 30 second. Add beans and tomatoes. Bring to boiling; reduce heat. Cook, covered, for 10 minutes, stirring occasionally. Stir in pesto. Cook, covered, for 5 minutes more. Divide beans among six bowls.

PER SERVING: 156 cal., 4 g total fat (1 g sat. fat), 1 mg chol., 195 mg sodium, 24 g carb. (7 g fiber, 4 g sugars), 7 g pro. Exchanges: 0.5 vegetable, 1.5 starch, 0.5 fat.

Meal Total (per plate):
376 cal., 9 g total fat (2 g sat. fat), 60 mg chol., 386 mg sodium, 40 g carb. (12 g fiber, 8 g sugars), 35 g pro.Exchanges: 1.5 vegetable, 2.5 starch, 3 lean meat, 0.5 fat.

The crisp-coated green beans are delicious served alongside the pork and cannellini, but they also make a fun finger-food snack.

¼ Plate

Starch, Grain, or Other Carb: panko, cannellini beans,

½ Plate

Nonstarchy Veggies: green beans, tomatoes, tomato pesto

¼ Plate

Protein: pork, egg, cannellini beans

143

Seafood

From flaky fish to assorted shellfish, seafood has many health benefits. Try to incorporate at least two servings each week.

Simple
Salmon Supper

It's so easy—while the potatoes and asparagus are roasting in the oven, you can turn your attention to the salmon searing on the stove top.

½ Plate

Nonstarchy Veggies: asparagus, leek, sweet pepper, mushrooms, shallot

¼ Plate

Starch, Grain, or Other Carb: potatoes, white wine

¼ Plate

Protein: salmon

Seared Salmon with Mushroom-Shallot Sauce
Carb. per serving 2 g

SERVINGS 4 (1 salmon fillet and about 2 tablespoons sauce each)
START TO FINISH 30 minutes

4	4-ounce fresh or frozen skinless salmon fillets
1/4	teaspoon black pepper
1/8	teaspoon salt
2	teaspoons olive oil
1	cup sliced fresh mushrooms
1	medium shallot, finely chopped
1/3	cup dry white wine or reduced-sodium chicken broth
1	tablespoon Dijon-style mustard
2	teaspoons snipped fresh thyme or 1/2 teaspoon dried thyme, crushed

1. Thaw fish, if frozen. Rinse fish and pat dry with paper towels. Sprinkle with pepper and salt. Measure thickness of fillets. In a large nonstick skillet cook salmon in hot oil over medium heat for 4 to 6 minutes per 1/2-inch thickness or until salmon flakes easily when tested with a fork, carefully turning once halfway through cooking. Remove from skillet; cover and keep warm.
2. Add mushrooms and shallot to the same skillet. Cook for 3 to 5 minutes over medium heat or until tender, stirring occasionally. Remove from heat and carefully add wine, mustard, and thyme. Return to heat; cook and stir for 1 to 2 minutes or until well combined and heated through. Place salmon on four serving plates and top with mushroom sauce.

PER SERVING: 284 cal., 17 g total fat (4 g sat. fat), 62 mg chol., 232 mg sodium, 2 g carb. (0 g fiber, 1 g sugars), 24 g pro. Exchanges: 3.5 medium-fat meat.

Meal Total (per plate): 438 cal., 24 g total fat (5 g sat. fat), 62 mg chol., 472 mg sodium, 23 g carb. (3 g fiber, 5 g sugars), 27 g pro. Exchanges: 1.5 vegetable, 1 starch, 3.5 medium-fat meat, 1 fat.

Quick Roasted Asparagus
CARB. PER SERVING 2 g
SERVINGS 4 (8 or 9 spears each) PREP 10 minutes
ROAST 8 minutes

1	pound fresh asparagus, trimmed
1	tablespoon olive oil
1/8	teaspoon salt
1/8	teaspoon black pepper

1. Preheat oven to 425°F. Place asparagus in a shallow roasting pan. Drizzle with oil and sprinkle with salt and pepper; toss to coat. Arrange asparagus in an even layer.
2. Roast, uncovered, for 8 to 10 minutes or until crisp-tender, tossing once. Divide among plates.

PER SERVING: 42 cal., 3 g total fat (0 g sat. fat), 0 mg chol., 74 mg sodium, 2 g carb. (1 g fiber, 1 g sugars), 1 g pro. Exchanges: 1 vegetable, 0.5 fat.

Roasted Potatoes and Leeks
CARB. PER SERVING 19 g
SERVINGS 4 (3/4 cup each) PREP 15 minutes ROAST 35 minutes

	Nonstick cooking spray
12	ounces tiny new potatoes, scrubbed and quartered
1	tablespoon olive oil
1/4	teaspoon salt
1/8	teaspoon black pepper
1	medium red sweet pepper, cut into bite-size strips
1	medium leek, trimmed and cut into 1/4-inch-thick slices (white part only)

1. Preheat oven to 425°F. Coat a 13×9×2-inch baking pan with cooking spray; add potatoes to pan. Drizzle with oil and sprinkle with salt and black pepper; toss to coat.
2. Roast, uncovered, for 25 minutes, stirring once. Add sweet pepper and leek; toss to combine. Roast about 10 minutes more or until potatoes are tender and browned on the edges and sweet pepper pieces are just tender. Divide among plates.

PER SERVING: 112 cal., 4 g total fat (1 g sat. fat), 0 mg chol., 166 mg sodium, 19 g carb. (2 g fiber, 3 g sugars), 2 g pro. Exchanges: 0.5 vegetable, 1 starch, 0.5 fat.

Taco-Style Tilapia

Chipotle-Cilantro Tilapia
Carb. per serving 15 g

SERVINGS 4 (2 tortillas, 1 fillet, and about
2 tablespoons sauce each)
START TO FINISH 25 minutes

- 4   4-ounce fresh or frozen skinless tilapia fillets
- 1/4 teaspoon salt
- 1/4 teaspoon ground cumin
- 1/8 teaspoon chipotle chile powder
- 1/8 teaspoon black pepper
- 2   teaspoons canola oil
- 1/2 cup plain fat-free yogurt
- 2   tablespoons snipped fresh cilantro
- 1/2 to 1 teaspoon chipotle chile peppers in adobo sauce,
  minced (see tip, *page 155*)
- 8   6-inch corn tortillas, warmed

1. Thaw fish, if frozen. Rinse fish and pat dry with paper towels.
Sprinkle with salt, cumin, chile powder, and black pepper.
2. In a very large nonstick skillet heat oil over medium heat. Add
fish fillets. Cook for 6 to 8 minutes or until fish flakes easily when
tested with a fork, turning once halfway through cooking.
3. Meanwhile, for yogurt sauce, in a small bowl combine yogurt,
cilantro, and chipotle peppers in adobo sauce. To serve, place
1 fish fillet, 2 warmed tortillas, and about 2 tablespoons yogurt
sauce on each of four serving plates.

PER SERVING: 207 cal., 5 g total fat (1 g sat. fat), 57 mg chol.,
235 mg sodium, 15 g carb. (1 g fiber, 2 g sugars), 26 g pro.
Exchanges: 1 starch, 3.5 lean meat, 0.5 fat.

Carrot-Cucumber Salad
CARB. PER SERVING 8 g
SERVINGS 4 (1 cup each) PREP 20 minutes CHILL 2 hours

- 1/4 cup rice vinegar
- 2   tablespoons snipped fresh cilantro
- 1   tablespoon toasted sesame oil
- 1/4 teaspoon salt
- 1/8 teaspoon chipotle chile powder
- 1/8 teaspoon black pepper
- 1   medium cucumber, halved lengthwise and
  cut into 1/4-inch slices (12 ounces)
- 2   medium carrots, cut into matchstick-size pieces (1 cup)
- 1/2 of a small red onion, thinly sliced (1/2 cup)

1. In a large bowl whisk together vinegar, cilantro, oil, salt, chile
powder, and black pepper. Stir in cucumber, carrots, and red
onion. Toss to coat. Cover and chill for 2 to 4 hours before
serving. Divide salad among plates.

PER SERVING: 60 cal., 4 g total fat (1 g sat. fat), 0 mg chol.,
200 mg sodium, 8 g carb. (1 g fiber, 3 g sugars), 1 g pro.
Exchanges: 1 vegetable, 0.5 fat.

Meal Total (per plate):
267 cal., 9 g total fat (2 g sat. fat),
57 mg chol., 435 mg sodium,
23 g carb. (2 g fiber, 5 g sugars),
27 g pro. Exchanges: 1 vegetable,
1 starch, 3.5 lean meat, 1 fat.

For casual fare, turn this knife-and-fork meal into finger food by wrapping the fish and salad in the tortillas to eat like tacos.

¼ Plate

Starch or Grain: corn tortillas

¼ Plate

Protein: tilapia, yogurt

½ Plate

Nonstarchy Veggies: cucumber, carrots, onion

149

A Fresh Take on
Tuna Salad

Cooking fresh tuna steaks is like cooking beef steaks. The tuna stays moist and flavorful when cooked until pink in the center, but it dries out if cooked longer.

½ Plate

Nonstarchy Veggies: watercress, cabbage, jicama, radishes, onion

¼ Plate

Starch, Grain, or Other Carb: brown rice

¼ Plate

Protein: tuna, cashews

Asian Tuna and Watercress
Carb. per serving 27 g or 25 g

SERVINGS 4 (2 cups salad, $1/3$ cup rice, 1 tuna steak, and 2 tablespoons dressing each)
START TO FINISH 45 minutes

- 3 cups watercress
- 3 cups shredded napa cabbage or Chinese cabbage
- 1 cup jicama, peeled and cut into matchstick-size pieces
- 1 cup sliced radishes
- $1/4$ of a medium red onion, thinly sliced
- $1/2$ cup rice vinegar
- 1 tablespoon sugar*
- 1 tablespoon reduced-sodium soy sauce
- 4 teaspoons toasted sesame oil
- $1/2$ teaspoon ground ginger
- $1/8$ to $1/4$ teaspoon crushed red pepper
- 4 4- to 5-ounce tuna steaks, about 1 inch thick
- $1/8$ teaspoon ground coriander
- $1^{1/3}$ cups hot cooked brown rice
- 2 tablespoons chopped cashews
  Lime wedges (optional)

1. In a very large bowl combine watercress, cabbage, jicama, radishes, and red onion; set aside.
2. For dressing, in a screw-top jar combine rice vinegar, sugar, soy sauce, 2 teaspoons of the toasted sesame oil, half of the ginger, and the crushed red pepper. Cover and shake well.
3. In a large nonstick skillet heat remaining 2 teaspoons toasted sesame oil over medium-high heat. Sprinkle tuna steaks with $1/4$ teaspoon *salt*, $1/4$ teaspoon *black pepper,* the coriander, and remaining ginger. Rub spices into tuna steaks. Add tuna to skillet.

Cook for 8 to 10 minutes or until tuna is browned but still slightly pink on the inside, turning once halfway through cooking.
4. To serve, toss watercress mixture with $1/4$ cup of the dressing. Divide watercress mixture among four serving plates. Spoon rice over the watercress, dividing evenly. Thinly slice tuna. Arrange tuna slices over the salad and rice mixture. Sprinkle with cashews. Pass remaining dressing. If desired, serve with lime wedges.
*SUGAR SUBSTITUTES: Choose from Splenda Granular, Sweet'N Low bulk or packets, or Equal Spoonful or packets. Follow package directions to use product amount equivalent to 1 tablespoon sugar.

PER SERVING: 321 cal., 8 g total fat (1 g sat. fat), 44 mg chol., 374 mg sodium, 27 g carb. (4 g fiber, 6 g sugars), 32 g pro. Exchanges: 2 vegetable, 1 starch, 4 lean meat, 1 fat.

PER SERVING WITH SUBSTITUTE: Same as above, except 310 cal., 25 g carb. (3 g sugars).

Meal Total (per plate): 321 cal., 8 g total fat (1 g sat. fat), 44 mg chol., 374 mg sodium, 27 g carb. (4 g fiber, 6 g sugars), 32 g pro. Exchanges: 2 vegetable, 1 starch, 4 lean meat, 1 fat.

30-Minute
Mediterranean Meal

Mediterranean Cod with Roasted Tomatoes
Carb. per serving 7 g

SERVINGS 4 (1 fish portion and $^1/_2$ cup tomato mixture each)
PREP 20 minutes BAKE 8 minutes

- 4 4-ounce fresh or frozen skinless cod fillets, $^3/_4$ to 1 inch thick
- 2 teaspoons snipped fresh oregano
- 1 teaspoon snipped fresh thyme
- $^1/_2$ teaspoon salt
- $^1/_4$ teaspoon garlic powder
- $^1/_4$ teaspoon paprika
- $^1/_4$ teaspoon black pepper
- Nonstick cooking spray
- 3 cups cherry tomatoes
- 2 cloves garlic, sliced
- 1 tablespoon olive oil
- 2 tablespoons sliced pitted ripe olives
- 2 teaspoons capers
- Fresh oregano and/or thyme leaves

1. Preheat oven to 450°F. Thaw fish, if frozen. Rinse fish and pat dry with paper towels. In a small bowl combine snipped oregano, snipped thyme, salt, garlic powder, paprika, and pepper. Sprinkle half of the oregano mixture over both sides of each fish fillet.
2. Line a 15×10×1-inch baking pan with foil. Coat foil with cooking spray. Place fish on one side of the foil-lined pan. Add tomatoes and garlic slices to the other side of the foil-lined pan. Combine remaining oregano mixture with oil. Drizzle oil mixture over tomatoes; toss to coat. Bake for 8 to 12 minutes or until fish flakes easily when tested with a fork, stirring tomato mixture once. Stir olives and capers into cooked tomato mixture.
3. Divide fish and roasted tomato mixture evenly among four serving plates. Garnish with fresh oregano and/or thyme leaves.

PER SERVING: 157 cal., 5 g total fat (1 g sat. fat), 49 mg chol., 429 mg sodium, 7 g carb. (2 g fiber, 4 g sugars), 22 g pro. Exchanges: 1 vegetable, 3 lean meat, 1 fat.

Israeli Couscous
In a small saucepan combine 1 cup water and $^2/_3$ cup Israeli (large pearl) couscous. Bring to boiling; reduce heat. Simmer, covered, for 12 to 15 minutes or until tender. Divide evenly among plates. Makes 4 servings ($^1/_3$ cup each).

PER SERVING: 86 cal., 0 g total fat, 0 mg chol., 0 mg sodium, 18 g carb. (1 g fiber, 1 g sugars), 3 g pro. Exchanges: 1 starch.

Meal Total (per plate):
243 cal., 5 g total fat (1 g sat. fat), 49 mg chol., 429 mg sodium, 25 g carb. (3 g fiber, 5 g sugars), 25 g pro. Exchanges: 1 vegetable, 1 starch, 3 lean meat, 1 fat.

Each bite is blissful when you combine the flavors of the roasted tomatoes and herb-topped fish with the pearly couscous.

½ Plate

Nonstarchy Veggies: tomatoes

¼ Plate

Starch or Grain: Israeli couscous

¼ Plate

Protein: cod

Seaside Tacos

These slaw-topped fish tacos make a hearty yet low-cal meal. The spicy cabbage slaw doubles as a filling and a salad on the side. Because it starts with a bagged mix, the slaw takes just minutes to make.

¼ Plate

Starch, Grain, or Other Carb: corn tortillas, Greek yogurt

¼ Plate

Protein: fish, avocado, Greek yogurt

½ Plate

Nonstarchy Veggies: coleslaw mix

Fish Tacos with Spicy Cabbage Slaw
Carb. per serving 37 g

SERVINGS 4 (2 tacos and 1¼ cups slaw each)
PREP 30 minutes MARINATE 15 minutes BAKE 4 minutes

- 1½ pounds fresh or frozen mahi mahi, cod, or tilapia
- 2 tablespoons fresh lime juice
- 2 tablespoons orange juice
- 1 tablespoon olive oil
- 2 cloves garlic, minced
- ½ teaspoon ground ancho chile pepper or chili powder
- ¼ teaspoon salt
- ⅛ teaspoon black pepper
- 1 14-ounce package shredded cabbage with carrot (coleslaw mix)
- 1 to 2 fresh jalapeño chile peppers, finely chopped*
- 2 tablespoons chopped fresh cilantro
- 1 6-ounce container plain fat-free Greek yogurt
- ⅓ cup fat-free mayonnaise
- 1 tablespoon fresh lime juice
- 1 teaspoon ground cumin
- ¼ teaspoon salt
  Nonstick cooking spray
- 8 6-inch corn tortillas, warmed
- 1 ripe avocado, halved, seeded, peeled, and cut into 8 slices
  Lime wedges (optional)

1. Thaw fish, if frozen. Rinse fish and pat dry with paper towels. Measure thickness of the fish; place fish in a shallow dish.
2. For marinade, in a small bowl whisk together the 2 tablespoons lime juice, the orange juice, olive oil, garlic, ancho chile pepper, ¼ teaspoon salt, and the black pepper; pour mixture over fish. Marinate at room temperature for 15 minutes.
3. Meanwhile, for cabbage slaw, in a large bowl combine cabbage, chopped jalapeño, and cilantro. In a small bowl whisk together yogurt, mayonnaise, the 1 tablespoon lime juice, the cumin, and ¼ teaspoon salt. Stir dressing into cabbage mixture. Cover and chill until serving time.
4. Preheat oven to 450°F. Coat a 15×10×1-inch baking pan with cooking spray. Remove fish from marinade; discard marinade. Place fish in a single layer in prepared pan. Bake for 4 to 6 minutes per ½-inch thickness of fish or until fish begins to flake when tested with a fork, turning once. (Or grill fish directly over medium heat for 4 to 6 minutes per ½-inch thickness, turning once.)
5. To serve, divide fish among the warmed tortillas. Add an avocado slice and 2 tablespoons of the slaw to each taco. Serve with remaining slaw on the side. If desired, serve with lime wedges.

*TEST KITCHEN TIP: Because chile peppers contain volatile oils that can burn your skin and eyes, avoid direct contact with them as much as possible. When working with chile peppers, wear plastic or rubber gloves. If your bare hands do touch the peppers, wash your hands and nails well with soap and warm water.

PER SERVING: 418 cal., 12 g total fat (2 g sat. fat), 126 mg chol., 682 mg sodium, 37 g carb. (9 g fiber, 8 g sugars), 41 g pro. Exchanges: 2 vegetable, 1.5 starch, 4 lean meat, 1.5 fat.

Meal Total (per plate):
418 cal., 12 g total fat (2 g sat. fat), 126 mg chol., 682 mg sodium, 37 g carb. (9 g fiber, 8 g sugars), 41 g pro. Exchanges: 2 vegetable, 1.5 starch, 4 lean meat, 1.5 fat.

Grab-&-Eat Salads

Thai Halibut Lettuce Wraps
Carb. per serving 21 g

SERVINGS 4 (2 or 3 lettuce leaves, $1/2$ cup noodles, $3/4$ cup vegetables, 1 tablespoon vinegar mixture, and about 5 pieces halibut each)
PREP 30 minutes **COOK** 8 minutes

- 1 pound fresh or frozen halibut steaks, 1 inch thick
- 2 ounces thin rice noodles or rice sticks
- $1/4$ teaspoon salt
- $1/4$ teaspoon black pepper
- 1 tablespoon sesame oil
- 2 tablespoons rice vinegar
- 1 tablespoon fish sauce
- 1 tablespoon lime juice
- 1 tablespoon packed brown sugar*
- $1/2$ to 1 teaspoon crushed red pepper
- 1 medium carrot, cut into matchstick- size pieces
- 1 cup snow peas, trimmed and very thinly sliced
- $1/4$ cup thinly sliced green onions
- $1/4$ cup canned bean sprouts, drained
- $1/4$ cup chopped fresh cilantro
- $1/4$ cup chopped fresh mint
- 8 to 12 leaves butterhead (Boston or Bibb) or romaine lettuce
- 4 teaspoons chopped unsalted peanuts

1. Thaw fish, if frozen. Rinse fish and pat dry with paper towels. Cut fish into 1-inch pieces; set aside.
2. Bring a large saucepan of water to boiling. Add rice noodles and cook about 3 minutes or until just tender. Drain and rinse under cold water. Gently squeeze noodles to remove most of the water. Snip noodles with kitchen shears into 2- to 3-inch pieces.

3. Meanwhile, sprinkle halibut with the salt and black pepper. In a large skillet heat sesame oil over medium heat. Add fish to skillet. Cook for 8 to 12 minutes or until fish flakes easily when tested with a fork, turning frequently to brown all sides.
4. In a small bowl combine rice vinegar, fish sauce, lime juice, brown sugar, and crushed red pepper.
5. Place one-fourth of the halibut on each of four dinner plates. Divide rice noodles, carrot, snow peas, green onions, bean sprouts, cilantro, mint, and lettuce among the four plates.
6. To serve, spoon fish, noodles, vegetables, and herbs into lettuce leaves. Drizzle with vinegar mixture and sprinkle with peanuts. Roll up.

*SUGAR SUBSTITUTE: We do not recommend using a sugar substitute for this recipe.

PER SERVING: 244 cal., 7 g total fat (1 g sat. fat), 56 mg chol., 634 mg sodium, 21 g carb. (2 g fiber, 6 g sugars), 24 g pro. Exchanges: 1 vegetable, 1 starch, 3 lean meat, 1 fat.

> **Meal Total (per plate):** 244 cal., 7 g total fat (1 g sat. fat), 56 mg chol., 634 mg sodium, 21 g carb. (2 g fiber, 6 g sugars), 24 g pro. Exchanges: 1 vegetable, 1 starch, 0.5 carb., 3 lean meat, 1 fat.

Depending on the type of lettuce you choose, the wraps will be tender and delicate (butterhead) or crisp and sturdy (romaine).

Make It Mine If you're not a fan of fish, use skinless, boneless chicken breast instead of the halibut. Breast is done when 165°F and no longer pink in the center.

½ Plate

Nonstarchy Veggies: carrot, snow peas, lettuce, green onions

¼ Plate

Protein: halibut, peanuts

¼ Plate

Starch or Grain: rice noodles

157

Italian-Style
Fish Steaks

Halibut with Eggplant Peperonata
Carb. per serving 13 g

SERVINGS 4 (1 halibut steak, 1 cup spinach, and ½ cup eggplant each)
START TO FINISH 45 minutes

    4   4-ounce fresh or frozen halibut steaks
    ½   of a medium sweet onion, thinly sliced
    1   tablespoon olive oil
    1   small eggplant (about 10 ounces), cut into 1-inch pieces (3 cups)
    1   large yellow or red sweet pepper, seeded and thinly sliced
    4   cloves garlic, minced
    1   teaspoon snipped fresh rosemary or ½ teaspoon dried rosemary, crushed
    ½   teaspoon salt
    ¼   teaspoon black pepper
    4   cups fresh spinach

1. Thaw fish, if frozen. Rinse fish and pat dry with paper towels; set aside.

2. In a large skillet cook onion in hot oil over medium heat for 5 minutes, stirring occasionally. Add eggplant, sweet pepper, garlic, rosemary, and ¼ teaspoon of the salt. Cook for 10 to 12 minutes more or until vegetables are very tender, stirring occasionally. Remove mixture from skillet and keep warm.

3. Add about 1 inch of water to the same skillet. Insert a steamer basket and bring water to boiling over high heat. Sprinkle halibut steaks with remaining ¼ teaspoon salt and the black pepper. Add halibut to steamer basket. Cover and steam over medium heat for 6 to 8 minutes or until fish flakes easily when tested with a fork.

4. Arrange a bed of spinach on each of four serving plates. Place halibut and eggplant mixture on spinach.

PER SERVING: 189 cal., 5 g total fat (1 g sat. fat), 56 mg chol., 396 mg sodium, 13 g carb. (4 g fiber, 5 g sugars), 23 g pro. Exchanges: 2 vegetable, 3 lean meat, 0.5 fat.

Whole Grain Bread
Cut 4 ounces of a whole grain bread loaf into eight slices. Place two slices on each plate. Makes 4 servings (2 slices each).

PER SERVING: 70 cal., 1 g total fat (0 g sat. fat), 0 mg chol., 120 mg sodium, 13 g carb. (1 g fiber, 1 g sugars), 2 g pro. Exchanges: 1 starch.

Meal Total (per plate): 259 cal., 6 g total fat (1 g sat. fat), 56 mg chol., 516 mg sodium, 26 g carb. (5 g fiber, 6 g sugars), 25 g pro. Exchanges: 2 vegetable, 1 starch, 3 lean meat, 0.5 fat.

Peperonata is a classic slow-cooked Italian dish made with peppers, onion, and garlic. This quick version features eggplant, too, to add more vegetable goodness to this meal.

¼ Plate

Starch or Grain: whole grain bread

½ Plate

Nonstarchy Veggies: eggplant, sweet pepper, onion, spinach

¼ Plate

Protein: halibut

Plate o' Pasta
& Greens

Flavors of lemon and basil brighten this sauceless pasta dish. For a more powerful pucker, serve lemon wedges on the side.

½ Plate

Nonstarchy Veggies: asparagus, sweet peppers, greens, onions

¼ Plate

Protein: shrimp

¼ Plate

Starch, Grain, or Other Carb: linguine, oranges

Basil-Lemon Shrimp Linguine
Carb. per serving 39 g

SERVINGS 4 (1$\frac{1}{2}$ cups each)
START TO FINISH 30 minutes

   1   pound fresh or frozen large shrimp in shells
   6   ounces dried linguine or fettuccine
   8   ounces fresh asparagus spears, trimmed
       and cut diagonally into 1-inch pieces
       Nonstick cooking spray
   2   cloves garlic, minced
   1   cup thin red, yellow, and/or green sweet pepper strips
   $\frac{1}{4}$ cup snipped fresh basil or 1 tablespoon
       dried basil, crushed
   1   teaspoon finely shredded lemon peel
   $\frac{1}{4}$ teaspoon black pepper
   $\frac{1}{8}$ teaspoon salt
   $\frac{1}{4}$ cup sliced green onions (2)
   2   tablespoons lemon juice
   1   tablespoon olive oil
       Fresh basil sprigs (optional)
       Lemon wedges (optional)

1. Thaw shrimp, if frozen. Peel and devein shrimp, leaving tails intact if desired. Rinse shrimp and pat dry with paper towels; set aside.
2. Cook pasta according to package directions, adding asparagus the last 3 minutes of cooking; drain and return to pan. Cover and keep warm.
3. Meanwhile, lightly coat an unheated large nonstick skillet with cooking spray. Heat over medium heat. Add garlic; cook and stir for 15 seconds. Add sweet pepper strips; cook and stir about 2 minutes or until crisp-tender. Add shrimp, dried basil (if using),

lemon peel, black pepper, and salt. Cook and stir for 3 minutes or until shrimp turn opaque. Remove from heat.
4. Add shrimp mixture to pasta mixture. Add snipped fresh basil (if using), green onions, lemon juice, and oil; toss gently to coat. Divide among four serving plates. If desired, garnish each serving with basil sprigs and/or lemon wedges.

PER SERVING: 286 cal., 5 g total fat (1 g sat. fat), 121 mg chol., 620 mg sodium, 39 g carb. (4 g fiber, 4 g sugars), 21 g pro. Exchanges: 1 vegetable, 2 starch, 2.5 lean meat, 0.5 fat.

Baby Greens with Oranges
CARB. PER SERVING 12 g **SERVINGS** 4 (1$\frac{1}{2}$ cups each)
START TO FINISH 15 minutes

   6   cups mesclun or other mild salad greens
   2   tablespoons olive oil
   1   tablespoon blood orange juice or orange juice
   1   tablespoon balsamic vinegar
   4   thin slices red onion, separated into rings
   1   cup blood orange and/or orange sections
       (4 blood oranges or 3 oranges)
   2   tablespoons mixed country olives or regular
       Kalamata olives
       Dash salt
       Dash black pepper

1. Place greens in a salad bowl. For dressing, in a small bowl whisk together oil, orange juice, and vinegar. Pour dressing over greens; toss gently to coat.
2. Divide greens mixture among plates. Top with onion rings, orange sections, and olives. Lightly sprinkle with salt and pepper.

PER SERVING: 118 cal., 8 g total fat (1 g sat. fat), 0 mg chol., 116 mg sodium, 12 g carb. (3 g fiber, 7 g sugars), 2 g pro. Exchanges: 1 vegetable, 0.5 fruit, 1.5 fat.

Meal Total (per plate): 404 cal., 13 g total fat (2 g sat. fat), 121 mg chol., 736 mg sodium, 51 g carb. (7 g fiber, 11 g sugars), 23 g pro. Exchanges: 2 vegetable, 0.5 fruit, 2 starch, 2.5 lean meat, 2 fat.

Mixed Miso Skewers
& Vermicelli Salad

Hot-off-the-grill kabobs and a cool Asian noodle salad make a pleasing summertime meal.

½ Plate

Nonstarchy Veggies: fennel, carrots, green onions, watercress

¼ Plate

Starch or Grain: rice vermicelli, edamame

¼ Plate

Protein: shrimp, chicken, edamame

Miso-Marinated Shrimp and Chicken Skewers
Carb. per serving 3 g

SERVINGS 4 (1 shrimp skewer and 1 chicken skewer each)
PREP 25 minutes MARINATE 1 hour GRILL 6 minutes

- 12 ounces fresh or frozen large shrimp in shells
- 8 ounces skinless, boneless chicken breast halves
- 1 teaspoon finely shredded lime peel
- 2 tablespoons lime juice
- 2 tablespoons rice vinegar
- 2 tablespoons canola oil
- 2 tablespoons miso (soybean paste)
- 1 teaspoon grated fresh ginger

1. Thaw shrimp, if frozen. Peel and devein shrimp, leaving tails intact if desired. Rinse shrimp and pat dry with paper towels. Place shrimp in a large resealable plastic bag set in a shallow bowl; set aside. Cut chicken breast halves lengthwise into $1/2$-inch-thick strips. Place chicken strips in another large resealable plastic bag set in a shallow bowl; set aside.
2. For marinade, in a small bowl whisk together lime peel, lime juice, vinegar, oil, miso, and ginger. Pour half of the marinade over shrimp in bag. Pour remaining half of marinade over chicken in bag. Seal bags, turning to coat shrimp and chicken, and marinate in the refrigerator for 1 to 2 hours, turning bags once or twice.
3. Drain shrimp and chicken; discard marinade. Thread shrimp onto four 10-inch skewers,* leaving $1/4$-inch spaces between shrimp pieces. Thread chicken strips accordion-style onto four 10-inch skewers,* leaving $1/4$-inch spaces.
4. For a charcoal grill, place shrimp and chicken skewers on the grill rack directly over medium coals. Grill, uncovered, for 6 to 10 minutes or until shrimp turn opaque and chicken is no longer pink, turning skewers once halfway through grilling. Remove skewers from the grill as they are done and keep warm. (For a gas grill, preheat grill. Reduce heat to medium. Place skewers on grill rack over heat. Cover and grill as directed.) Place one shrimp skewer and one chicken skewer on each of four serving plates.

*TEST KITCHEN TIP: If using wooden skewers, soak skewers in enough water to cover for 30 minutes before using.

PER SERVING: 166 cal., 7 g total fat (1 g sat. fat), 108 mg chol., 614 mg sodium, 3 g carb. (0 g fiber, 1 g sugars), 21 g pro. Exchanges: 3 lean meat, 1 fat.

Edamame, Vermicelli, and Watercress Salad
CARB. PER SERVING 23 g

SERVINGS 4 (1 cup watercress and about 1 cup noodle mixture each) START TO FINISH 30 minutes

- 2 ounces dried rice vermicelli or angel hair pasta
- 1 medium fennel bulb, trimmed, cored, and cut into thin strips
- 1 cup frozen shelled sweet soybeans (edamame), thawed
- 1 cup purchased coarsely shredded carrots
- 2 green onions, thinly sliced
- 3 tablespoons rice vinegar
- 1 tablespoon toasted sesame oil
- $1/4$ teaspoon crushed red pepper
- $1/8$ teaspoon salt
- 4 cups fresh watercress, tough stems removed

1. Prepare vermicelli according to package directions; drain. Place the noodles in a large bowl. Add fennel, edamame, carrots, and green onions.
2. For dressing, in a screw-top jar combine vinegar, oil, crushed red pepper, and salt. Cover and shake well. Pour over edamame mixture; toss gently to coat.
3. To serve, divide watercress among plates and top with edamame mixture.

PER SERVING: 177 cal., 6 g total fat (1 g sat. fat), 0 mg chol., 160 mg sodium, 23 g carb. (5 g fiber, 3 g sugars), 7 g pro. Exchanges: 1 vegetable, 1 starch, 1 fat.

Meal Total (per plate): 343 cal., 13 g total fat (2 g sat. fat), 108 mg chol., 774 mg sodium, 26 g carb. (5 g fiber, 4 g sugars), 28 g pro. Exchanges: 1 vegetable, 1 starch, 3 lean meat, 2 fat.

163

Jazz 'n' Jambalaya

Shrimp Jambalaya
Carb. per serving 32 g

SERVINGS 4 (1¹/₄ cups jambalaya with about 6 shrimp and ¹/₃ cup rice each)
PREP 30 minutes COOK 16 minutes

- 1 pound fresh or frozen medium shrimp
- 1 to 2 tablespoons olive oil
- 2 teaspoons salt-free Cajun seasoning
- 2 cups chopped green sweet peppers
- 1 cup chopped onion
- 1 cup chopped celery
- 2 cloves garlic, minced
- 2 cups chopped tomatoes
- 1 cup reduced-sodium chicken broth
- ¹/₄ cup no-salt-added tomato paste
- ¹/₄ teaspoon bottled hot pepper sauce
- ¹/₈ teaspoon salt
- 1 tablespoon lemon juice
- 1¹/₃ cups hot cooked brown rice
- ¹/₄ cup sliced green onions
- Salt-free Cajun seasoning (optional)

1. Thaw shrimp, if frozen. Peel and devein shrimp, leaving tails intact if desired. Rinse shrimp and pat dry with paper towels. In a very large skillet heat 1 tablespoon of the oil over medium heat. Toss shrimp with 1 teaspoon of the Cajun seasoning to coat. Cook shrimp in hot oil for 2 to 4 minutes or until shrimp are opaque, stirring frequently. Remove shrimp from skillet; keep warm.

2. If needed, heat an additional 1 tablespoon oil over medium heat. Cook the sweet peppers, onion, celery, and garlic in the hot oil for 8 to 10 minutes or until vegetables are tender, stirring occasionally. Stir in tomatoes, chicken broth, tomato paste, the remaining 1 teaspoon Cajun seasoning, the hot pepper sauce, and salt. Bring to boiling; reduce heat. Simmer, uncovered, about 6 minutes, stirring occasionally. Stir in shrimp and lemon juice; heat through.

3. Evenly divide rice among four shallow serving bowls. Evenly divide jambalaya among bowls. Top each serving with 1 tablespoon of the green onions. If desired, sprinkle with additional Cajun seasoning.

PER SERVING: 245 cal., 5 g total fat (1 g sat. fat), 121 mg chol., 712 mg sodium, 32 g carb. (6 g fiber, 9 g sugars), 18 g pro. Exchanges: 2 vegetable, 1 starch, 2 lean meat, 1 fat.

Meal Total (per plate): 245 cal., 5 g total fat (1 g sat. fat), 121 mg chol., 712 mg sodium, 32 g carb. (6 g fiber, 9 g sugars), 18 g pro. Exchanges: 2 vegetable, 1 starch, 2 lean meat, 1 fat.

Set the scene with a little jazz playing in the background when you dish up this healthful take on a Southern classic.

½ Plate

Nonstarchy Veggies: sweet peppers, onions, celery, tomatoes

¼ Plate

Starch or Grain: brown rice

¼ Plate

Protein: shrimp

Time-Saver Rather than cooking your own rice, start with a bag of cooked brown rice and heat according to the package directions.

Grilled Goodness
from the Sea

Grilled Dijon Scallops and Squash
Carb. per serving 9 g

SERVINGS 4 (3 scallops, $^1/_2$ cup squash, and
$^1/_2$ cup zucchini each)
PREP 20 minutes GRILL 4 minutes

  12 fresh or frozen sea scallops (about 1$^1/_4$ pounds total)
    1 tablespoon olive oil
    1 tablespoon Dijon-style mustard
    1 tablespoon honey
    1 tablespoon snipped fresh parsley
    1 clove garlic, minced
$^1/_4$ teaspoon black pepper
    1 medium yellow summer squash, sliced lengthwise
       into planks
    1 medium zucchini, sliced lengthwise into planks
      Fresh parsley leaves
      Lemon wedges

1. Thaw scallops, if frozen. Rinse scallops and pat dry with paper towels.

2. In a small bowl combine olive oil, mustard, honey, snipped parsley, garlic, and pepper. Brush the squash and zucchini planks with half of the olive oil mixture. Brush scallops with remaining half of the mixture.

3. For a charcoal grill, place scallops and vegetables on the greased grill rack directly over medium-hot coals. Grill, uncovered, for 4 to 6 minutes or until scallops turn opaque and vegetables are crisp-tender, turning occasionally to cook evenly. (For a gas grill, preheat grill. Reduce heat to medium-high. Place scallops and vegetables on greased grill rack directly over heat. Cover and grill as directed.)

4. Divide scallops among four serving plates. Cut up grilled squash planks and divide into four servings. Sprinkle the scallops and vegetables with additional fresh parsley and serve with lemon wedges.

PER SERVING: 155 cal., 4 g total fat (1 g sat. fat), 31 mg chol., 371 mg sodium, 9 g carb. (2 g fiber, 6 g sugars), 20 g pro. Exchanges: 1 vegetable, 3 lean meat, 0.5 fat.

Italian White Bean Salad
CARB. PER SERVING 16 g
SERVINGS 4 ($^1/_2$ cup each) PREP 15 minutes

    2 tablespoons lemon juice
    1 tablespoon olive oil
    2 cloves garlic, minced
    1 teaspoon dried rosemary, crushed
$^1/_4$ teaspoon black pepper
$^1/_8$ teaspoon salt
    1 15-ounce can no-salt-added white kidney beans
       (cannellini beans), rinsed and drained
    1 medium tomato, chopped ($^1/_2$ cup)
    2 tablespoons snipped fresh parsley
    1 teaspoon capers, drained

1. In a medium bowl whisk together lemon juice, olive oil, garlic, rosemary, pepper, and salt. Stir in beans, tomato, parsley, and capers. Divide among plates.

PER SERVING: 121 cal., 4 g total fat (1 g sat. fat), 0 mg chol., 129 mg sodium, 16 g carb. (5 g fiber, 1 g sugars), 5 g pro. Exchanges: 1 starch, 1 fat.

Meal Total (per plate):
276 cal., 8 g total fat (2 g sat. fat),
31 mg chol., 500 mg sodium,
25 g carb. (7 g fiber, 7 g sugars),
25 g pro. Exchanges: 1 vegetable,
1 starch, 3 lean meat, 1.5 fat.

Sweet and succulent sea scallops vary in size. Look for those that are about $1\frac{1}{2}$ inches across (about $1\frac{1}{2}$ ounces each).

½ Plate

Nonstarchy Veggies: zucchini, yellow summer squash, tomatoes

¼ Plate

Protein: scallops

¼ Plate

Starch or Grain: cannellini beans

167

Citrus-Splashed
Orzo & Shrimp

With a meal total of just 272 calories and 5 grams of fat, this plateful will leave you feeling full but not weighed down.

¼ Plate

Starch, Grain, or Other Carb: orzo, orange juice

½ Plate

Nonstarchy Veggies: tomatoes, zucchini

¼ Plate

Protein: shrimp, cheese

Orange-Balsamic Marinated Shrimp
Carb. per serving 6 g

SERVINGS 4 (5 shrimp each) PREP 20 minutes
MARINATE 1 hour BROIL 4 minutes

- 1 pound fresh or frozen extra-large shrimp in shells
- 2 tablespoons white balsamic vinegar
- ½ teaspoon finely shredded orange peel
- 2 tablespoons orange juice
- 2 tablespoons finely chopped shallot or onion
- 1 tablespoon olive oil
- ¼ teaspoon salt
- Finely shredded orange peel

1. Thaw shrimp, if frozen. Peel and devein shrimp, leaving tails intact if desired. Rinse shrimp and pat dry with paper towels. Place shrimp in a large resealable plastic bag set in a shallow bowl.
2. In a small bowl combine vinegar, the ½ teaspoon orange peel, the orange juice, shallot, olive oil, and salt. Pour over shrimp in bag. Seal bag, turning to coat shrimp, and marinate in the refrigerator for 1 to 4 hours, turning bag once.
3. Preheat broiler. Remove shrimp from marinade; discard marinade. Arrange shrimp on the unheated rack of a broiler pan. Broil 4 to 5 inches from the heat for 4 to 6 minutes or until shrimp are opaque, turning once halfway through broiling. Divide shrimp among four serving plates. Sprinkle with additional orange peel before serving.

PER SERVING: 120 cal., 4 g total fat (1 g sat. fat), 121 mg chol., 606 mg sodium, 6 g carb. (0 g fiber, 5 g sugars), 13 g pro. Exchanges: 0.5 fruit, 2 lean meat, 0.5 fat.

Flavor Boost Give the entire plate a squeeze of fresh orange juice and light sprinkling of snipped fresh basil or Italian (flat-leaf) parsley.

Herbed Orzo
CARB. PER SERVING 24 g
SERVINGS 4 (½ cup each) START TO FINISH 20 minutes

- ¾ cup whole wheat or regular orzo
- ½ cup halved cherry tomatoes or grape tomatoes
- ¼ cup crumbled reduced-fat feta cheese
- 2 tablespoons orange juice or reserved pasta water
- 1 tablespoon snipped fresh basil or Italian (flat-leaf) parsley
- ½ teaspoon snipped fresh thyme

1. In a medium saucepan cook orzo according to package directions, omitting any salt or oil. Drain orzo, reserving 2 tablespoons pasta cooking water if not using orange juice. Return orzo to the pan. Stir in tomatoes, feta cheese, orange juice or reserved pasta cooking water, the basil, and thyme. Heat through. Divide among plates.

PER SERVING: 135 cal., 1 g total fat (1 g sat. fat), 3 mg chol., 119 mg sodium, 24 g carb. (5 g fiber, 1 g sugars), 6 g pro. Exchanges: 1.5 starch, 0.5 fat.

Grilled Zucchini
Cut 2 medium zucchini in half lengthwise. Coat cut sides of zucchini with nonstick cooking spray. Grill or broil until just tender. To serve, slice the zucchini and sprinkle with black pepper. Divide among plates. Makes 4 servings (½ cup each).

PER SERVING: 17 cal., 0 g total fat, 0 mg chol., 8 mg sodium, 3 g carb. (1 g fiber, 2 g sugars), 1 g pro. Exchanges: 1 vegetable.

Meal Total (per plate):
272 cal., 5 g total fat (2 g sat. fat), 124 mg chol., 733 mg sodium, 33 g carb. (6 g fiber, 8 g sugars), 20 g pro. Exchanges: 1 vegetable, 0.5 fruit, 1.5 starch, 2 lean meat, 1 fat.

Soup, Salad & **Salmon**

Roasted Onion and Beet Soup with Tomato-Blue Cheese Salad
Carb. per serving 22 g

SERVINGS 4 (1 cup soup and 1$\frac{1}{4}$ cups salad each)
PREP 35 minutes ROAST 50 minutes

- 12 ounces beets, trimmed, peeled, and cut into 1-inch wedges
- $\frac{3}{4}$ cup 1-inch pieces peeled rutabaga (about 4 ounces)
- $\frac{1}{2}$ small sweet onion, cut into thin wedges (about $\frac{3}{4}$ cup)
- 1 tablespoon olive oil
- 2 medium tomatoes, cored and cut into 1-inch wedges
- 2 cups low-sodium vegetable broth
- 3 cups torn romaine lettuce
- 2 cups packaged spring salad greens mix
- $\frac{1}{4}$ cup crumbled reduced-fat blue cheese
- $\frac{1}{4}$ cup reduced-fat balsamic vinaigrette
- 2 tablespoons light sour cream
- 2 tablespoons snipped fresh chives

1. Preheat oven to 425°F. In a 3-quart rectangular baking dish combine beets, rutabaga, and onion. Drizzle with olive oil and toss to coat. Cover; roast for 35 to 40 minutes or until vegetables are nearly tender, stirring twice. Add tomato wedges to dish. Roast, uncovered, for 15 to 20 minutes more or until vegetables are tender, stirring once halfway through. Remove about half of the tomato wedges; set aside. Cool vegetables slightly.
2. Transfer beet mixture to a blender. Add vegetable broth and $\frac{1}{8}$ teaspoon *black pepper.* Cover; blend until smooth. Transfer to a medium saucepan. Heat soup through over medium heat.
3. To serve, divide greens among four plates. Top with reserved tomato wedges; sprinkle with cheese. Drizzle with vinaigrette.
4. Ladle soup into small bowls. Spoon sour cream on soup and sprinkle with chives. Place soup bowls on plates with the salad.

PER SERVING: 163 cal., 6 g total fat (2 g sat. fat), 6 mg chol., 361 mg sodium, 22 g carb. (6 g fiber, 14 g sugars), 6 g pro. Exchanges: 3.5 vegetable, 1 fat.

Spice-Rubbed Salmon
CARB. PER SERVING 0 g
SERVINGS 4 (1 portion salmon)
PREP 10 minutes BAKE 15 minutes

- 1 pound fresh or frozen salmon fillet (with skin)
- $\frac{1}{2}$ teaspoon ground coriander
- $\frac{1}{4}$ teaspoon fennel seeds, crushed

1. Thaw fish, if frozen; set aside. Preheat oven to 425°F. Line a 2-quart rectangular baking dish with foil; lightly grease foil. Rinse salmon with cold water; pat dry. Place salmon in prepared dish, skin side down. Combine coriander, fennel seeds, $\frac{1}{4}$ teaspoon *salt,* and $\frac{1}{4}$ teaspoon *black pepper.* Sprinkle evenly over salmon. Bake for 15 to 20 minutes or until salmon flakes easily.
2. Cut salmon into four portions; place one portion to each plate.

PER SERVING: 162 cal., 7 g total fat (1 g sat. fat), 62 mg chol., 196 mg sodium, 0 g carb. (0 g fiber, 0 g sugars), 20 g pro. Exchanges: 3 lean meat, 0.5 fat.

Garlic Toast
Thinly cut 4 ounces crusty whole grain bread into 8 slices; toast. Halve 1 clove garlic. Rub toast slices lightly with the cut sides of the garlic halves. Divide toast slices among plates. Makes 4 servings (2 slices each).

PER SERVING: 75 cal., 1 g total fat (0 g sat. fat), 0 mg chol., 111 mg sodium, 14 g carb. (2 g fiber, 2 g sugars), 3 g pro. Exchanges: 1 starch.

Meal Total (per plate): 400 cal., 14 g total fat (3 g sat. fat), 72 mg chol., 678 mg sodium, 36 g carb. (8 g fiber, 16 g sugars), 31 g pro. Exchanges: 3.5 vegetable, 1 starch, 3 lean meat, 1.5 fat.

Salmon is loaded with heart-healthy omega-3 fats. When teamed with veggies, it's a nutrition knockout.

¼ **Plate**

Starch or Grain: whole grain bread

½ **Plate**

Nonstarchy Veggies: beets, rutabaga, onion, tomatoes, romaine, greens

¼ **Plate**

Protein: salmon, blue cheese

171

Farmer's Market
Fish Dish

When garden-fresh veggies are in abundance at the market, gather them to create this colorful, nutritent-rich plate.

¼ Plate

Protein: grouper, feta

¼ Plate

Starch, Grain, or Other Carb: whole grain bread, corn

Nonstarchy Veggies: artichoke hearts, sweet pepper, shallot, broccoli, tomatoes

½ Plate

Grouper with Mint-Artichoke Salad
Carb. per serving 15 g

SERVINGS 4 (1 fish fillet and about $^2/_3$ cup salad each)
PREP 20 minutes BAKE 4 minutes

- 4   4- to 6-ounce fresh or frozen skinless grouper or cod fillets
- $^1/_2$ teaspoon paprika
- 2   slices whole grain bread, torn into pieces
- 2   tablespoons olive oil
- 2   6- to 6.5-ounce jars marinated artichoke hearts
- 1   medium red sweet pepper, cut into thin bite-size strips
- $^1/_4$ cup pitted Kalamata olives, coarsely chopped
- 1   tablespoon snipped fresh mint
- 1   teaspoon snipped fresh rosemary
- 1   clove garlic, minced

1. Thaw fish, if frozen. Preheat oven to 425°F. Rinse fish; pat dry. Place fish on a lightly greased baking sheet. Measure thickness of fish. In a small bowl combine paprika, $^1/_4$ teaspoon *black pepper*, and $^1/_8$ teaspoon *salt;* sprinkle over fish.
2. Place bread in a food processor; cover and pulse to make very large crumbs. You should have about $1^1/_2$ cups. Transfer crumbs to a bowl and add oil; toss to coat. Spoon bread crumbs over fish.
3. Bake fish for 4 to 6 minutes per $^1/_2$-inch thickness or until fish flakes easily when tested with a fork, tenting with foil toward the end of baking time, if needed, to avoid overbrowning.
4. Meanwhile, for artichoke salad, drain artichoke hearts reserving 1 tablespoon of the marinade. Coarsely chop artichoke hearts. In a small bowl combine artichoke hearts, reserved marinade, sweet pepper, olives, mint, rosemary, and garlic.
5. Place one fish fillet on each of four serving plates. Divide artichoke salad among plates.

PER SERVING: 280 cal., 14 g total fat (1 g sat. fat), 42 mg chol., 509 mg sodium, 15 g carb. (2 g fiber, 2 g sugars), 25 g pro. Exchanges: 1 starch, 3 lean meat, 2 fat.

Meal Total (per plate): 455 cal., 22 g total fat (3 g sat. fat), 43 mg chol., 698 mg sodium, 38 g carb. (6 g fiber, 9 g sugars), 31 g pro. Exchanges: 1 vegetable, 2 starch, 3 lean meat, 3.5 fat.

Pepper-Shallot Corn
CARB. PER SERVING 17 g
SERVINGS 4 ($^1/_3$ cup each) PREP 10 minutes COOK 7 minutes

- 2   tablespoons chopped shallot
- 2   cloves garlic, minced
- 1   tablespoon olive oil
- 2   cups fresh or frozen whole kernel corn
- $^1/_4$ cup snipped fresh parsley and/or basil
- 2   tablespoons lemon juice

1. In a medium nonstick skillet cook and stir shallot and garlic in hot oil over medium heat for 3 to 5 minutes or until just tender. Add corn; cook for 4 to 6 minutes or until corn is tender, Remove from heat. Stir in parsley, lemon juice, $^1/_4$ teaspoon *black pepper,* and pinch *salt*. Divide among plates.

PER SERVING: 105 cal., 4 g total fat (1 g sat. fat), 0 mg chol., 87 mg sodium, 17 g carb. (2 g fiber, 5 g sugars), 3 g pro. Exchanges: 1 starch, 0.5 fat.

Broccoli and Tomatoes with Feta
CARB. PER SERVING 6 g
SERVINGS 4 (1 cup each) PREP 15 minutes COOK 8 minutes

- 3   cups fresh broccoli florets
- 1   tablespoon olive oil
- 1   cup grape tomatoes or cherry tomatoes
- 2   tablespoons crumbled reduced-fat feta cheese

1. In a large skillet cook broccoli, covered, in boiling water for 3 to 5 minutes or until broccoli is crisp-tender. Drain well. Carefully wipe skillet dry.
2. Add oil to the same skillet. Heat over medium heat. Add the tomatoes. Cook and stir for 2 minutes. Add the broccoli. Cook for 3 to 5 minutes more or until broccoli is tender and tomatoes are just softened. Sprinkle with $^1/_8$ teaspoon *black pepper* and pinch *salt;* toss to coat. Divide broccoli mixture among plates. Sprinkle with feta.

PER SERVING: 70 cal., 4 g total fat (1 g sat. fat), 1 mg chol., 102 mg sodium, 6 g carb. (2 g fiber, 2 g sugars), 3 g pro. Exchanges: 1 vegetable, 1 fat.

Crab Cakes
Salad

This main-dish salad is not short on seafood; each serving includes three crisp golden cakes.

¼ Plate

Starch, Grain, or Other Carb: bread crumbs, brown rice, grapefruit

½ Plate

Nonstarchy Veggies: green onions, spinach

¼ Plate

Protein: egg, crabmeat

Spinach Salad with Grapefruit, Avocado, and Crab Cakes

Carb. per serving 38 g

SERVINGS 4 (1^1/$_2$ cups salad and 3 crab cakes each)
PREP 25 minutes **COOK** 16 minutes

- ^{3}/$_4$ cup refrigerated or frozen egg product, thawed, or 1 egg, lightly beaten
- 3 cloves garlic, minced
- ^{1}/$_4$ teaspoon crushed red pepper
- 18 ounces cooked lump crabmeat, coarsely flaked, or three 6-ounce cans crabmeat, drained, flaked, and cartilage removed
- 1^1/$_2$ cups soft whole wheat bread crumbs
- 1 cup cooked brown rice
- 3 green onions, thinly sliced
- Nonstick cooking spray
- 6 cups packaged fresh baby spinach
- 2 small red or pink grapefruit, peeled and sectioned
- 1 medium avocado, halved, seeded, peeled, and thinly sliced
- 1 recipe Lime-Ginger Vinaigrette *(right)*
- Bias-sliced green onions (optional)

1. In a large bowl combine egg, garlic, and crushed red pepper. Add crabmeat, bread crumbs, rice, and green onions. Gently mix until well combined. Using moistened hands, shape crab mixture into twelve ^{3}/$_4$-inch-thick patties, using about ^{1}/$_3$ cup for each patty.

Time-Saver Skip the task of peeling and sectioning grapefruit. Use 1^1/$_2$ cups refrigerated grapefruit sections instead.

2. Coat an unheated nonstick griddle or very large nonstick skillet with cooking spray. Heat griddle or skillet over medium heat. Add crab cakes, half at a time if necessary. Cook for 8 to 10 minutes or until golden brown and heated through, turning once. If crab cakes brown too quickly, reduce heat to medium-low.

3. Divide spinach among four serving plates. Top evenly with grapefruit sections and sliced avocado. Top each salad with three crab cakes. Shake Lime-Ginger Vinaigrette and drizzle over salads. If desired, garnish with bias sliced green onions.

LIME-GINGER VINAIGRETTE: In a small screw-top jar combine 2 tablespoons lime juice, 2 tablespoons sesame oil, 1 tablespoon honey, ^{1}/$_2$ teaspoon grated fresh ginger or ^{1}/$_4$ teaspoon ground ginger, and dash salt. Cover and shake well.

PER SERVING: 434 cal., 15 g total fat (2 g sat. fat), 97 mg chol., 698 mg sodium, 38 g carb. (7 g fiber, 12 g sugars), 39 g pro. Exchanges: 1 vegetable, 0.5 fruit, 1.5 starch, 4.5 lean meat, 1 fat.

Meal Total (per plate):

434 cal., 15 g total fat (2 g sat. fat), 97 mg chol., 698 mg sodium, 38 g carb. (7 g fiber, 12 g sugars), 39 g pro. Exchanges: 1 vegetable, 0.5 fruit, 1.5 starch, 4.5 lean meat, 1 fat.

Crispy Baked
Coconut Fish

Cod skips the frying pan for a soak in coconut milk beverage, a bread crumb-coconut coating, and a quick bake.

¹/₂ Plate

Nonstarchy Veggies: jicama, mushrooms, sweet pepper, onion, spinach

¹/₄ Plate

Starch, Grain, or Other Carb: panko, coconut, mango, orzo, kiwifruit

¹/₄ Plate

Protein: cod

Coconut-Crusted Cod with Mango-Kiwi Salsa
Carb. per serving 14 g

SERVINGS 4 (1 fish fillet with $1/4$ cup salsa each)
PREP 30 minutes MARINATE 2 hours BAKE 4 minutes

- 4 4- to 5-ounce fresh or frozen skinless cod fillets
- 1 cup refrigerated coconut milk beverage, such as Silk brand
-    Nonstick cooking spray
- $1/3$ cup whole wheat or regular panko bread crumbs
- 3 tablespoons shredded coconut
- $1/2$ cup chopped, peeled jicama or daikon
- $1/3$ cup chopped, peeled mango or pineapple
- $1/4$ cup chopped, peeled kiwifruit
- 2 teaspoons snipped fresh chives
- $1/8$ teaspoon crushed red pepper (optional)

1. Thaw fish, if frozen. Rinse fish; pat dry with paper towels. Place fish in a large resealable plastic bag. Add coconutmilk. Seal bag and turn gently to coat fish. Place bag with fish in a large bowl. Place in the refrigerator. Marinate fish for 2 to 4 hours, turning bag occasionally.

2. Preheat oven to 425°F. Line a large baking sheet with foil and coat foil with cooking spray; set aside. In a shallow dish combine bread crumbs and coconut. Drain fish, discarding the coconutmilk. Place fish on the prepared baking sheet. Measure thickness of fish. Sprinkle fish with $1/2$ teaspoon *salt* and $1/4$ teaspoon *black pepper*. Sprinkle bread crumb mixture over fish, pressing coating onto fish to adhere. Lightly coat top of fish with cooking spray.

3. Bake fish for 4 to 6 minutes per $1/2$-inch thickness or until fish flakes easily when tested with a fork, tenting with foil toward the end of baking time, if needed, to avoid overbrowning.

Meal Total (per plate): 406 cal., 15 g total fat (4 g sat. fat), 49 mg chol., 696 mg sodium, 41 g carb. (9 g fiber, 9 g sugars), 28 g pro. Exchanges: 1.5 vegetable, 1 starch, 1 carb., 3 lean meat, 2 fat.

4. Meanwhile, for salsa, in a small bowl combine jicama, mango, kiwifruit, chives, and, if desired, crushed red pepper. Place one fish fillet on each of four serving plates. Serve salsa over fish.

PER SERVING: 180 cal., 4 g total fat (3 g sat. fat), 49 mg chol., 383 mg sodium, 14 g carb. (2 g fiber, 6 g sugars), 22 g pro. Exchanges: 1 carb., 3 lean meat.

Vegetable and Cilantro Pesto Orzo Salad
CARB. PER SERVING 27 g
SERVINGS 4 (1 cup salad each) PREP 25 minutes
COOK 5 minutes COOL 10 minutes

- $3/4$ cup dried whole wheat or regular orzo (4 ounces)
- 2 cups sliced fresh button mushrooms
- 1 medium red or yellow sweet pepper, cut into bite-size strips
- $1/2$ cup chopped onion
- 1 tablespoon olive oil
- $3/4$ cup firmly packed fresh cilantro
- $1/4$ cup firmly packed fresh mint
- $1/4$ cup firmly packed fresh Italian (flat-leaf) parsley
- 3 cloves garlic, minced
- 2 tablespoons olive oil
- 1 tablespoon water
- 2 cups chopped fresh spinach, arugula, and/or watercress (about 4 ounces)

1. Cook orzo according to package directions. Drain and rinse with cold water. Drain well; set aside.

2. Meanwhile, in a large skillet cook mushrooms, sweet pepper, and onion in hot oil over medium heat for 5 to 8 minutes or until crisp-tender and edges are starting to brown, stirring occasionally. Remove from heat and let cool about 10 minutes; set aside.

3. For pesto, in a food processor combine cilantro, mint, parsley, garlic, $1/2$ teaspoon *salt,* and $1/4$ teaspoon *black pepper*. Cover and pulse with several on-off turns until herb mixture is very finely chopped. Add oil and water. Cover and process until nearly smooth but still a little chunky.

4. In a large bowl combine orzo, vegetables, and pesto. Add spinach and stir gently to mix. Divide among plates.

PER SERVING: 226 cal., 11 g total fat (1 g sat. fat), 0 mg chol., 313 mg sodium, 27 g carb. (7 g fiber, 3 g sugars), 6 g pro. Exchanges: 1.5 vegetable, 1 starch, 2 fat.

Meatless

Every meal need not include meat. Eggs, tofu, and grains can step in as the lean protein. And they are ultimately healthful and filling.

179

Salad in a Wrap

Making your own hummus helps control the amount of sodium in the spread. Serve the extra with vegetable dippers as a snack.

½ Plate

Nonstarchy Veggies: greens, tomato, onion, cucumber, banana peppers

¼ Plate

Protein: cheese, hummus

¼ Plate

Starch or Grain: wrap

Mediterranean Veggie Wrap
Carb. per serving 35 g

SERVINGS 4 (1 wrap each)
START TO FINISH 20 minutes

- 4 cups mixed baby greens
- ½ of a large cucumber, halved lengthwise and sliced (1 cup)
- 1 cup chopped tomato
- ½ cup thinly sliced red onion
- ¼ cup crumbled reduced-fat feta cheese
- 2 tablespoons bottled sliced mild banana peppers
- 1 tablespoon balsamic vinegar
- 1 tablespoon olive oil
- 1 clove garlic, minced
- ¼ teaspoon black pepper
- 4 8-inch light tomato-flavor oval multigrain wraps
- ⅔ cup Cilantro Hummus *(below)*

1. In a large bowl combine greens, cucumber, tomato, red onion, feta cheese, and banana peppers. In a small bowl whisk together vinegar, olive oil, garlic, and black pepper. Pour dressing mixture over greens mixture. Toss to combine.

2. Spread each wrap with about 2½ tablespoons of the Cilantro Hummus. Top each with one-fourth of the dressed greens mixture. Roll up. Serve immediately.

CILANTRO HUMMUS: With the motor running, drop 1 clove peeled garlic through the feed tube of a food processor fitted with a steel blade attachment; process until finely minced. Scrape down sides of bowl. Rinse and drain one 15-ounce can no-salt-added garbanzo beans (chickpeas). Add garbanzo beans, 3 tablespoons lemon juice, 2 tablespoons olive oil, 1 tablespoon tahini (sesame seed paste), ¼ teaspoon salt, and ¼ teaspoon white pepper. Process until smooth, stopping to scrape down sides as necessary. Add ¼ cup fresh cilantro leaves. Pulse until cilantro is evenly distributed and chopped. Chill any remaining hummus for up to 3 days and serve with vegetable dippers.

PER SERVING: 269 cal., 12 g total fat (2 g sat. fat), 3 mg chol., 574 mg sodium, 35 g carb. (13 g fiber, 3 g sugars), 16 g pro. Exchanges: 2 vegetable, 1.5 starch, 1.5 lean meat, 2 fat

Flavor Boost Add a pinch of crushed red pepper to the dressing mixture. For even more heat, add a bit of the pepper to the hummus, too.

Meal Total (per plate): 269 cal., 12 g total fat (2 g sat. fat), 3 mg chol., 547 mg sodium, 35 g carb. (13 g fiber, 3 g sugars), 16 g pro. Exchanges: 2 vegetable, 1.5 starch, 1.5 lean meat, 2 fat.

Caribbean
Tofu & Beans

Caribbean Tofu with Black Beans and Rice
Carb. per serving 31 g

SERVINGS 4 (1 slice tofu and $^2/_3$ cup rice mixture each)
PREP 20 minutes **MARINATE** 30 minutes **COOK** 16 minutes

- 1 8-ounce can pineapple tidbits (juice pack)
- $^1/_4$ cup snipped fresh cilantro
- 2 tablespoons tamarind paste
- 2 tablespoons canola oil
- 2 cloves garlic, minced
- $^1/_4$ teaspoon salt
- $^1/_4$ teaspoon black pepper
- 16 to 18 ounces firm or extra-firm water-pack tofu (fresh bean curd), drained and cut into 4 lengthwise slices
- $^1/_3$ cup quick-cooking brown rice
- $^2/_3$ cup water
- 1 cup canned lower-sodium black beans, rinsed and drained
- 2 green onions, thinly sliced
- $^1/_4$ teaspoon crushed red pepper
  Lime wedges (optional)
  Fresh cilantro sprigs (optional)

1. Drain pineapple, reserving juice. In a 2-quart shallow baking dish combine pineapple juice, 2 tablespoons of the snipped cilantro, the tamarind, oil, garlic, salt, and black pepper. Add tofu; turn to coat. Marinate at room temperature for 30 minutes, turning tofu once halfway through.

2. Meanwhile, in a small saucepan combine rice and the water. Bring to boiling; reduce heat. Simmer, covered, for 10 to 12 minutes or until rice is done.

3. Coat an unheated nonstick grill pan with *nonstick cooking spray*. Preheat over medium-high heat. Transfer tofu slices to grill pan, reserving marinade in the baking dish. Cook tofu about 6 minutes or until heated through and browned, turning once halfway through cooking.

4. Add drained pineapple, the reserved marinade from dish, the black beans, green onions, the remaining snipped cilantro, and the crushed red pepper to cooked rice in saucepan, stirring to combine. Return to heat to warm.

5. Place tofu slices on four serving plates. Serve with rice mixture. If desired, garnish with lime wedges and cilantro sprigs.

PER SERVING: 282 cal., 12 g total fat (1 g sat. fat), 0 mg chol., 314 mg sodium, 31 g carb. (5 g fiber, 9 g sugars), 15 g pro. Exchanges: 0.5 fruit, 1.5 starch, 2 lean meat, 1.5 fat.

Steamed Sugar Snap Peas

Remove strings and tips from 3 cups sugar snap peas (about 9 ounces). Place steamer basket in a saucepan. Add water to just below the bottom of the basket. Bring water to boiling. Add snap peas to steamer basket. Cover pan; reduce heat. Steam peas for 2 to 4 minutes or until crisp-tender. Spoon snap peas onto plates. Makes 4 servings ($^3/_4$ cup each).

PER SERVING: 20 cal., 0 g total fat, 0 mg chol., 2 mg sodium, 4 g carb. (1 g fiber, 2 g sugars), 1 g pro. Exchanges: 1 vegetable.

Meal Total (per plate):
302 cal., 12 g total fat (1 g sat. fat), 0 mg chol., 316 mg sodium, 35 g carb. (6 g fiber, 11 g sugars), 16 g pro. Exchanges: 1 vegetable, 0.5 fruit, 1.5 starch, 2 lean meat, 1.5 fat.

If you don't own a stove-top grill pan, cook the tofu in a large nonstick skillet. The slices will have seared browned sides instead of grill marks to lock in the flavor.

¼ Plate

Starch, Grain, or Other Carb: brown rice, pineapple, black beans

¼ Plate

Protein: tofu, black beans

½ Plate

Nonstarchy Veggies: sugar snap peas

183

Italian-Style Brunch

Radicchio is an Italian red-leaf head lettuce that has a sharp, almost bitter flavor. If you can't find it, substitute red cabbage or other leafy greens.

¼ Plate

Starch, Grain, or Other Carb: bread, pear

½ Plate

Nonstarchy Veggies: radicchio, spinach, onions, sweet pepper, tomato

¼ Plate

Protein: eggs, cheese, pine nuts

Tomato and Olive Dinner Frittata
Carb. per serving 7 g

SERVINGS 4 (^{1}/4 of the frittata each) **PREP** 20 minutes
COOK 10 minutes **BROIL** 2 minutes **STAND** 5 minutes

- ^{3}/4 cup bite-size strips red sweet pepper
- ^{1}/2 cup chopped onion
- 1 tablespoon olive oil
- 1^1/2 cups refrigerated or frozen egg product, thawed, or 6 eggs, lightly beaten
- ^{1}/2 cup finely shredded Parmesan cheese (2 ounces)
- 2 tablespoons snipped fresh parsley
- 1 tablespoon snipped fresh oregano
- ^{1}/4 cup pitted Kalamata olives, thinly sliced
- 1 medium roma tomato, thinly sliced

1. Preheat broiler. In a small broilerproof nonstick skillet cook sweet pepper and onion in hot oil over medium heat just until tender. In a bowl combine eggs, half of the cheese, the parsley, oregano, and ^{1}/4 teaspoon *black pepper*. Pour egg mixture over sweet pepper mixture. Stir in olives. Cook over medium heat. As mixture sets, run a spatula around edge, lifting egg mixture so uncooked portion flows underneath. Continue cooking and lifting edge until egg mixture is almost set (surface will be moist). Arrange tomato slices on top. Sprinkle with remaining cheese.
2. Broil 4 to 5 inches from the heat for 2 to 3 minutes or until center is set. Let stand for 5 minutes. Cut into four wedges to serve.

PER SERVING: 152 cal., 7 g total fat (2 g sat. fat), 7 mg chol., 440 mg sodium, 7 g carb. (2 g fiber, 4 g sugars), 14 g pro. Exchanges: 1 vegetable, 2 lean meat, 1 fat.

Radicchio-Red Onion Salad
CARB. PER SERVING 17 g

SERVINGS 4 (2 cups each) **START TO FINISH** 20 minutes

- 1 medium head radicchio, trimmed and coarsely chopped
- 3 cups packaged fresh baby spinach
- 1 medium pear, cored, quartered, and thinly sliced
- ^{1}/2 of a medium red onion, halved and thinly sliced
- ^{1}/4 cup white wine vinegar
- 1 tablespoon olive oil
- 1 tablespoon honey
- 1 teaspoon Dijon-style mustard
- ^{1}/4 cup pine nuts, toasted

1. In a large bowl combine radicchio, spinach, pear, and red onion. For dressing, in a screw-top jar combine vinegar, oil, honey, mustard, and ^{1}/8 teaspoon *salt*. Cover and shake well. Pour over radicchio mixture; toss to coat. Divide salad among plates. Sprinkle with nuts.

PER SERVING: 160 cal., 9 g total fat (1 g sat. fat), 0 mg chol., 147 mg sodium, 17 g carb. (3 g fiber, 10 g sugars), 3 g pro. Exchanges: 1 vegetable, 0.5 fruit, 2 fat.

Baguette Slices
Cut 4 ounces whole grain baguette-style bread into eight slices; toast. Place two slices on each plate. Makes 4 servings (2 slices each).

PER SERVING: 70 cal., 1 g total fat (0 g sat. fat), 0 mg chol., 120 mg sodium, 13 g carb. (1 g fiber, 1 g sugars), 2 g pro. Exchanges: 1 starch.

Meal Total (per plate): 382 cal., 17 g total fat (3 g sat. fat), 7 mg chol., 707 mg sodium, 37 g carb. (6 g fiber, 15 g sugars), 19 g pro. Exchanges: 2 vegetable, 0.5 fruit, 1 starch, 2 lean meat, 3 fat.

Peanutty Stir-Fry & Quinoa Bowls

Quinoa is a cholesterol-free and low-fat source of protein, making it a great substitute for cooked rice in any stir-fried meal.

Spicy Peanut-Sauced Tofu Stir-Fry
Carb. per serving 26 g

SERVINGS 4 ($1^1/2$ cups stir-fry each)
START TO FINISH 30 minutes

- 12 to 14 ounces light extra-firm tofu (fresh bean curd), drained
- 1 tablespoon olive oil
- $^1/2$ cup cold water
- 2 teaspoons cornstarch
- $^1/3$ cup creamy peanut butter
- $^1/4$ cup reduced-sodium soy sauce
- $^1/4$ cup rice vinegar
- 2 tablespoons honey
- 1 tablespoon grated fresh ginger
- $^1/4$ teaspoon crushed red pepper
- 2 cloves garlic, minced
- 2 medium red sweet peppers, cut into strips
- 1 medium red onion, cut into thin wedges
- 4 cups sliced bok choy
- Crushed red pepper (optional)

1. Drain tofu; pat dry with paper towels. Cut tofu into 1-inch cubes. In a very large skillet heat 1 teaspoon of the olive oil. Add tofu cubes; cook on one side about 6 minutes or until browned and slightly crisp. Gently turn over the tofu and add another 1 teaspoon of the oil. Continue cooking until all sides are browned and slightly crisp. Using a spatula, transfer tofu to a bowl.

2. For peanut sauce, in a small saucepan stir the cold water into the cornstarch. Stir in peanut butter, soy sauce, rice vinegar, honey, ginger, and the $^1/4$ teaspoon crushed red pepper. Cook and stir over medium heat until thickened and bubbly; cook and stir for 1 minute more. Set aside.

3. In the same skillet heat the remaining 1 teaspoon oil over medium-high heat. Add garlic, sweet peppers, and red onion; cook and stir for 5 minutes. Add bok choy; cook and stir for 2 to 3 minutes more. Add the browned tofu and the peanut sauce; stir gently to coat and heat through. Divide the tofu mixture among four serving plates. If desired, sprinkle with additional crushed red pepper.

PER SERVING: 292 cal., 15 g total fat (3 g sat. fat), 0 mg chol., 770 mg sodium, 26 g carb. (4 g fiber, 18 g sugars), 13 g pro. Exchanges: 2 vegetable, 0.5 starch, 0.5 carb., 1.5 lean meat, 2.5 fat.

Quinoa

In a medium saucepan bring $1^1/2$ cups water to boiling. Add $^3/4$ cup rinsed and drained quinoa. Reduce heat. Cover and simmer about 15 minutes or until done. Drain any excess water. Divide quinoa among plates. Makes 4 servings ($^1/2$ cup each).

PER SERVING: 117 cal., 2 g total fat (0 g sat. fat), 0 mg chol., 4 mg sodium, 20 g carb. (2 g fiber, 0 g sugars), 5 g pro. Exchanges: 1.5 starch.

Meal Total (per plate): 409 cal., 17 g total fat (3 g sat. fat), 0 mg chol., 774 mg sodium, 46 g carb. (6 g fiber, 18 g sugars), 18 g pro. Exchanges: 2 vegetable, 2 starch, 0.5 carb., 1.5 lean meat, 2.5 fat.

Make It Mine To vary the color and flavor, swap farro or red quinoa for the quinoa and trade small broccoli florets for the bok choy.

¼ Plate

Protein: tofu, peanut butter, quinoa

¼ Plate

Starch or Grain: quinoa

½ Plate

Nonstarchy Veggies: sweet peppers, onion, bok choy

187

Summertime
Salad Plate

Fresh Egg Salad
Carb. per serving 4 g

SERVINGS 4 (1/2 cup each)
START TO FINISH 15 minutes

4 hard-cooked eggs, chopped
1 cup chopped cucumber
1/2 cup sliced green onions (4)
1/3 cup plain low-fat Greek yogurt
1 teaspoon dried dill weed, crushed
1/4 teaspoon salt
1/4 teaspoon black pepper

1. In a medium bowl stir together eggs, cucumber, green onions, yogurt, dill weed, salt, and pepper. Serve immediately or cover and chill for up to 2 hours. Divide among four serving plates.

PER SERVING: 101 cal., 6 g total fat (2 g sat. fat), 188 mg chol., 218 mg sodium, 4 g carb. (1 g fiber, 2 g sugars), 9 g pro. Exchanges: 1 vegetable, 1 medium-fat meat.

Rye Cocktail Bread
Place 3 slices whole grain rye cocktail bread on each plate.

PER SERVING: 80 cal., 2 g total fat (0 g sat. fat), 0 mg chol., 180 mg sodium, 14 g carb. (2 g fiber, 2 g sugars), 3 g pro. Exchanges: 1 starch.

Cucumber-Tomato Salad
CARB. PER SERVING 12 g
SERVINGS 4 (2 cups each) **START TO FINISH** 20 minutes

4 cups cucumber chunks
4 cups halved cherry tomatoes
1/4 cup bottled red wine vinaigrette
Dash black pepper

1. In a large bowl combine cucumbers and tomatoes. Drizzle with vinaigrette and toss to coat. Divide among plates. Sprinkle individual servings with pepper.

PER SERVING: 93 cal., 5 g total fat (0 g sat. fat), 0 mg chol., 251 mg sodium, 12 g carb. (3 g fiber, 7 g sugars), 2 g pro. Exchanges: 2 vegetable, 1 fat.

Meal Total (per plate): 274 cal., 13 g total fat (2 g sat. fat), 188 mg chol., 649 mg sodium, 30 g carb. (6 g fiber, 11 g sugars), 14 g pro. Exchanges: 3 vegetable, 1 starch, 1 medium-fat meat, 1 fat.

Two fresh and flavorful salads combine to create a colorful, no-cook summertime meal.

¼ Plate

Starch or Grain: rye bread

½ Plate

Nonstarchy Veggies: tomatoes, cucumbers, green onions

¼ Plate

Protein: egg, Greek yogurt

Time-Saver Wash and prep the vegetables; place in bags or covered containers and refrigerate. Toss the mixture just before serving.

189

Sizzlin' Burgers & Slaw

Cooked lentils provide lean protein and meatlike texture in these pan-fried burgers.

½ Plate

Nonstarchy Veggies: broccoli slaw mix, onion, tomato, lettuce

¼ Plate

Starch or Grain: whole wheat bun

¼ Plate

Protein: lentils, almonds, egg

Almond-Lentil Burgers
Carb. per serving 31 g

SERVINGS 4 (1 burger patty and 1 bun each)
PREP 25 minutes **STAND** 20 minutes **COOK** 10 minutes

- 1 medium carrot
- 1/4 of a medium red onion
- 5 teaspoons olive oil
- 1 stalk celery, finely chopped
- 3 cloves garlic, minced
- 5 low-calorie whole wheat hamburger buns (such as Sara Lee Delightful Wheat brand)
- 1/3 cup sliced almonds, toasted
- 2 teaspoons fresh oregano leaves
- 1 teaspoon finely shredded lemon peel
- 3/4 cup cooked lentils*
- 1 egg or 1/4 cup refrigerated or frozen egg product, thawed
- 4 lettuce leaves
- 4 tomato slices
- 4 thin slices red onion

1. Using a large-hole grater, grate the carrot and the one-fourth onion. In a small skillet heat 2 teaspoons of the oil over medium heat. Cook and stir grated vegetables, celery, and garlic in hot oil for 4 to 5 minutes or until just crisp-tender. Remove from heat; set aside.

2. In a food processor process one of the hamburger buns to coarse crumbs. Measure out 1/2 cup; discard any remaining crumbs. Return the 1/2 cup crumbs to the food processor along with the almonds, oregano, lemon peel, half of the lentils, and 1/4 teaspoon each *salt* and *black pepper*. Process until finely ground.

3. In a large bowl whisk egg. Add processed mixture, unprocessed lentils, and cooked carrot mixture; mix until combined. Let mixture stand for 20 minutes. Divide mixture into four portions; roll into balls and flatten into 3/4-inch-thick patties.

4. Toast remaining 4 buns. In a large nonstick skillet heat remaining 3 teaspoons oil. Add burger patties. Cook over medium heat for 6 to 8 minutes or until crisp and browned and internal temperature reaches 160°F, turning once halfway through cooking time. To serve, place burgers on toasted bun bottoms and top with lettuce leaves, tomato slices, onion slices, and toasted bun tops..

***TEST KITCHEN TIP:** Cook lentils according to package directions.

PER SERVING: 274 cal., 12 g total fat (2 g sat. fat), 47 mg chol., 372 mg sodium, 31 g carb. (12 g fiber, 6 g sugars), 12 g pro. Exchanges: 1 vegetable, 1.5 starch, 1 lean meat, 2 fat.

Lemony Broccoli Slaw
CARB. PER SERVING 12 g

SERVINGS 4 (1 cup each) **PREP** 15 minutes **CHILL** 1 hour

- 2 tablespoons light mayonnaise
- 2 tablespoons plain low-fat yogurt
- 1 tablespoon honey
- 1/4 teaspoon finely shredded lemon peel
- 1 teaspoon lemon juice
- 1 teaspoon cider vinegar
- 4 cups packaged shredded broccoli (broccoli slaw mix)
- 1/4 cup thinly sliced red onion
- 2 tablespoons snipped fresh parsley
- 1 tablespoon sliced almonds, toasted

1. In a large bowl combine mayonnaise, yogurt, honey, lemon peel, lemon juice, vinegar, and 1/4 teaspoon each *salt* and *black pepper*. Add broccoli, red onion, and parsley. Stir until combined. Cover; chill for 1 to 4 hours.

2. To serve, divide mixture evenly among plates and sprinkle with almonds.

PER SERVING: 84 cal., 3 g total fat (1 g sat. fat), 3 mg chol., 225 mg sodium, 12 g carb. (2 g fiber, 8 g sugars), 3 g pro. Exchanges: 2 vegetable, 0.5 fat.

Meal Total (per plate):
358 cal., 15 g total fat (3 g sat. fat), 50 mg chol., 597 mg sodium, 43 g carb. (14 g fiber, 14 g sugars), 15 g pro. Exchanges: 3 vegetable, 1.5 starch, 1 lean meat, 2.5 fat.

Risotto
Veggie Bowls

Farro Risotto with Butternut Squash
Carb. per serving 36 g

SERVINGS 4 (^{3}/4 cup each)
PREP 25 minutes SOAK 30 minutes COOK 35 minutes

- ^{2}/3 cup farro
- 4 cups water
- 3 cups low-sodium vegetable broth
- 1 tablespoon olive oil
- 1 tablespoon butter
- 2 cups chopped, peeled butternut squash
- 1 small onion, chopped
- 3 cloves garlic, minced
- ^{1}/3 cup white wine or low-sodium vegetable broth
- ^{1}/3 cup finely shredded Parmesan cheese
- 1 tablespoon snipped fresh sage
- Fresh sage leaves and/or finely shredded Parmesan cheese (optional)

1. In a medium bowl mix together farro and the water. Soak for 30 minutes. Drain well.

2. In a medium saucepan heat the 3 cups broth and keep warm over low heat.

3. In a large saucepan heat olive oil and butter over medium heat. Add squash, onion, garlic, ^{1}/4 teaspoon *salt,* and ^{1}/4 teaspoon *black pepper;* cook and stir for 5 to 6 minutes or until onion is just softened. Add the drained farro and cook, stirring constantly, about 3 minutes or until toasted. Add wine and stir constantly about 2 minutes or until liquid is evaporated. Add ^{1}/2 cup of the hot broth and stir constantly until completely absorbed. Continue adding the remaining broth, ^{1}/2 cup at a time, until the farro is creamy and just tender, about 25 minutes total. Remove from heat and stir in the ^{1}/3 cup shredded Parmesan cheese and 1 tablespoon snipped fresh sage.

4. Spoon risotto onto four serving plates. If desired, garnish with additional fresh sage and/or finely shredded Parmesan cheese.

PER SERVING: 267 cal., 8 g total fat (3 g sat. fat), 12 mg chol., 415 mg sodium, 36 g carb. (5 g fiber, 4 g sugars), 8 g pro. Exchanges: 1 vegetable, 2 starch, 0.5 lean meat, 1.5 fat.

Vegetable Medley
CARB. PER SERVING 12 g
SERVINGS 4 (1^1/2 cups each)
PREP 25 minutes ROAST 25 minutes

- 1 small eggplant, cut into 1-inch cubes (about 1 pound)
- 2 cups fresh mushrooms, halved (6 ounces)
- 1 medium red sweet pepper, cut into bite-size strips
- 1 medium red onion, sliced
- 1 tablespoon olive oil
- 3 cloves garlic, minced
- 2 teaspoons snipped fresh sage or ^{1}/2 teaspoon dried sage, crushed
- ^{1}/4 teaspoon salt
- ^{1}/4 teaspoon black pepper

1. Preheat oven to 425°F. In a 15×10×1-inch baking pan place eggplant, mushrooms, sweet pepper, and red onion. In a small bowl combine olive oil, garlic, sage, salt, and black pepper. Drizzle over vegetables, tossing to coat.

2. Roast, uncovered, about 25 minutes or until vegetables are tender, stirring twice.

PER SERVING: 87 cal., 4 g total fat (1 g sat. fat), 0 mg chol., 152 mg sodium, 12 g carb. (5 g fiber, 6 g sugars), 3 g pro. Exchanges: 2 vegetable, 0.5 fat.

Meal Total (per plate):
354 cal., 12 g total fat (4 g sat. fat), 12 mg chol., 567 mg sodium, 48 g carb. (10 g fiber, 10 g sugars), 11 g pro. Exchanges: 3 vegetable, 2 starch, 0.5 lean meat, 2 fat.

Farro, a grain with a nutty flavor similar to brown rice, takes the place of traditional Arborio rice in this squash-studded risotto.

½ **Plate**

Nonstarchy Veggies: eggplant, onions, mushrooms, sweet pepper

¼ **Plate**

Starch, Grain, or Other Carb: farro, squash, white wine

¼ **Plate**

Protein: farro, cheese

A Squash
Full of Yum

Vegetable lovers will dig this baked squash half that's brimming with spiced, pan-roasted veggies.

¼ Plate

Starch, Grain, or Other Carb: acorn squash

½ Plate

Nonstarchy Veggies: cauliflower, onion, Swiss chard

¼ Plate

Protein: pine nuts, tofu

Spiced Acorn Squash with Pan-Roasted Cauliflower and Greens
Carb. per serving 31 g

SERVINGS 4 (1 squash half, 1¼ cups cauliflower mixture, about ½ cup chard, and ½ tablespoon pine nuts each)
PREP 35 minutes **BAKE** 40 minutes **COOK** 13 minutes

2	1- to 1¼-pound acorn squash, halved and scooped out
½	teaspoon ground coriander
¼	teaspoon crushed red pepper
¼	teaspoon ground allspice
¼	teaspoon ground cumin
1½	tablespoons canola oil
6	cups cauliflower florets
1	small onion, cut into thin wedges
8	cups coarsely torn Swiss chard
1	clove garlic, minced
⅓	cup reduced-fat unsweetened coconut milk
2	tablespoons pine nuts, toasted, or roasted unsalted pistachio nuts
2	ounces reduced-fat feta cheese, crumbled (optional)

1. Preheat oven to 350°F. Line a shallow baking pan with parchment paper or foil. Place squash halves, cut sides down, in prepared pan. Bake for 30 minutes.
2. Combine coriander, ¼ teaspoon *salt,* red pepper, allspice, and cumin. Turn squash cut sides up. Sprinkle with spice mixture. Bake, uncovered, for 10 to 15 minutes more or until tender.
3. Meanwhile, add oil to a very large nonstick skillet; preheat over medium heat. Add cauliflower and onion; sprinkle with ¼ teaspoon *black pepper* and ⅛ teaspoon *salt.* Cook cauliflower, covered, over medium heat for 5 minutes, stirring once. Uncover and cook for 5 to 8 minutes more or until cauliflower is just tender, stirring occasionally. Remove cauliflower mixture from the pan and keep warm.
4. Add chard and garlic to the same pan. Cook about 2 minutes or until chard is tender, tossing occasionally with tongs. Remove from heat. Add coconut milk. To serve, place one squash half, cut side up, on each of four serving plates. Spoon chard mixture evenly into squash bowls and top with cauliflower mixture. Sprinkle evenly with pine nuts and, if desired, feta cheese.

PER SERVING: 217 cal., 10 g total fat (2 g sat. fat), 0 mg chol., 427 mg sodium, 31 g carb. (7 g fiber, 5 g sugars), 7 g pro. Exchanges: 2.5 vegetable, 1 starch, 2 fat.

Miso-Sesame Grilled Tofu
CARB. PER SERVING 6 g
SERVINGS 4 (2 slices each) **PREP** 15 minutes
MARINATE 2 hours **GRILL** 4 minutes

1	18-ounce package firm tofu (fresh bean curd)
⅓	cup rice vinegar
2	tablespoons sesame oil
1	tablespoon white miso paste
2	cloves garlic, minced
¼	teaspoon crushed red pepper
1	teaspoon sesame seeds, toasted

1. Place a large resealable plastic bag in a shallow baking dish. Drain tofu and pat dry with paper towels. Cut tofu crosswise into four slices; cut each slice in half to make a total of eight slices. Place tofu in the bag. In a small bowl whisk together vinegar, oil, miso paste, garlic, and crushed red pepper. Drizzle evenly over tofu. Seal bag. Turn to coat tofu with marinade. Marinate in the refrigerator for 2 to 3 hours, turning tofu occasionally.
2. Coat an unheated stove-top grill pan with *nonstick cooking spray.* Heat pan over medium heat. Drain tofu, discarding excess marinade. Add tofu to hot pan. Grill for 4 to 6 minutes or until tofu is heated through and browned, turning once. Sprinkle with sesame seeds and divide among plates.

PER SERVING: 164 cal., 11 g total fat (2 g sat. fat), 0 mg chol., 165 mg sodium, 6 g carb. (0 g fiber, 3 g sugars), 9 g pro. Exchanges: 0.5 carb., 1.5 lean meat, 1.5 fat.

Meal Total (per plate): 381 cal., 21 g total fat (4 g sat. fat), 0 mg chol., 592 mg sodium, 37 g carb. (7 g fiber, 8 g sugars), 16 g pro. Exchanges: 2.5 vegetable, 0.5 carb., 1 starch, 1.5 lean meat, 3.5 fat.

So-Easy
Egg Sandwiches

Open-Face English Muffin Omelet Sandwiches
Carb. per serving 23 g

SERVINGS 4 (1 sandwich each)
PREP 20 minutes **COOK** 14 minutes

  1 large red, yellow, or orange sweet pepper, cut into bite-size strips
  1 medium zucchini, trimmed, quartered lengthwise, and thinly sliced crosswise
  1 small red onion, chopped
  2 tablespoons olive oil
  8 ounces fresh asparagus, trimmed and cut into 1-inch pieces
  2 cups trimmed, chopped fresh kale or Swiss chard
  1/4 teaspoon salt
  1/4 teaspoon black pepper
  1/3 cup light semisoft cheese with garlic and fine herbs
  2 tablespoons fat-free milk
  6 eggs*
  2 egg whites*
  1/3 cup water
  2 whole wheat English muffins, split and toasted

1. In a large nonstick skillet with flared sides cook sweet pepper, zucchini, and onion in 1 tablespoon of the olive oil over medium heat for 5 minutes, stirring occasionally. Add asparagus, kale, salt, and black pepper. Cook for 3 to 5 minutes more or until vegetables are just tender, stirring occasionally. Remove vegetables from skillet and keep warm.

2. Meanwhile, in a small saucepan combine cheese and milk. Stir over medium-low heat until warm. Keep warm.

3. In a medium bowl combine eggs, egg whites, and the water. Using a fork, beat until combined but not frothy. Heat the same large skillet over medium-high heat until skillet is hot.

4. Add half of the remaining oil to the hot skillet. Add half of the egg mixture and 1/2 cup of the vegetable mixture to the skillet; reduce heat to medium. Immediately begin stirring the egg mixture gently but continuously with a wooden or plastic spatula until mixture resembles small pieces of cooked egg surrounded by liquid egg. Stop stirring. Cook for 30 to 60 seconds more or until egg is set and shiny.

5. Using a butter knife, carefully cut the omelet in half. With a spatula, lift and fold each omelet half in half. Remove the folded omelet pieces from the skillet and keep warm. Repeat with remaining oil, remaining egg mixture, and 1/2 cup more of the vegetable mixture.

6. To serve, place an English muffin half on each of four serving plates. Top with remaining vegetable mixture, dividing evenly. Top each with a folded omelet half. Drizzle with cheese sauce and serve warm.

*TEST KITCHEN TIP: If desired, omit the eggs and egg whites and substitute 1 3/4 cups refrigerated or frozen egg product, thawed.

PER SERVING: 333 cal., 19 g total fat (6 g sat. fat), 293 mg chol., 527 mg sodium, 23 g carb. (5 g fiber, 9 g sugars), 19 g pro. Exchanges: 1 vegetable, 1 starch, 1.5 lean meat, 3 fat.

Meal Total (per plate): 333 cal., 19 g total fat (6 g sat. fat), 293 mg chol., 527 mg sodium, 23 g carb. (5 g fiber, 9 g sugars), 19 g pro. Exchanges: 1 vegetable, 1 starch, 1.5 lean meat, 3 fat.

Grab a knife and fork—this open-face sandwich is stacked; no picking up necessary!

¼ Plate

Protein: eggs, cheese

½ Plate

Nonstarchy Veggies: sweet pepper, zucchini, red onion, asparagus, kale

¼ Plate

Starch or Grain: whole wheat English muffin

197

Fresh Falafels

Lemon mayo brightens each bite of these classically crunchy chickpea patties.

½ Plate

Nonstarchy Veggies: carrots, red onion, summer squash, asparagus, spinach, green onions

¼ Plate

Protein: garbanzo beans, pistachio nuts

¼ Plate

Starch, Grain, or Other Carb: garbanzo beans, panko

Olive-Pistachio Falafels with Lemon Mayonnaise
Carb. per serving 38 g

SERVINGS 6 (3 falafels and 2 tablespoons mayonnaise each)
PREP 40 minutes **BAKE** 15 minutes

- 3 cups rinsed and drained canned no-salt-added garbanzo beans (chickpeas)
- 1/2 cup thinly sliced green onions (4)
- 1/4 cup chopped pitted Kalamata olives
- 1/4 cup chopped pimiento-stuffed green olives
- 1/4 cup snipped fresh Italian (flat-leaf) parsley
- 3 tablespoons whole wheat pastry flour or all-purpose flour
- 3 cloves garlic, minced
- 1/4 teaspoon salt
- 1/4 teaspoon ground cumin
- 1/4 teaspoon black pepper
- 2 egg whites
- 2 tablespoons water
- 1/2 cup whole wheat or regular panko bread crumbs
- 1/2 cup very finely chopped roasted, shelled pistachio nuts
- Nonstick cooking spray
- 1 recipe Lemon Mayonnaise *(right)*
- 1/2 cup snipped fresh basil

1. Preheat oven to 400°F. Lightly grease a 15×10×1-inch baking pan; set aside. In a food processor combine the beans, green onions, olives, parsley, flour, garlic, salt, cumin, and black pepper. Cover and process until finely chopped and mixture holds together (should have some visible pieces of garbanzo beans and olives).
2. Shape mixture evenly into 18 balls, using about 1 1/2 tablespoons per ball; set aside.
3. In a shallow dish beat egg whites and the water until foamy. In another shallow dish combine panko and pistachio nuts. Dip falafels in egg whites, turning to coat; allow excess to drip off. Roll falafels in panko mixture. Place falafels in prepared baking pan. Flatten each ball to about 1/2 inch thick. Lightly coat tops with cooking spray.
4. Bake falafels for 15 to 20 minutes or until heated through and lightly browned. Place three falafels on each of six serving plates. Drizzle with Lemon Mayonnaise. Sprinkle with basil.

LEMON MAYONNAISE: In a small bowl combine 1/2 cup light mayonnaise, 1 teaspoon finely shredded lemon peel, 2 tablespoons lemon juice, and 1/8 teaspoon cayenne pepper. Add enough milk (1 to 2 tablespoons) to make drizzling consistency.

PER SERVING: 327 cal., 14 g total fat (2 g sat. fat), 7 mg chol., 487 mg sodium, 38 g carb. (8 g fiber, 3 g sugars), 13 g pro. Exchanges: 1.5 starch, 1 carb., 1.5 lean meat, 2 fat.

Roasted Vegetables
CARB. PER SERVING 10 g
SERVINGS 6 (1 cup vegetables each)
PREP 20 minutes **ROAST** 40 minutes

- 4 medium carrots, halved lengthwise and cut crosswise into 2-inch pieces (2 cups)
- 1 medium red onion, cut into 1-inch wedges (1 cup)
- Nonstick cooking spray
- 1 large yellow summer squash, trimmed, halved lengthwise and cut crosswise, and cut into 1/2-inch-thick slices (1 3/4 cups)
- 12 ounces fresh asparagus, trimmed and cut into 2-inch pieces (3 cups)
- 1/4 teaspoon salt
- 1/4 teaspoon black pepper
- 4 cups packaged fresh baby spinach

1. Preheat oven to 400°F. In a 3-quart rectangular baking dish combine carrots and red onion. Spray vegetables with cooking spray and toss to coat. Cover and roast for 25 minutes or until carrots are almost tender, stirring once.
2. Add squash, asparagus, salt, and pepper to carrot mixture. Toss to combine. Roast, uncovered, for 15 to 20 minutes more or until vegetables are just tender and lightly browned. Just before serving, stir in the spinach. Divide vegetables among six serving plates.

PER SERVING: 50 cal., 0 g total fat, 0 mg chol., 156 mg sodium, 10 g carb. (4 g fiber, 4 g sugars), 3 g pro. Exchanges: 2 vegetable.

Meal Total (per plate): 377 cal., 14 g total fat (2 g sat. fat), 7 mg chol., 643 mg sodium, 48 g carb. (12 g fiber, 7 g sugars), 16 g pro. Exchanges: 2 vegetable, 1 carb., 1.5 starch, 1.5 lean meat, 2 fat.

199

Wrap-It-Up
Egg Salad

Chunky Egg Salad Lettuce Wraps
Carb. per serving 28 g

SERVINGS 4 (3 lettuce leaves, $1/2$ cup bulgur, and 1 cup egg salad each)
PREP 30 minutes **COOK** 10 minutes

- $3/4$ cup dry bulgur
- $3/4$ cup water
- $1/8$ teaspoon salt
- 6 hard-cooked eggs, peeled and chopped
- 1 medium avocado, halved, seeded, peeled, and chopped
- $3/4$ cup coarsely shredded carrots
- $1/4$ cup matchstick-size radish pieces
- $1/4$ cup thinly sliced green onions (2)
- $1/4$ cup chopped celery
- $1/4$ cup cider vinegar
- 2 tablespoons snipped fresh cilantro or parsley
- 1 tablespoon light mayonnaise
- 1 tablespoon honey mustard
- 1 tablespoon olive oil
- 3 cloves garlic, minced
- $1/2$ teaspoon salt
- $1/4$ teaspoon black pepper
- 12 butterhead (Boston or Bibb) lettuce leaves

1. In a medium saucepan bring the bulgur, water, and $1/8$ teaspoon salt to boiling; reduce heat. Cover and simmer for 5 minutes. Remove from the heat. Let stand, covered, for 10 minutes. Stir and let cool for 10 minutes.

2. In a large bowl gently combine eggs, avocado, carrots, radishes, green onions, and celery.

3. In a small bowl whisk together vinegar, cilantro, mayonnaise, mustard, oil, garlic, $1/2$ teaspoon salt, and the pepper. Pour over egg mixture and stir gently to combine.

4. Divide lettuce leaves, bowl sides up, among four serving plates. Spoon bulgur evenly into lettuce leaves. Top evenly with egg salad.

PER SERVING: 327 cal., 18 g total fat (4 g sat. fat), 280 mg chol., 534 mg sodium, 28 g carb. (8 g fiber, 3 g sugars), 14 g pro. Exchanges: 1 vegetable, 1.5 starch, 1 lean meat, 2.5 fat.

Meal Total (per plate): 327 cal., 18 g total fat (4 g sat. fat), 280 mg chol., 534 mg sodium, 28 g carb. (8 g fiber, 3 g sugars), 14 g pro. Exchanges: 1 vegetable, 1.5 starch, 1 lean meat, 2.5 fat.

The cup-shape butterhead lettuce leaves make perfect bowls to nestle the veggie- and bulgur-loaded egg salad. Pick them up to eat like a taco or use a knife and fork to eat like a salad.

Nonstarchy Veggies: carrot, radishes, green onions, celery, lettuce
½ Plate

¼ Plate
Starch or Grain: bulgur

¼ Plate
Protein: eggs

201

Celebration
Luncheon

This rich and creamy tortellini soup adds an exclamation to a celebration! Bottled dressing makes the salad an easy serve-along.

½ Plate

Nonstarchy Veggies: romaine, kohlrabi, sweet pepper, mushrooms, onion, broccoli, sugar snap peas

¼ Plate

Starch, Grain, or Other Carb: tortellini, salad dressing

¼ Plate

Protein: cheese, cream cheese, milk

Broccoli Cheese Tortellini Soup
Carb. per serving 33 g

SERVINGS 6 (1^{1}/$_{3}$ cups soup each)
PREP 20 minutes **COOK** 20 minutes

- 2 cups thinly sliced fresh mushrooms, such as button, cremini, or stemmed shiitake
- ^{1}/$_{2}$ cup chopped onion
- 3 cloves garlic, minced
- 1 tablespoon olive oil
- 1^{1}/$_{2}$ cups low-sodium vegetable broth or stock
- 1 cup water
- 1 9-ounce package refrigerated whole wheat three-cheese tortellini
- 1 tablespoon snipped fresh sage or 1 teaspoon dried sage, crushed
- 1^{1}/$_{2}$ cups small fresh broccoli florets
- 1 cup fresh sugar snap peas, trimmed
- 3 cups low-fat (1%) milk
- 2 tablespoons cornstarch
- 6 ounces reduced-fat cream cheese (Neufchâtel), cut into cubes and softened
- Fresh sugar snap peas, very thinly sliced lengthwise (optional)

1. In a 4-quart Dutch oven cook mushrooms, onion, and garlic in hot oil over medium heat for 5 minutes, stirring occasionally. Carefully add broth, water, tortellini, and dried sage (if using). Bring to boiling; reduce heat. Simmer, covered, for 4 minutes.
2. Add broccoli; return to simmering. Cook, covered, for 2 minutes. Add 1 cup peas; cook for 2 to 3 minutes more or until tortellini is just tender.

3. In a medium bowl whisk together milk and cornstarch until smooth. Add all at once to the soup. Cook and stir until thickened and bubbly.
4. Place cream cheese in a small bowl; microwave on 100 percent power (high) for 30 seconds or until melted. Stir until smooth. Add melted cream cheese and fresh sage (if using) to the soup. Cook and stir until soup is smooth. Ladle into six warm serving bowls. If desired, garnish with thinly sliced peas.

PER SERVING: 321 cal., 15 g total fat (6 g sat. fat), 53 mg chol., 412 mg sodium, 33 g carb. (5 g fiber, 11 g sugars), 15 g pro. Exchanges: 0.5 milk, 1 vegetable, 1.5 starch, 0.5 lean meat, 2 fat.

Kohlrabi Chopped Salad
CARB. PER SERVING 7 g
SERVINGS 6 (1^{1}/$_{4}$ cups salad each)
START TO FINISH 15 minutes

- 6 cups chopped romaine lettuce
- ^{3}/$_{4}$ cup coarsely shredded, peeled kohlrabi or carrots
- ^{1}/$_{2}$ cup bite-size red sweet pepper strips
- 1 ounce Parmesan cheese, shaved
- 6 tablespoons bottled light honey-Dijon salad dressing

1. Divide romaine among six serving plates. Top with kohlrabi, sweet pepper, and cheese. Drizzle with dressing.

PER SERVING: 71 cal., 4 g total fat (1 g sat. fat), 6 mg chol., 208 mg sodium, 7 g carb. (2 g fiber, 4 g sugars), 3 g pro. Exchanges: 1 vegetable, 1 fat.

Meal Total (per plate): 392 cal., 19 g total fat (7 g sat. fat), 59 mg chol., 620 mg sodium, 40 g carb. (7 g fiber, 15 g sugars), 18 g pro. Exchanges: 0.5 milk, 2 vegetable, 1.5 starch, 0.5 lean meat, 3 fat.

Plate Extras

As your calorie and carb allowance permits, choose one of these beverages or fruit dishes to serve alongside your plate.

What are plate extras?

Beyond the plate, you can enjoy a beverage, dairy, or fruit serving if the calorie and carb totals in your meal plan allow.

As you know, the plate method of eating is a visual guide to help you identify the composition of a healthful plate of food. Because lean protein, nonstarchy vegetables, and starch or grain fill quadrants on the plate, you may wonder where these other foods fit in.

Beverages, fruit, and dairy items are served in glasses or bowls on the side. For a delicious extra, mix and match the recipes on the following pages to serve with one or two meals each day to round out your menus and keep you satisfied.

Spiced Apples
Carb. per serving 27 g

SERVINGS 6 (^{2}/₃ cup each)
START TO FINISH 18 minutes

- 5 medium red-skin cooking apples, such as Jonathon or Rome, cored, quartered, and thinly sliced (about 7 cups slices)
- ¼ cup water
- ½ teaspoon ground cinnamon
- ⅛ teaspoon ground nutmeg
- 2 tablespoons honey

1. In a large skillet combine apple slices and water. Sprinkle with cinnamon and nutmeg. Bring to boiling; reduce heat. Simmer, covered, about 3 minutes or until apples are just tender, stirring once or twice. Drizzle with honey and toss to coat. Serve warm in six small serving bowls.

PER SERVING: 101 cal., 0 g total fat, 0 mg chol., 2 mg sodium, 27 g carb. (4 g fiber, 22 g sugars), 0 g pro. Exchanges: 1 fruit, 1 carb.

Grapefruit with Maple-Pomegranate Syrup
Carb. per serving 18 g

SERVINGS 4 (½ grapefruit with 1 tablespoon syrup each)
START TO FINISH 10 minutes

- 2 medium grapefruit, halved horizontally
- ⅓ cup pomegranate juice
- ½ teaspoon cornstarch
- 1 tablespoon light maple-flavor syrup

1. Preheat oven to 375°F. Place grapefruit, cut sides up, in 2-quart square baking dish; add ¼ cup *water*. Cover; bake 10 minutes or until warmed and starting to soften.
2. In a small saucepan combine juice and cornstarch. Cook and stir over medium-low heat until bubbly; cook and stir 2 minutes more. Remove from heat; stir in syrup. Drizzle mixture over grapefruit.

PER SERVING: 71 cal., 0 g total fat, 0 mg chol., 14 mg sodium, 18 g carb. (2 g fiber, 13 g sugars), 1 g pro. Exchanges: 1 fruit.

warm fruit

Ginger-Tea Pineapple
Carb. per serving 14 g

SERVINGS 6 (1 skewer each)
PREP 15 minutes **STAND** 4 minutes
MARINATE 2 hours **BROIL** 4 minutes

 4 green tea bags
 1 1-inch piece fresh ginger, peeled
 and thinly sliced
 4 cups $1\frac{1}{2}$-inch pieces fresh
 pineapple
 $\frac{1}{3}$ cup snipped fresh mint

1. In a pan heat $1\frac{1}{2}$ cups *water* to
boiling. Remove from heat; add tea bags
and ginger. Cover; steep for 4 minutes.
Remove bags, squeezing out all water.
Set tea aside to cool.
2. Place pineapple in a bowl; add tea
and ginger; toss to coat. Cover; marinate
for 2 to 6 hours, stirring occasionally.
3. Preheat broiler. Drain pineapple;
discard ginger. Thread pineapple loosely
onto six 8-inch skewers. Place skewers
on the unheated rack of a broiler pan.
4. Broil 5 to 6 inches from heat for 4 to
6 minutes or until heated through, turning
once. Sprinkle with mint before serving.

PER SERVING: 54 cal., 0 g total fat,
0 mg chol., 3 mg sodium, 14 g carb.
(2 g fiber, 10 g sugars), 1 g pro.
Exchanges: 1 fruit.

Roasted Grapes
Carb. per serving 10 g

SERVINGS 6 (1 cluster each)
PREP 10 minutes **ROAST** 20 minutes

 12 ounces seedless red grapes on
 the stem, cut into 6 clusters
 1 tablespoon lemon juice
 1 tablespoon olive oil
 $\frac{1}{8}$ teaspoon salt

1. Preheat oven to 325°F. Place grapes
in a 2-quart baking dish. Whisk together
lemon juice, oil, and salt; brush about
half over grape clusters.
2. Roast, uncovered, about 20 minutes
or until grapes are softened and skins
are starting to split, brushing with
remaining juice mixture halfway
through roasting.

PER SERVING: 60 cal., 2 g total fat
(0 g sat. fat), 0 mg chol., 50 mg sodium,
10 g carb. (1 g fiber, 9 g sugars), 0 g pro.
Exchanges: 0.5 fruit, 0.5 fat.

Grilled Pears
Carb. per Serving 14 g

SERVINGS 4 (1 pear half and
1 tablespoon topping each)
PREP 10 minutes **COOK** 4 minutes

 2 medium just-ripe pears, halved
 and cored
 1 tablespoon light butter or tub-
 style vegetable oil spread, melted
 $\frac{1}{8}$ teaspoon ground cinnamon
 $\frac{1}{4}$ cup thawed frozen whipped
 dessert topping

1. Brush pear halves all over with
melted butter. Sprinkle cinnamon
evenly over pears.
2. Heat grill pan over medium heat.
Add pear halves. Cook for 4 to
6 minutes or until lightly browned,
turning once. Top each pear half with
1 tablespoon dessert topping. Sprinkle
with dash *ground nutmeg*.

PER SERVING: 73 cal., 2 g total fat
(2 g sat. fat), 4 mg chol., 26 mg sodium,
14 g carb. (3 g fiber, 9 g sugars), 0 g pro.
Exchanges: 1 fruit, 0.5 fat.

Mint-Berry Spritzer
Carb. per serving 10 g

SERVINGS 4 (8 ounces each)
PREP 10 minutes CHILL 2 hours

- 3 tablespoons fresh mint leaves
- 3 cups light cranberry-raspberry juice or light cranberry juice
- 1 cup club soda, chilled
  Ice cubes
- ½ cup fresh raspberries

1. Place the mint leaves in a pitcher. Use the back of a large spoon to lightly bruise leaves. Stir in cranberry-raspberry juice. Cover and chill for 2 to 4 hours.
2. Strain mint from juice and discard the mint. Stir club soda into juice. Pour into four ice-filled glasses. Divide fresh berries among glasses and garnish with additional fresh mint leaves.

PER SERVING: 41 cal., 0 g total fat, 0 mg chol., 67 mg sodium, 10 g carb. (1 g fiber, 8 g sugars), 0 g pro. Exchanges: 0.5 fruit.

Golden Sparklers
Carb. per serving 11 g

SERVINGS 10 (4 ounces each)
PREP 15 minutes FREEZE 2 hours

- 10 thin lemon or lime wedges
- 1½ cups orange juice, chilled
- 1½ cups apricot nectar, chilled
- 1 cup ice cubes
- 1½ cups sparkling water or club soda

1. For ice cubes, place a citrus wedge in each ice cube tray compartment. Fill tray with *water;* freeze 2 hours or until firm.
2. Pour juice and nectar over 1 cup ice cubes in a pitcher or punch bowl. Add sparkling water; stir gently. Place a fruited ice cube in each glass. Add juice mixture.

PER SERVING: 44 cal., 0 g total fat, 0 mg chol., 9 mg sodium, 11 g carb. (1 g fiber, 10 g sugars), 1 g pro. Exchanges: 0.5 fruit.

Easy Strawberry Soda
Carb. per serving 11 g

SERVINGS 6 (8 ounces each)
START TO FINISH 10 minutes

- 1½ cups sliced fresh strawberries
- ½ cup low-sugar or sugar-free strawberry preserves
- 4 cups club soda, chilled
  Ice cubes
- 6 small fresh strawberries (optional)

1. In a blender or food processor combine strawberries and preserves. Cover and blend or process until smooth.
2. To serve, divide strawberry mixture among six tall, ice-filled glasses. Slowly pour in club soda. Stir gently to mix. If desired, garnish with a whole strawberry.

PER SERVING: 45 cal., 0 g total fat, 0 mg chol., 34 mg sodium, 11 g carb. (1 g fiber, 8 g sugars), 0 g pro. Exchanges: 1 carb.

fizzy drinks

Fruit Sparklers
Carb. per serving 6 g

SERVINGS 6 (8 ounces each)
START TO FINISH 5 minutes

    Ice cubes
3 cups low-calorie grape juice or low-calorie cranberry juice
3 cups sparkling water
³/₄ cup halved fresh cranberries, halved fresh grapes, or fresh raspberries (optional)

1. Half fill six tall glasses with ice cubes. Divide grape juice evenly among glasses. Pour sparkling water into glasses, dividing evenly. Stir gently. If desired, float fresh fruit in drinks.

PER SERVING: 23 cal., 0 g total fat, 0 mg chol., 39 mg sodium, 6 g carb. (0 g fiber, 6 g sugars), 0 g pro. Exchanges: 0.5 fruit.

Orange-Lime Ginger Fizz
Carb. per serving 6 g

SERVINGS 4 (8 ounces each)
START TO FINISH 10 minutes

3 medium oranges
3 limes
1 1-inch piece fresh ginger, peeled and thinly sliced
3 cups diet ginger ale

1. Using a vegetable peeler, remove the peel from the oranges and limes in 12 long strips. Set aside. Cut oranges and limes in half. Juice enough of the halves to get ³/₄ cup orange juice and ¹/₄ cup lime juice. (Reserve remaining orange and lime halves for another use.)
2. Combine orange juice and lime juice. Half-fill four 16-ounce glasses with *ice cubes*. Evenly divide orange and lime peel strips and ginger slices among glasses. Fill with more ice. Pour orange juice mixture evenly into glasses. Slowly pour ginger ale into glasses.

PER SERVING: 25 cal., 0 g total fat, 0 mg chol., 61 mg sodium, 6 g carb. (0 g fiber, 4 g sugars), 0 g pro. Exchanges: 0.5 fruit.

Pineapple-Coconut Fizz
Carb. per serving 18 g

SERVINGS 4 (6 ounces each)
PREP 10 minutes **CHILL** 2 hours
FREEZE 2 hours

8 ounces fresh pineapple, cut into 1-inch chunks (about 1¹/₂ cups)
1 cup unsweetened pineapple juice
³/₄ cup coconut water
¹/₄ cup lime juice
1 cup club soda, chilled
4 small pineapple wedges with peel on (optional)

1. Line a large baking pan with waxed paper. Place pineapple chunks in pan in a single layer. Cover and freeze.
2. Combine pineapple juice, coconut water, and lime juice. Chill 2 to 24 hours.
3. Divide frozen pineapple and 1 cup *ice cubes* among four 10-ounce glasses. Pour juice mixture evenly into glasses. Add club soda to each glass. Stir gently. If desired, garnish with pineapple wedge.

PER SERVING: 74 cal., 0 g total fat, 0 mg chol., 62 mg sodium, 18 g carb. (1 g fiber, 13 g sugars), 1 g pro. Exchanges: 1 fruit.

Citrus-Infused Strawberries
Carb. per serving 15 g

SERVINGS 4 (1 cup each)
PREP 15 minutes **CHILL** 1 hour

- 4 cups trimmed and halved fresh strawberries
- 2 tablespoons orange juice
- 1/2 teaspoon finely shredded lemon peel
- 1 tablespoon lemon juice
- 1 tablespoon orange liqueur or orange juice
- 1 teaspoon honey
  Finely shredded lemon peel

1. In a medium bowl combine strawberries, orange juice, 1/2 teaspoon lemon peel, lemon juice, orange liqueur, and honey. Cover and chill for 1 to 4 hours. Divide among four serving bowls. Garnish with additional lemon peel.

PER SERVING: 66 cal., 0 g total fat, 0 mg chol., 2 mg sodium, 15 g carb. (3 g fiber, 9 g sugars), 1 g pro. Exchanges: 1 fruit.

Orange-Cinnamon Figs
Carb. per serving 21 g

SERVINGS 4 (2 figs or 2/3 cup grapes each)
START TO FINISH 10 minutes

- 8 medium fresh figs or 2 3/4 cups grapes
- 1/2 teaspoon finely shredded orange peel
- 1/4 cup orange juice
- 1/8 teaspoon ground cinnamon

1. Remove stems from figs or cut grapes in half. Divide figs or grapes evenly among four serving bowls. In a small bowl whisk together orange peel, orange juice, and cinnamon. Drizzle over fruit in bowls.

PER SERVING: 81 cal., 0 g total fat, 0 mg chol., 1 mg sodium, 21 g carb. (3 g fiber, 18 g sugars), 1 g pro. Exchanges: 1.5 fruit.

Orange-Balsamic Berries
Carb. per serving 17 g

SERVINGS 6 (1 cup berries each)
PREP 15 minutes **MARINATE** 2 hours

- 2 teaspoons finely shredded orange peel
- 3/4 cup orange juice
- 3 tablespoons white balsamic vinegar
- 2 tablespoons honey
- 2 cups fresh raspberries
- 2 cups fresh blackberries
- 2 cups fresh blueberries

1. In a large bowl combine orange peel, orange juice, vinegar, and honey. Stir until honey is dissolved. Add berries and toss gently to combine. Marinate berries in the refrigerator for 2 to 4 hours, stirring occasionally.

2. Drain berries, discarding marinade. Divide berries among six serving bowls.

PER SERVING: 73 cal., 1 g total fat (0 g sat. fat), 0 mg chol., 1 mg sodium, 17 g carb. (6 g fiber, 10 g sugars), 2 g pro. Exchanges: 1 fruit.

citrus

Cardamom-Spiced Kiwi and Pineapple with Coconut
Carb. per serving 21 g

SERVINGS 4 (³/4 cup fruit mixture and 1 tablespoon coconut each)
START TO FINISH 10 minutes

- 2 cups cubed fresh pineapple
- 3 medium kiwifruits, peeled and thinly sliced crosswise
- ¼ teaspoon ground cardamom
- ¼ cup shredded coconut, lightly toasted

1. In a medium bowl combine pineapple cubes and kiwifruit slices. Sprinkle with cardamom and toss gently to coat. Divide fruit mixture among four serving dishes. Sprinkle with coconut.

PER SERVING: 103 cal., 2 g total fat (2 g sat. fat), 0 mg chol., 18 mg sodium, 21 g carb. (3 g fiber, 15 g sugars), 1 g pro. Exchanges: 1.5 fruit, 0.5 fat.

Blackberry Salads
Carb. per serving 32 g or 27 g

SERVINGS 4 (³/4 cup each)
PREP 15 minutes COOK 3 minutes
COOL 20 minutes CHILL 4 hours

- 4 cups fresh or frozen blackberries
- 2 tablespoons sugar*
- 1 envelope unflavored gelatin
- 2 cups frozen light whipped dessert topping, thawed

1. In a pan combine 3½ cups of the berries and 2 tablespoons *water*. Bring to boiling, stirring often. Cook, covered, 3 to 4 minutes or until soft, stirring often. Transfer to blender. Cover; blend until smooth. Press through fine-mesh sieve; discard seeds. Return strained berries to pan.
2. Combine sugar and gelatin. Add to pan. Cook and stir over medium heat until dissolved. Transfer to bowl; cool 20 minutes, stirring occasionally. Layer berry mixture and topping in four glasses. Cover; chill 4 to 24 hours. Garnish with remaining berries and, if desired, *fresh mint*.
***SUGAR SUBSTITUTES:** Choose from Splenda Granular or Sweet'N Low bulk or packets. Follow package directions to use product amount equivalent to 2 tablespoons sugar.

PER SERVING: 176 cal., 5 g total fat (4 g sat. fat), 0 mg chol., 2 mg sodium, 32 g carb. (8 g fiber, 17 g sugars), 6 g pro. Exchanges: 1 fruit, 1 starch, 0.5 fat.

PER SERVING WITH SUBSTITUTE: Same as above, except 155 cal., 27 g carb. (12 g sugars).

Honey-Rosemary Orange Slices
Carb. per serving 20 g

SERVINGS 4 (1 orange and about 1 teaspoon honey mixture each)
START TO FINISH 10 minutes

- 1 tablespoon honey
- 2 teaspoons lemon juice
- ½ teaspoon snipped fresh rosemary
- 4 medium oranges

1. In a small bowl combine honey, lemon juice, and rosemary; stir until honey is dissolved. Trim ends off each orange. Place each orange on a cutting board with a flat end down. Using a sharp knife, cut off the peel, making sure to cut off the white pith. Set the orange on its side and cut crosswise into thin slices.
2. Divide half the orange slices among four serving bowls. Drizzle with half of the honey mixture. Top with remaining orange slices and drizzle with remaining honey mixture.

PER SERVING: 78 cal., 0 g total fat, 0 mg chol., 0 mg sodium, 20 g carb. (3 g fiber, 17 g sugars), 1 g pro. Exchanges: 1 fruit, 0.5 starch.

Cottage Cheese and Blueberries
Carb. per serving 15 g

SERVINGS 4 ($^1/_2$ cup cottage cheese and $^1/_2$ cup berries each)
START TO FINISH 5 minutes

  2 cups low-fat cottage cheese
  2 cups fresh blueberries

1. For each serving, spoon $^1/_2$ cup cottage cheese and $^1/_2$ cup berries into a dish.

PER SERVING: 139 cal., 3 g total fat (1 g sat. fat), 11 mg chol., 374 mg sodium, 15 g carb. (2 g fiber, 11 g sugars), 14 g pro. Exchanges: 1 fruit, 2 lean meat.

Fruit and Feta
Carb. per serving 16 g

SERVINGS 4 (1 cup fruit and $^1/_2$ tablespoon cheese each)
START TO FINISH 15 minutes

  3 cups cubed watermelon
1$^1/_3$ cups fresh blueberries
  2 tablespoons crumbled reduced-fat feta cheese

1. In a bowl combine watermelon and blueberries. Divide among four dishes. Sprinkle with feta cheese.

PER SERVING: 71 cal., 1 g total fat (0 g sat. fat), 1 mg chol., 60 mg sodium, 16 g carb. (2 g fiber, 12 g sugars), 2 g pro. Exchanges: 1 fruit.

Sweet and Spicy Yogurt and Fruit
Carb. per serving 18 g

SERVINGS 6 ($^1/_2$ cup fruit and $^1/_4$ cup yogurt each)
START TO FINISH 20 minutes

1$^1/_2$ cups plain fat-free or low-fat Greek yogurt
  2 tablespoons honey
  2 teaspoons finely shredded lemon peel
    Dash cayenne pepper
  1 cup bite-size pieces fresh pineapple
$^3/_4$ cup fresh blueberries
  2 medium kiwifruits, peeled, halved lengthwise, and thinly sliced crosswise

1. Combine yogurt, honey, lemon peel, and pepper. Combine fruit. Spoon yogurt mixture and fruit into glasses.

PER SERVING: 94 cal., 0 g total fat, 0 mg chol., 23 mg sodium, 18 g carb. (2 g fiber, 15 g sugars), 7 g pro. Exchanges: 0.5 fruit, 0.5 carb., 1 lean meat.

rich & fruity

Savory Goat Cheese Stuffed Apricots
Carb. per serving 6 g

SERVINGS 4 (3 apricot halves each)
START TO FINISH 25 minutes

    3 ounces soft goat cheese (chèvre)
    2 tablespoons light tub-style
       cream cheese
    1 teaspoon finely shredded
       lemon peel
  1/2 teaspoon snipped fresh thyme
    6 medium fresh apricots
       (about 12 ounces)

1. In a bowl stir together goat cheese, cream cheese, lemon peel, and thyme.
2. Cut apricots in half. Remove the pits and place apricots, cut sides up, on a serving dish. Spoon or pipe goat cheese mixture evenly on top of apricot halves.

PER SERVING: 99 cal., 6 g total fat (4 g sat. fat), 15 mg chol., 114 mg sodium, 6 g carb. (1 g fiber, 6 g sugars), 5 g pro.
Exchanges: 0.5 fruit, 1 lean meat, 1 fat.

Melon-Berry Bowls with Sweet and Sour Cream
Carb. per serving 18 g

SERVINGS 6 (1 cup fruit and 1^2/$_3$ tablespoons cream each)
START TO FINISH 15 minutes

    2 cups cubed cantaloupe
    2 cups fresh raspberries
    2 cups cubed
       honeydew melon
  1/2 cup light sour cream
    2 tablespoons orange juice
    2 teaspoons finely chopped
       crystallized ginger
  1/4 teaspoon ground cinnamon

1. In a medium bowl combine cantaloupe, raspberries, and honeydew. Divide fruit mixture among six dishes.
2. In a small bowl combine sour cream, orange juice, ginger, and cinnamon. Drizzle evenly over fruit.

PER SERVING: 90 cal., 2 g total fat (1 g sat. fat), 6 mg chol., 31 mg sodium, 18 g carb. (4 g fiber, 11 g sugars), 2 g pro.
Exchanges: 1 fruit, 0.5 fat.

Yogurt and Strawberries
Carb. per serving 19 g

SERVINGS 4 (heaping 1/3 cup yogurt and 1/2 cup berries each)
START TO FINISH 5 minutes

  1 1/2 cups vanilla fat-free yogurt
      2 cups sliced fresh strawberries
         Chopped walnuts (optional)

1. For each serving, spoon a heaping 1/3 cup yogurt and 1/2 cup berries into a glass. If desired, sprinkle with nuts.

PER SERVING: 93 cal., 0 g total fat, 0 mg chol., 60 mg sodium, 19 g carb. (1 g fiber, 16 g sugars), 4 g pro.
Exchanges: 0.5 fruit, 1 starch.

213

Virgin Marys
Carb. per serving 10 g

SERVINGS 8 (6 ounces each)
PREP 15 minutes CHILL 4 hours

- 6 cups low-sodium vegetable juice
- ½ cup lime juice
- 2 tablespoons Worcestershire sauce
- 1 to 1½ teaspoons bottled hot pepper sauce
- ½ teaspoon black pepper
- 8 small cucumber spears (optional)

1. In an 8-cup glass measure combine vegetable juice, lime juice, Worcestershire sauce, hot pepper sauce, and pepper. Cover; chill 4 to 6 hours.
2. If desired, place cucumber spears in eight tall glasses. Add *ice cubes* to the glasses. Stir juice mixture and pour evenly into ice-filled glasses.

PER SERVING: 45 cal., 0 g total fat, 0 mg chol., 151 mg sodium, 10 g carb. (2 g fiber, 6 g sugars), 2 g pro. Exchanges: 2 vegetable.

Easy Homemade Shandy
Carb. per serving 8 g

SERVINGS 4 (9 ounces each)
START TO FINISH 10 minutes

- 2 12-ounce bottles nonalcoholic light beer, chilled
- 1 12-ounce can light lemonade, chilled
- Ice cubes
- Lemon and lime slices

1. In a pitcher combine beer and lemonade. Pour into four ice-filled glasses. Add lemon and lime slices.

PER SERVING: 35 cal., 0 g total fat, 0 mg chol., 35 mg sodium, 8 g carb. (1 g fiber, 1 g sugars), 0 g pro. Exchanges: 0.5 starch.

Peach Sunrise Refresher
Carb. per serving 12 g

SERVINGS 4 (8 ounces each)
START TO FINISH 5 minutes

- 2 cups ice cubes
- 1⅓ cups diet cranberry juice drink
- 1⅓ cups peach nectar
- Fresh peach slices (optional)

1. Place ½ cup ice in each of four glasses. Add ⅓ cup of the cranberry juice to each glass. Slowly fill each glass with ⅓ cup of the peach nectar. If desired, garnish with peach slices.

PER SERVING: 46 cal., 0 g total fat, 0 mg chol., 24 mg sodium, 12 g carb. (0 g fiber, 12 g sugars), 0 g pro. Exchanges: 1 carb.

mock libations

Mock Sangria
Carb. per serving 19 g

SERVINGS 4 (10 ounces each)
PREP 10 minutes **CHILL** 4 hours

- 1 cup pomegranate juice
- 2/3 cup low-calorie cranberry juice
- 1/3 cup orange juice
- 1 1/2 cups fresh fruit, such as cut-up strawberries or mango and/or whole blueberries or raspberries
- 2 cups club soda, chilled

1. In a large bowl combine pomegranate juice, cranberry juice, and orange juice. Add fruit. Cover and chill for 4 to 24 hours.
2. Fill four tall glasses half full of *ice cubes*. Remove fruit from juice mixture using a slotted spoon; divide fruit among glasses. Pour in juice mixture. Pour club soda into glasses; stir gently.

PER SERVING: 80 cal., 0 g total fat, 0 mg chol., 38 mg sodium, 19 g carb. (1 g fiber, 17 g sugars), 1 g pro. Exchanges: 1.5 fruit.

Citrus Martini
Carb. per serving 22 g

SERVINGS 4 (4 ounces each)
START TO FINISH 10 minutes

- 3/4 cup reduced-calorie orange juice
- 3/4 cup lime juice
- 1/4 cup agave nectar or honey
  Ice cubes
- 4 1/4-inch-thick slices lime

1. In a cocktail shaker combine 6 tablespoons of the orange juice, 6 tablespoons of the lime juice, and 2 tablespoons of the agave nectar. Add 3/4 cup ice cubes. Cover and shake very well. Strain liquid into two chilled martini glasses. Discard ice cubes from the cocktail shaker. Repeat with remaining orange juice, lime juice, agave, and 3/4 cup fresh ice cubes. Pour into two glasses. Garnish each with a lime slice.

PER SERVING: 81 cal., 0 g total fat, 0 mg chol., 3 mg sodium, 22 g carb. (1 g fiber, 18 g sugars), 0 g pro. Exchanges: 1.5 carb.

Monkey Tail Freeze
Carb. per serving 20 g

SERVINGS 4 (12 ounces each)
START TO FINISH 10 minutes

- 2 cups refrigerated coconut milk beverage
- 1 cup brewed espresso or strong coffee, chilled
- 1 medium banana, peeled and cut up
- 1 6-ounce carton vanilla fat-free Greek yogurt
- 1/4 cup reduced-calorie chocolate-flavor syrup
- 2 cups small ice cubes

1. In a blender combine coconut milk, espresso, banana, yogurt, and syrup. Cover and blend until well combined, scraping sides of container occasionally. Add ice cubes. Cover and blend until slushy. Pour into four tall, chilled glasses. Serve immediately.

PER SERVING: 124 cal., 3 g total fat (3 g sat. fat), 0 mg chol., 60 mg sodium, 20 g carb. (1 g fiber, 15 g sugars), 5 g pro. Exchanges: 1.5 starch.

Warm Pear-Apple Cider
Carb. per serving 8 g

SERVINGS 4 (10 ounces each)
PREP 20 minutes **COOK** 20 minutes

- 2 medium ripe pears, quartered, cored, and thinly sliced
- 2 medium red-skin cooking apples, quartered, cored, and thinly sliced
- 2 3- to 4-inch sticks cinnamon
- 1 1-inch piece fresh ginger, peeled and thinly sliced
- 1 teaspoon whole cloves
- 2 tablespoons sugar
- $\frac{1}{4}$ teaspoon ground cinnamon
- $\frac{1}{4}$ teaspoon ground ginger

1. In a pot combine 6 cups *water* and the fruit. Place cinnamon sticks, ginger slices, and whole cloves on an 8-inch square of double-thickness cheesecloth. Pull up corners; tie with 100 percent cotton kitchen string. Add bag of spices to the pot with sugar and ground cinnamon and ginger. Bring to boiling; reduce heat. Simmer, covered, 20 to 25 minutes or until fruit is tender. Remove spice bag; discard.
2. Pour mixture through a fine-mesh sieve into a clean saucepan. Press on fruit to remove juice. Heat through. Serve in mugs. If desired, garnish with additional pear slices.

PER SERVING: 31 cal., 0 g total fat, 0 mg chol., 11 mg sodium, 8 g carb. (0 g fiber, 7 g sugars), 0 g pro. Exchanges: 0.5 fruit.

Orange-Ginger Tea
Carb. per serving 3 g

SERVINGS 4 (8 ounces each)
PREP 10 minutes **STAND** 4 minutes

- 4 cups water
- 4 green tea bags
- 1 1-inch piece fresh ginger, peeled and thinly sliced
- $\frac{1}{4}$ cup orange juice

1. In a medium saucepan bring water to boiling. Remove from heat. Add tea bags and ginger slices. Cover and steep for 4 minutes. Remove tea bags and discard. Stir in orange juice. If desired, remove ginger slices or leave them in for a more intense flavor. Ladle tea into four cups.

PER SERVING: 11 cal., 0 g total fat, 0 mg chol., 7 mg sodium, 3 g carb. (0 g fiber, 1 g sugars), 0 g pro. Exchanges: Free

Warm Honey Green Tea
Carb. per serving 5 g

SERVINGS 4 (7 ounces each)
PREP 10 minutes **COOK** 10 minutes
STAND 1 minutes

- 4 lemon peel strips ($2\frac{1}{2}$×1 inches each)
- 4 orange peel strips ($2\frac{1}{2}$×1 inches each)
- 4 green tea bags
- 2 teaspoons honey
- 4 lemon slices

1. In a medium saucepan stir together the 4 cups *water*, lemon peel strips, and orange peel strips. Bring to boiling; reduce heat. Simmer, uncovered, for 10 minutes. Remove lemon and orange strips; discard.
2. Place tea bags in a teapot; immediately add simmering water mixture. Cover and steep according to directions (1 to 3 minutes). Remove tea bags, squeezing gently; discard. Stir in honey. Pour tea into four cups; garnish each with a lemon slice.

PER SERVING: 16 cal., 0 g total fat, 0 mg chol., 8 mg sodium, 5 g carb. (1 g fiber, 3 g sugars), 0 g pro. Exchanges: Free

coffee shop

Chai-Spiced Lattes
Carb. per serving 11 g or 5 g

SERVINGS 4 (6 ounces each)
START TO FINISH 10 minutes

- 1½ cups fat-free milk
- 2 tablespoons sugar*
- ¼ to ½ teaspoon pumpkin pie spice
- 1½ cups hot brewed espresso or strong coffee

1. In a pan heat and stir milk, sugar, and pumpkin pie spice over medium heat until just simmering. Remove from heat. If desired, froth the milk with a milk frothing wand or immersion blender.
2. Pour espresso into four mugs. Pour in hot milk mixture, spooning frothed milk on top if using. If desired, garnish with additional pumpkin pie spice.
*SUGAR SUBSTITUTES: Choose Splenda Granular, Equal Spoonful or packets, or Sweet'N Low bulk or packets. Follow package directions to use product amount equivalent to 2 tablespoons sugar. If using Equal, add to milk after removing from the heat.

PER SERVING: 57 cal., 0 g total fat, 2 mg chol., 40 mg sodium, 11 g carb. (0 g fiber, 11 g sugars), 3 g pro. Exchanges: 0.5 milk, 0.5 starch

PER SERVING WITH SUBSTITUTE: 35 cal., 5 g carb. (5 g sugars). Exchanges: 0 starch.

Mango Ginger Lassi
Carb. per serving 24 g

SERVINGS 4 (6 ounces each)
START TO FINISH 10 minutes

- 1 medium mango, halved, seeded, peeled, and cut up
- ¾ cup cold water
- 1½ cups plain fat-free or low-fat yogurt
- 2 tablespoons honey
- 1 teaspoon grated, peeled fresh ginger

1. In a blender combine mango and the water. Cover and blend until smooth. Add yogurt, honey, and ginger. Cover and blend until well combined. Pour into four glasses filled with *ice cubes*.

PER SERVING: 115 cal., 0 g total fat, 2 mg chol., 73 mg sodium, 24 g carb. (1 g fiber, 23 g sugars), 6 g pro. Exchanges: 1.5 starch.

Watermelon-Hibiscus Iced Tea
Carb. per serving 6 g

SERVINGS 4 (8 ounces each)
PREP 10 minutes **CHILL** 2 hours

- 3 cups water
- 4 hibiscus herbal tea bags (such as Red Zinger brand)
- 2 cups chopped, seeded watermelon

1. In a small saucepan bring the water just to boiling. Remove from heat; add tea bags. Cover; steep for 4 minutes. Remove tea bags, squeezing gently. Transfer tea to a 4-cup glass measure. Cover and chill for 2 hours to 3 days.
2. When ready to serve, place watermelon in a blender. Cover and blend until smooth. Stir watermelon into chilled tea. Strain mixture through a fine-mesh sieve; discard solids. Pour into four glasses filled with *ice cubes*.

PER SERVING: 25 cal., 0 g total fat, 0 mg chol., 3 mg sodium, 6 g carb. (0 g fiber, 5 g sugars), 0 g pro. Exchanges: 0.5 fruit.

217

Low-Cal Desserts

You deserve a treat once in a while. With about 200 calories or less, these yummy recipes promise sensible sweetness.

Lemon-Blueberry Angel Cake Dessert

Carb. per serving 14 g

SERVINGS 12 (1/2 cup each)
PREP 25 minutes FREEZE 4 hours

  1/2 of a 7- to 8-inch purchased angel food cake (5 ounces)
  1 8-ounce tub light cream cheese
  1 1/2 teaspoons finely shredded lemon peel
  2 tablespoons lemon juice
  1 1/2 cups frozen light whipped dessert topping, thawed
  2 cups fresh blueberries
  Lemon peel strips (optional)

1. Cut cake into 1/2-inch cubes. (You should have about 4 1/2 cups cubes.) Place half of the cubes in a 2-quart soufflé dish.
2. In a medium bowl beat cream cheese with an electric mixer on medium speed until smooth. Add lemon juice, beating until smooth. Stir in finely shredded lemon peel. Fold in about 1/4 cup of the dessert topping until combined. Fold in the remaining dessert topping. Divide the mixture in half; stir 1 1/2 cups of the blueberries into one portion of the cream cheese mixture. Spoon over cake cubes in dish.

Top with the remaining cake cubes and the remaining plain cream cheese mixture. Cover and freeze about 4 hours or until firm.
3. Sprinkle with the remaining blueberries before serving. If desired, garnish with lemon peel strips.

PER SERVING: 100 cal., 4 g total fat (3 g sat. fat), 9 mg chol., 177 mg sodium, 14 g carb. (1 g fiber, 8 g sugars), 3 g pro. Exchanges: 1 carb., 0.5 fat.

Carrot Cupcakes

Carb. per serving 30 g or 24 g

SERVINGS 15 (1 cupcake each)
PREP 30 minutes BAKE 18 minutes COOL 5 minutes

Nonstick cooking spray
1 cup all-purpose flour
1 cup whole wheat flour
3/4 cup packed brown sugar*
1 teaspoon baking powder
1 teaspoon baking soda
3/4 teaspoon ground cinnamon
1/4 teaspoon salt
1/4 teaspoon ground ginger
2 eggs, lightly beaten
2 cups shredded carrots (4 medium)
1 cup unsweetened applesauce
1/3 cup canola oil
6 ounces reduced-fat cream cheese (Neufchâtel)
3 tablespoons agave nectar or honey
5 tablespoons finely shredded carrot

1. Preheat oven to 350°F. Line fifteen 2 1/2-inch muffin cups with paper bake cups. Lightly coat paper cups with cooking spray; set aside.

2. In a large bowl stir together flours, brown sugar, baking powder, baking soda, cinnamon, salt, and ginger; set aside.

3. In a medium bowl combine eggs, 2 cups carrots, applesauce, and oil. Add egg mixture to flour mixture. Stir until combined. Spoon batter into the prepared muffin cups, filling each three-fourths full.

4. Bake for 18 to 20 minutes or until a toothpick inserted near centers comes out clean. Cool in muffin cups on a wire rack for 5 minutes. Remove from muffin cups. Cool completely on a wire rack.

5. For frosting, in a small bowl beat cream cheese with an electric mixer on medium speed until smooth. Add agave nectar; beat for 1 minute more. Spread frosting on cupcakes. Top each cupcake with 1 teaspoon of the finely shredded carrots.

SUGAR SUBSTITUTE: Choose Splenda Brown Sugar Blend. Follow package directions to use product amount equivalent to 3/4 cup brown sugar.

PER SERVING: 207 cal., 8 g total fat (2 g sat. fat), 37 mg chol., 218 mg sodium, 30 g carb. (2 g fiber, 17 g sugars), 4 g pro. Exchanges: 2 starch, 1 fat.

PER SERVING WITH SUBSTITUTE: Same as above, except 189 cal., 215 mg sodium, 24 g carb.(11 g sugars). Exchanges: 1.5 starch.

Grilled Angel Food Cake with Strawberry Sauce

Carb. per serving 33 g or 32 g

SERVINGS 6 (1 cake slice, ¼ cup ice cream, and about ⅓ cup sauce each)
PREP 25 minutes COOK 5 minutes

- ¾ cup water
- 1 hibiscus and rosehip herbal tea bag
- 2½ cups small fresh strawberries, hulled
- 1 tablespoon sugar*
- 1½ teaspoons cornstarch
- 1 tablespoon tub-style vegetable oil spread
- 6 ounces purchased angel food cake, cut into 6 equal slices
- Butter-flavor nonstick cooking spray
- 1½ cups light strawberry ice cream
- Fresh mint leaves (optional)

1. In a small saucepan bring water just to boiling. Remove from heat and add the tea bag. Cover and let steep for 5 minutes. Remove the tea bag, pressing out all the tea; discard tea bag.

2. Meanwhile, in a small bowl use a potato masher or pastry blender to mash 1 cup of the strawberries until well mashed. Thinly slice remaining strawberries. Add the sugar and cornstarch to the mashed strawberries and stir until combined. Add to the brewed tea in the saucepan. Cook and stir until thickened and bubbly. Cook and stir for 2 minutes more. Remove from heat and stir in the vegetable oil spread and sliced strawberries. Set aside to cool slightly.

3. Lightly coat both sides of the angel food cake slices with cooking spray. Heat an indoor grill pan or griddle over medium-high heat. Add cake slices. Cook for 2 to 3 minutes or until cake is golden brown, turning once halfway through cooking.

4. To serve, place one cake slice on each of six dessert dishes or plates. Spoon strawberry sauce over cake. Top each with a ¼-cup scoop of ice cream. If desired, garnish with mint leaves.

*SUGAR SUBSTITUTES: Choose from Splenda Granular, Sweet'N Low bulk or packets, or Equal Spoonful or packets. Follow package directions to use product amount equivalent to 1 tablespoon sugar. If using Equal, add to the sauce with the vegetable oil spread.

PER SERVING: 171 cal., 3 g total fat (1 g sat. fat), 6 mg chol., 258 mg sodium, 33 g carb. (2 g fiber, 21 g sugars), 4 g pro. Exchanges: 0.5 fruit, 1.5 carb., 0.5 fat.

PER SERVING WITH SUBSTITUTE: Same as above, except 164 cal., 32 g carb. (19 g sugars).

Cinnamon-Banana Cake with Chocolate Ganache

Carb. per serving 34 g or 27 g

SERVINGS 16 (1 slice each)
PREP 15 minutes BAKE 45 minutes COOL 10 minutes

2 cups all-purpose flour
$\frac{1}{2}$ cup whole wheat pastry flour
$\frac{1}{2}$ cup granulated sugar*
$\frac{1}{2}$ cup packed brown sugar*
$1\frac{1}{4}$ teaspoons baking powder
1 teaspoon ground cinnamon
$\frac{1}{2}$ teaspoon salt
$\frac{1}{2}$ teaspoon baking soda
$\frac{3}{4}$ cup fat-free milk
$\frac{2}{3}$ cup mashed banana
$\frac{1}{2}$ cup refrigerated or frozen egg product, thawed, or 2 eggs, lightly beaten
$\frac{1}{4}$ cup canola oil
1 teaspoon vanilla
3 ounces dark chocolate, chopped
$\frac{1}{4}$ cup fat-free half-and-half

1. Preheat oven to 325°F. Generously grease and flour a 10-inch fluted tube pan; set aside. In large mixing bowl stir together flours, granulated and brown sugars, baking powder, cinnamon, salt, and baking soda.
2. In a medium bowl combine milk, banana, eggs, oil, and vanilla. Add egg mixture all at once to flour mixture. Beat with an electric mixer on medium to high speed for 2 minutes. Spoon batter into the prepared pan; spread evenly.
3. Bake for 45 to 55 minutes or until a wooden toothpick inserted near the center comes out clean. Cool in pan on a wire rack for 10 minutes. Remove cake from pan. Cool completely on wire rack.
4. For ganache, in a small microwave-safe bowl combine chocolate and half-and-half. Microwave, uncovered, on 50 percent power (medium) for 1 minute. Let stand for 5 minutes. Stir until completely smooth. Let stand to thicken slightly. Spoon evenly over top of cooled cake.

*SUGAR SUBSTITUTES: Choose Splenda Sugar Blend for Baking to substitute for the granulated sugar. Choose Splenda Brown Sugar Blend for Baking to substitute for the brown sugar. Follow package directions to use product amounts equivalent to $\frac{1}{2}$ cup granulated sugar and $\frac{1}{2}$ cup brown sugar.

PER SERVING: 197 cal., 5 g total fat (1 g sat. fat), 1 mg chol., 177 mg sodium, 34 g carb. (2 g fiber, 17 g sugars), 4 g pro. Exchanges: 1.5 starch, 1 carb., 1 fat.

PER SERVING WITH SUBSTITUTES: Same as above, except 177 cal., 27 g carb. (10 g sugars), 175 mg sodium. Exchanges: 0.5 carb.

223

Pistachio-Apple Baklava

Carb. per serving 14 g

SERVINGS 18 (1 triangle each)
PREP 30 minutes BAKE 40 minutes

- 2 large cooking apples, cored and finely chopped (2 cups)
- ½ teaspoon finely shredded lemon peel
- 1 tablespoon lemon juice
- 1 tablespoon honey
- ¼ teaspoon ground allspice
- ¾ cup lightly salted pistachio nuts, toasted pecans, or toasted hazelnuts, finely chopped
- ½ cup snipped dried cranberries
  Butter-flavor nonstick cooking spray
- ½ of a 16-ounce package frozen phyllo dough, thawed (twenty 14×9-inch sheets)

1. Preheat oven to 325°F. In a large bowl combine apples, lemon peel, lemon juice, honey, and allspice. Stir in pistachios and cranberries. Set aside.

2. Coat a 2-quart square baking dish with cooking spray. Unroll phyllo dough. Using kitchen shears or a long knife, cut the whole stack of phyllo in half crosswise to make forty 9×7-inch sheets. Keep phyllo covered with plastic wrap, removing sheets as needed.

3. Using one sheet of the phyllo dough at a time, layer 10 phyllo sheets in the dish, coating the top of each sheet with cooking spray and folding over any extra. Turn every other sheet a quarter turn to make even layers. Spread about 1 cup of the apple mixture over phyllo in dish.

Repeat layers twice. Layer remaining 10 phyllo dough sheets over apple mixture, coating the top of each sheet with cooking spray.

4. Using a sharp knife, cut through phyllo and apple mixture to make nine squares; cut each square in half diagonally to make triangles. (Do not remove the pieces from dish.) Bake for 40 to 45 minutes or until golden brown. Cool completely on a wire rack.

PER SERVING: 88 cal., 3 g total fat (0 g sat. fat), 0 mg chol., 85 mg sodium, 14 g carb. (1 g fiber, 5 g sugars), 2 g pro. Exchanges: 1 carb., 0.5 fat.

Peach-Blackberry Crisp with Oatmeal-Coconut Topping

Carb. per serving 25 g or 18 g

SERVINGS 6 (²/₃ cup fruit mixture and 2 tablespoons topping each)
START TO FINISH 35 minutes

- 2 tablespoons butter
- ¼ cup chopped pecans
- ¼ cup regular rolled oats
- 3 tablespoons packed brown sugar*
- 2 tablespoons sweetened shredded coconut
- ⅛ teaspoon ground cinnamon
- 4 firm, ripe peaches, pitted and sliced
- 1 tablespoon lemon juice
- 1 cup fresh blackberries
- 1½ cups low-fat or light vanilla ice cream or frozen yogurt (optional)

1. For the topping, in a large nonstick skillet melt 1 tablespoon of the butter over medium heat. Stir in pecans, oats, 1 tablespoon of the brown sugar, the coconut, and cinnamon. Cook and stir for 6 to 8 minutes or until mixture begins to brown. Spread topping evenly on a baking sheet; set aside. Wipe out the skillet with a paper towel.

2. In the same skillet melt the remaining 1 tablespoon butter over medium-high heat. Add peaches, the remaining 2 tablespoons brown sugar, and the lemon juice. Bring to boiling; reduce heat. Simmer, uncovered, about 5 minutes or until juices are slightly thickened. Fold in blackberries.

3. To serve, spoon about ²/₃ cup of the peach mixture into each of six serving dishes. Sprinkle the topping over fruit. If desired, serve with ice cream.

*SUGAR SUBSTITUTES: Choose from Sugar Twin Granulated Brown or Sweet'N Low Brown. Follow package directions to use product amount equivalent to 3 tablespoons brown sugar.

PER SERVING: 179 cal., 9 g total fat (4 g sat. fat), 10 mg chol., 36 mg sodium, 25 g carb. (4 g fiber, 17 g sugars), 3 g pro. Exchanges: 1 fruit, 0.5 carb., 2 fat.

PER SERVING WITH SUBSTITUTE: Same as above, except 152 cal., 18 g carb. (11 g sugars). Exchanges: 0 carb.

225

Apple Crumble with Oats

Carb. per serving 30 g or 26 g

SERVINGS 6 (²/₃ cup crumble each)
PREP 20 minutes BAKE 40 minutes

- ½ cup regular rolled oats
- 2 tablespoons whole wheat pastry flour
- 2 tablespoons packed brown sugar*
- ½ teaspoon ground cinnamon
- 1 tablespoon cold butter, cut into small pieces
- 3 medium Golden Delicious apples, cored and cut into thin wedges
- 2 tablespoons water
- 1 tablespoon fresh lemon juice
- 1 tablespoon packed brown sugar*

Frozen yogurt or low-fat vanilla yogurt (optional)

1. Preheat oven to 350°F. In a medium bowl combine oats, flour, 2 tablespoons brown sugar, and cinnamon. Mix with fork until combined. Add the butter and work it in with your fingers, the fork, or a pastry blender until the mixture begins to form clumps.

2. In a large bowl toss the apples with the water, lemon juice, and remaining 1 tablespoon brown sugar. Transfer apple mixture to a 9-inch pie plate. Sprinkle the oat mixture evenly over the apples. Bake for 40 to 45 minutes or until the topping is golden and the apples are tender. If desired, serve warm with yogurt.

TEST KITCHEN TIP: To make individual servings, prepare as above, except divide the apple mixture among six 6- to 8-ounce custard cups or ramekins. Sprinkle with oat mixture and bake about 35 minutes or until apples are tender. Serve as above.

*SUGAR SUBSTITUTE: Choose Splenda Brown Sugar Baking Blend. Follow package directions to use product amounts equivalent to 2 tablespoons and 1 tablespoon brown sugar.

PER SERVING: 148 cal., 3 g total fat (1 g sat. fat), 5 mg chol., 20 mg sodium, 30 g carb. (4 g fiber, 16 g sugars), 3 g pro. Exchanges: 1 fruit, 0.5 starch, 0.5 carb., 0.5 fat.

PER SERVING WITH SUBSTITUTE: Same as above, except 137 cal., 26 g carb. (13 g sugars), 18 mg sodium.

Bing Cherry Fool

Carb. per serving 25 g or 19 g

SERVINGS 8 ($^1/_2$ cup each)
PREP 30 minutes CHILL 2 hours

$^1/_4$ cup sugar*
  1 tablespoon cornstarch
 12 ounces fresh dark sweet cherries, stemmed, halved, and pitted
$^1/_2$ cup dry red wine or pomegranate juice
  1 tablespoon finely shredded orange peel
  1 8-ounce container frozen light whipped dessert topping, thawed
  1 6-ounce carton plain fat-free or low-fat Greek yogurt
  1 teaspoon vanilla
  8 fresh dark sweet cherries with stems (optional)

1. In a medium saucepan stir together sugar and cornstarch. Add the halved cherries and the wine, stirring until combined. Cook and stir over medium heat until thickened and bubbly. Cook and stir for 2 minutes more. Transfer cherry mixture to a medium bowl. Stir in orange peel. Cover and chill for 2 hours.

2. In a large bowl whisk together whipped topping, yogurt, and vanilla. Add 1$^1/_2$ cups of the chilled cherry mixture to the whipped topping mixture and fold gently to marble. Spoon into eight 6-ounce dessert dishes. Spoon the remaining cherry mixture evenly over desserts. Cover and chill for up to 4 hours. If desired, top each dessert with a cherry with a stem before serving.

*SUGAR SUBSTITUTES: Choose from Splenda Granular, Sweet'N Low bulk or packets, or Truvia Spoonable or packets. Follow package directions to use product amount equivalent to $^1/_4$ cup sugar.

PER SERVING: 143 cal., 3 g total fat (3 g sat. fat), 0 mg chol., 10 mg sodium, 25 g carb. (1 g fiber, 15 g sugars), 3 g pro. Exchanges: 0.5 fruit, 1 carb., 0.5 fat.

PER SERVING WITH SUBSTITUTE: Same as above, except 122 cal., 19 g carb. (10 g sugars). Exchanges: 0.5 carb.

Apricot-Vanilla Clafoutis

Carb. per serving 18 g or 15 g

SERVINGS 8 (³/₄ cup each)
PREP 20 minutes STAND 15 minutes
BAKE 25 minutes COOL 15 minutes

Nonstick cooking spray
1 vanilla bean, split lengthwise
1 cup evaporated low-fat milk
3 eggs
¹/₃ cup white whole wheat flour or all-purpose flour
¹/₄ cup granulated sugar*
2 tablespoons butter, melted
1 teaspoon vanilla
¹/₈ teaspoon salt
12 ounces ripe, yet firm, fresh apricots, sliced
1 teaspoon powdered sugar

1. Preheat oven to 375°F. Coat the bottom and sides of a 9-inch pie plate or quiche dish with cooking spray; set aside.

2. With the tip of a sharp knife, scrape seeds from vanilla bean. Place seeds in a small saucepan; add evaporated milk and the vanilla bean pod. Bring to simmering over medium heat; remove from heat. Let stand, uncovered, for 15 minutes. Discard vanilla bean pod.

3. In a blender or food processor combine eggs, flour, sugar, melted butter, vanilla extract, and salt. Add milk mixture. Cover and blend or process until combined.

4. Arrange the apricot slices in the prepared dish. Pour batter over apricots. Bake for 25 to 30 minutes or until puffed and lightly browned. Cool in dish on a wire rack for 15 minutes. Sift the powdered sugar over top. Serve warm.

*SUGAR SUBSTITUTE: Choose Splenda Sugar Blend for Baking. Follow package directions to use product amount equivalent to ¹/₄ cup granulated sugar.

PER SERVING: 142 cal., 5 g total fat (2 g sat. fat), 82 mg chol., 124 mg sodium, 18 g carb. (2 g fiber, 14 g sugars), 6 g pro. Exchanges: 0.5 fruit, 0.5 starch, 0.5 medium-fat meat, 1 fat.

PER SERVING WITH SUBSTITUTE: Same as above, except 133 cal., 15 g carb. (10 g sugars).

Grilled Peaches with Honey-Balsamic Syrup

Carb. per serving 25 g

SERVINGS 6 (1 peach half, 1 to 2 teaspoons balsamic syrup, scant 2 tablespoons dessert topping, and 1 gingersnap each)
PREP 15 minutes   GRILL 3 minutes

- 1 cup balsamic vinegar
- 1 tablespoon honey
- $\frac{1}{8}$ teaspoon ground cinnamon
- 3 ripe large peaches, halved and pitted
- 2 teaspoons canola oil
- $\frac{2}{3}$ cup frozen light whipped dessert topping, thawed
- 6 gingersnaps, coarsely crushed

1. In a small saucepan bring the vinegar to boiling. Reduce heat; simmer gently for 10 to 13 minutes or until reduced to about $\frac{1}{4}$ cup. Remove from the heat. Add honey and cinnamon; stir until honey is dissolved. Set aside to cool.

2. Brush peach halves lightly with oil. For a charcoal or gas grill, place peach halves, cut sides down, on grill rack directly over medium-high heat. Grill, covered, for 3 to 4 minutes or until just heated through and grill marks begin to form.

3. Place a peach half on each of six dessert plates. Drizzle each with 1 to 2 teaspoons balsamic syrup. Spoon dessert topping evenly over peaches and sprinkle with crushed gingersnaps. Cover any remaining balsamic syrup and use within 2 weeks.

PER SERVING: 135 cal., 3 g total fat (1 g sat. fat), 0 mg chol., 42 mg sodium, 25 g carb. (2 g fiber, 18 g sugars), 1 g pro.
Exchanges: 1 fruit, 0.5 carb., 0.5 fat.

Gingered Pears
Carb. per serving 26 g or 20 g

SERVINGS 4 (1 pear and about $1^{1}/_{2}$ tablespoons sauce each)
PREP 15 minutes COOK 7 minutes

4 small pears, cored (about $1^{1}/_{2}$ pounds total)
2 tablespoons sugar*
2 tablespoons water
1 teaspoon finely shredded lemon peel
2 tablespoons lemon juice
1 tablespoon butter
$^{1}/_{4}$ teaspoon ground ginger
1 tablespoon chopped crystallized ginger

1. Fill a large Dutch oven with water to a depth of 1 inch. Bring water to boiling. Place a steamer basket in the Dutch oven. Place pears in the steamer basket. Cover and steam for 7 to 9 minutes or until fruit is tender. Remove fruit from steamer basket.

2. Meanwhile, for lemon sauce, in a small saucepan heat and stir sugar, water, lemon peel, lemon juice, butter, and ground ginger over medium heat until butter is melted and sugar is dissolved.

3. To serve, place pears in four dessert dishes. Divide lemon sauce among the dishes and sprinkle with crystalized ginger.

*SUGAR SUBSTITUTES: Choose from Splenda Granular, Truvia Spoonable, or Sweet'N Low bulk or packets. Follow package directions to use product amount equivalent to 2 tablespoons sugar.

PER SERVING: 122 cal., 3 g total fat (2 g sat. fat), 8 mg chol., 27 mg sodium, 26 g carb. (4 g fiber, 17 g sugars), 1 g pro. Exchanges: 1 fruit, 0.5 carb., 0.5 fat.

PER SERVING WITH SUBSTITUTE: Same as above, except 101 cal., 20 g carb. (12 g sugars). Exchanges: 0 carb.

Berry-Topped Cheesecake

Carb. per serving 14 g

SERVINGS 12 (1 wedge each)
PREP 45 minutes BAKE 8 minutes CHILL 4 hours

1½ cups small pretzel twists (2 ounces; about 34)
2 tablespoons sliced almonds, toasted
3 tablespoons butter, melted
⅓ cup water
1 envelope unflavored gelatin
1½ 8-ounce tubs light cream cheese, softened
1 8-ounce carton light sour cream
¼ cup powdered sugar
½ teaspoon almond extract
½ of an 8-ounce container frozen light whipped dessert topping, thawed
1 cup quartered or halved fresh strawberries
1 cup fresh blackberries or blueberries

1. Preheat oven to 350°F. For crust, in a food processor combine pretzels and sliced almonds; cover and process until finely crushed. Add butter; cover and process until combined. Press pretzel mixture evenly onto the bottom of an 8- or 9-inch springform pan. Bake for 8 to 10 minutes or until lightly browned. Cool on a wire rack.

2. For filling, place the water in a small saucepan; sprinkle with gelatin (do not stir). Let stand for 5 minutes to soften. Stir over low heat until gelatin is dissolved. Remove from heat; set aside to cool slightly.

3. In a large bowl beat cream cheese, sour cream, powdered sugar, and almond extract with an electric mixer on medium speed until smooth; slowly beat in gelatin mixture until combined. Fold in whipped topping.

4. Spread half of the filling evenly over cooled crust. Top with half of the strawberries and half of the blackberries. Spread the remaining cream cheese

mixture over berries. Cover and chill for 4 to 24 hours or until set.

5. To serve, using a sharp knife, loosen cheesecake from pan; remove sides of pan. Cut cheesecake into 12 wedges. Top each serving with some of the remaining strawberries and blackberries.

PER SERVING: 176 cal., 11 g total fat (7 g sat. fat), 28 mg chol., 236 mg sodium, 14 g carb. (1 g fiber, 7 g sugars), 6 g pro. Exchanges: 1 carb., 2 fat.

No-Bake Chocolate Swirl Cheesecake

Carb. per serving 16 g or 13 g

SERVINGS 16 (1 wedge each)
PREP 45 minutes CHILL 6 hours

- ¹/₂ cup finely crushed graham crackers
- 2 tablespoons butter, melted
- ³/₄ cup fat-free milk
- 1 envelope unflavored gelatin
- 2 8-ounce packages reduced-fat cream cheese (Neufchâtel), softened
- 1 8-ounce package fat-free cream cheese, softened
- 1 8-ounce carton fat-free sour cream
- ¹/₃ cup sugar*
- 2 teaspoons vanilla
- 4 ounces semisweet chocolate, melted and cooled
- Chocolate curls (optional)

1. For crust, in a medium bowl stir together cracker crumbs and melted butter until crumbs are moistened. Press mixture evenly onto the bottom of an 8-inch springform pan (may not completely cover bottom). Cover and chill while preparing filling.

2. For filling, place the milk in a small saucepan; sprinkle with gelatin (do not stir). Let stand for 5 minutes to soften. Stir over low heat just until gelatin is dissolved. Remove from heat; set aside to cool about 15 minutes.

3. In a large bowl beat cream cheese with an electric mixer until smooth. Beat in sour cream, sugar, and vanilla until well mixed; slowly beat in gelatin mixture until combined. Divide mixture in half. Gradually stir melted chocolate into one portion.

4. Spread half of the chocolate mixture evenly over chilled crust. Carefully spoon half of the white mixture over chocolate mixture in small mounds. Using a narrow spatula or knife, swirl chocolate and white fillings. Top with remaining chocolate and white fillings, spreading each evenly. Swirl again. Cover and chill for 6 to 24 hours or until set.

5. To serve, using a sharp knife, loosen cheesecake from pan; remove sides of pan. Cut cheesecake into 16 wedges. If desired, garnish with chocolate curls.

*SUGAR SUBSTITUTES: Choose from Splenda Granular, Equal Spoonful or packets, or Sweet'N Low bulk or packets. Follow package directions to use product amount equivalent to ¹/₃ cup sugar.

PER SERVING: 187 cal., 11 g total fat (6 g sat. fat), 29 mg chol., 252 mg sodium, 16 g carb. (1 g fiber, 11 g sugars), 8 g pro. Exchanges: 1 starch, 2 fat.

PER SERVING WITH SUBSTITUTE: Same as above, except 173 cal., 13 g carb. (7 g sugars).

Key Lime Pie

Carb. per serving 17 g

SERVINGS 8 (1 wedge each)
PREP 30 minutes BAKE 8 minutes
CHILL 4 hours 30 minutes

1½ cups small pretzel twists (2 ounces; about 34)
2 tablespoons sliced almonds, toasted
3 tablespoons butter, melted
1 4-serving-size package sugar-free, low-calorie lime-flavor gelatin or regular lime-flavor gelatin
1 cup boiling water
2 6-ounce cartons low-fat Key lime pie-flavor yogurt
½ of an 8-ounce container frozen light whipped dessert topping, thawed
1 teaspoon finely shredded lime peel
Shredded lime peel and/or Key lime slices (optional)

1. Preheat oven to 350°F. For crust, in a food processor combine pretzels and sliced almonds; cover and process until finely crushed. Add butter; cover and process until combined. Press pretzel mixture evenly onto the bottom and up the sides of a 9-inch pie plate. Bake for 8 to 10 minutes or until lightly browned. Cool on a wire rack.

2. For filling, place gelatin in a medium bowl. Add the boiling water and stir until gelatin is dissolved (about 2 minutes). Cover and chill about 30 minutes or until mixture is partially set (the consistency of unbeaten egg whites). Fold in yogurt, whipped topping, and the 1 teaspoon lime peel. Pour into cooled crust. Cover and chill for at least 4 hours.

3. To serve, cut into eight wedges. If desired, top wedges with additional shredded lime peel and/or Key lime slices.

PER SERVING: 153 cal., 7 g total fat (5 g sat. fat), 13 mg chol., 180 mg sodium, 17 g carb. (0 g fiber, 10 g sugars), 3 g pro. Exchanges: 0.5 starch, 0.5 carb., 1.5 fat.

Tiramisu Brownie Parfaits

Carb. per serving 32 g

SERVINGS 6 (1 parfait each)
PREP 20 minutes BAKE 35 minutes STAND 10 minutes

Nonstick cooking spray
1   12.35-ounce package sugar-free fudge brownie mix
½   cup unsweetened applesauce
¼   cup refrigerated or frozen egg product, thawed
3   tablespoons canola oil
¼   cup strong brewed coffee
½   of an 8-ounce tub fat-free cream cheese (about ½ cup)
¼   cup fat-free milk
1   1.3-ounce envelope whipped dessert topping mix
½   teaspoon vanilla
1   tablespoon unsweetened cocoa powder
1   tablespoon shaved bittersweet chocolate (optional)

1. Preheat oven to 350°F. Lightly coat an 8×8×2-inch square baking pan with cooking spray. In a medium bowl combine brownie mix, applesauce, egg, and oil, stirring with a wooden spoon until well mixed.

2. Spread batter evenly into the prepared baking pan. Bake about 35 minutes or until a toothpick inserted near the center comes out clean. Cool completely in pan on a wire rack.

3. Cut half of the pan of brownies into 1-inch-square pieces. (Store the remaining half for another use.) Transfer the brownie pieces to a large bowl. Pour the coffee over brownie pieces; toss to coat lightly. Let stand for 10 minutes to allow brownies to soak up the coffee.

4. Meanwhile, in a medium bowl combine cream cheese, milk, dessert topping mix, and vanilla. Beat with an electric mixer on high speed until stiff peaks form (tips stand straight). Cover and chill until ready to assemble parfaits.

5. To serve, layer a few coffee-soaked brownie pieces in the bottom of each of six 4- to 6-ounce glasses. Top each with a spoonful of the whipped topping mixture. Layer with the remaining brownie pieces; top each with another spoonful of the whipped topping. Lightly sift cocoa powder over parfaits. If desired, garnish with shaved chocolate.

PER SERVING: 181 cal., 8 g total fat (2 g sat. fat), 3 mg chol., 240 mg sodium, 32 g carb. (3 g fiber, 5 g sugars), 5 g pro. Exchanges: 2 starch, 1 fat.

Mocha Cream Puffs

Carb. per serving 6 g

SERVINGS 20 (1 puff each)
PREP 30 minutes **BAKE** 25 minutes

      Nonstick cooking spray
  $3/4$ cup water
   3 tablespoons butter
   1 teaspoon instant coffee crystals
  $1/8$ teaspoon salt
  $3/4$ cup flour
   3 eggs
   1 recipe Mocha Filling *(below)*
      Fresh strawberries (optional)

1. Preheat oven to 400°F. Coat a very large baking sheet with cooking spray; set aside.
2. For cream puffs, in a medium saucepan combine the water, butter, coffee crystals, and salt. Bring to boiling. Add flour all at once, stirring vigorously. Cook and stir until a ball forms that doesn't separate. Cool for 5 minutes.
3. Add eggs, one at a time, beating with a wooden spoon after each addition until smooth. Drop into 20 small mounds on the prepared baking sheet. Bake about 25 minutes or until brown. Cool on wire rack. Split puffs; remove soft dough from insides. Prepare Mocha Filling.
4. Using a pastry bag fitted with a star tip or a spoon, pipe or spoon Mocha Filling into cream puff bottoms. Add cream puff tops. If desired, serve with fresh strawberries.

MOCHA FILLING: In a medium bowl combine $1/2$ cup low-fat vanilla yogurt, 2 tablespoons unsweetened cocoa powder, and 1 teaspoon instant coffee crystals. Fold in half of an 8-ounce container light whipped dessert topping, thawed. Pipe or spoon into cream puffs.

MAKE-AHEAD DIRECTIONS: Prepare and bake cream puffs as directed through Step 3; cover and store at room temperature for up to 24 hours. Prepare Mocha Filling as directed; cover and chill for up to 2 hours. Serve as directed in Step 4.

PER SERVING: 63 cal., 3 g total fat (2 g sat. fat), 37 mg chol., 42 mg sodium, 6 g carb. (0 g fiber, 1 g sugars), 2 g pro.
Exchanges: 0.5 carb., 0.5 fat.

Almond Cannoli with Lemon-Basil Ricotta Cream Filling

Carb. per serving 18 g

SERVINGS 8 (1 filled cannoli each)
PREP 30 minutes BAKE 5 minutes per batch

      2 egg whites
    1/3 cup sugar*
      3 tablespoons flour
      3 tablespoons ground almonds
    1/8 teaspoon salt
      2 tablespoons olive oil or almond oil
    1/2 teaspoon vanilla
      3 ounces reduced-fat cream cheese (Neufchâtel), softened
      2 tablespoons honey
      2 teaspoons finely shredded lemon peel
  1 1/4 cups light or part-skim ricotta cheese
      2 tablespoons snipped fresh basil
         Lemon peel strips and small fresh basil leaves (optional)

1. Preheat oven to 375°F. For cannoli,** line two cookie sheets with parchment paper; set aside. In a medium bowl use a rotary beater to beat egg whites until foamy. Add sugar and beat for 1 minute. Sprinkle with flour, almonds, and salt. Fold together gently. Drizzle with oil and vanilla. Fold together gently. Drop batter evenly into eight mounds, putting four mounds on each cookie sheet and separating the mounds by about 4 inches. Spread each mound to a 6-inch circle.

2. Bake one cookie sheet for 5 to 6 minutes or until bottoms of cookies are lightly browned. Immediately loosen cookies from cookie sheet. Turn over and wrap around metal cannoli forms or the straight metal handle of a whisk. Cool slightly and remove from cones or handle while still warm. Cool on a wire rack, seam sides down. (If cookies become too stiff to roll, return briefly to oven to soften.) Repeat with remaining cookie sheet.

3. For filling, in a medium bowl beat cream cheese with an electric mixer on medium speed until smooth. Beat in honey and lemon peel until smooth. Stir in ricotta cheese and basil.

4. To serve, pipe or spoon cheese mixture into cooled cannoli shells. If desired, garnish with lemon peel strips and/or basil leaves. Serve immediately.

*SUGAR SUBSTITUTES: We do not recommend using a sugar substitute for this recipe.

**TEST KITCHEN TIP: If desired, omit Steps 1 and 2 and substitute 8 full-size or 16 miniature purchased cannoli shells for the homemade shells. Prepare filling and fill shells as directed.

MAKE-AHEAD DIRECTIONS: Prepare cannoli shells and filling as directed through Step 3. Place shells in an airtight container and store at room temperature for up to 3 days. Place filling in an airtight container and chill for up to 3 days. To serve, let filling stand at room temperature for 30 minutes to soften slightly. Fill and garnish shells as directed in Step 4.

PER SERVING: 172 cal., 9 g total fat (3 g sat. fat), 17 mg chol., 120 mg sodium, 18 g carb. (0 g fiber, 15 g sugars), 6 g pro. Exchanges: 1 carb., 1 lean meat, 1.5 fat.

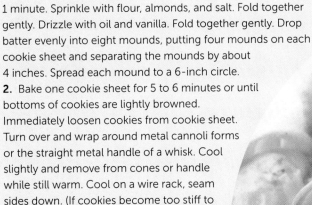

Pumpkin Bars

Carb. per serving 11 g

SERVINGS 25 (1 bar each)
PREP 25 minutes BAKE 12 minutes COOL 10 minutes

½ cup tub-style vegetable oil spread, softened
½ cup packed brown sugar*
½ teaspoon baking soda
½ teaspoon pumpkin pie spice
⅓ cup canned pumpkin
¼ cup refrigerated or frozen egg product, thawed, or 1 egg
1½ cups flour
½ of an 8-ounce package reduced-fat cream cheese (Neufchâtel), softened
1 cup frozen light whipped dessert topping, thawed
Freshly grated nutmeg (optional)

1. Preheat oven to 350°F. Grease and lightly flour a 9×9×2-inch baking pan; set aside.

2. In a large bowl combine vegetable oil spread, brown sugar, baking soda, and pumpkin pie spice; beat with an electric mixer on medium speed until well mixed. Beat in pumpkin and egg. Beat in as much of the flour as you can with the mixer. Using a wooden spoon, stir in any remaining flour.

3. Spread dough into prepared pan. Bake for 12 to 15 minutes or until a toothpick inserted near the center comes out clean. Cool in pan on a wire rack for 10 minutes. Remove from pan; cool completely on a wire rack.

4. Meanwhile, for frosting, in a medium bowl beat cream cheese with an electric mixer on medium speed until smooth. Beat in half of the dessert topping. Fold in remaining dessert topping. Spread over cooled pumpkin layer. If desired, sprinkle with nutmeg. Cut into bars. Store, covered, in the refrigerator for up to 3 days.

SUGAR SUBSTITUTE: We do not recommend using a sugar substitute for this recipe.

PER SERVING: 90 cal., 4 g total fat (2 g sat. fat), 3 mg chol., 75 mg sodium, 11 g carb. (0 g fiber, 5 g sugars), 1 g pro. Exchanges: 1 carb., 0 .5 fat.

237

Chocolate-Drizzled Peanut Butter Cheesecake Bars

Carb. per serving 13 g or 10 g

SERVINGS 24 (1 bar each)
PREP 30 minutes **BAKE** 25 minutes **COOL** 30 minutes
CHILL 4 hours

Nonstick cooking spray
1/2 cup regular rolled oats
1/2 cup whole wheat flour
1/4 cup packed brown sugar*
1/4 cup butter, melted
2 8-ounce packages fat-free cream cheese, softened
3/4 cup creamy peanut butter
1/3 cup granulated sugar*
3/4 cup refrigerated or frozen egg product, thawed
1/4 cup fat-free milk
1 teaspoon vanilla
2 ounces semisweet chocolate, chopped
2 to 3 tablespoons fat-free milk
3 tablespoons chopped peanuts (optional)

1. Preheat oven to 350°F. Lightly coat a 13x9x2-inch baking pan or 3-quart rectangular baking dish with cooking spray; set aside.
2. For crust, place oats in a food processor or blender. Cover; process or blend until coarsely ground. In a small bowl combine ground oats, flour, brown sugar, and melted butter. Pat mixture evenly onto bottom of prepared pan. Set aside.
3. Meanwhile, for cheesecake filling, in a large bowl combine cream cheese, peanut butter, and granulated sugar. Beat with an electric mixer on medium speed until combined. Add egg, the 1/4 cup milk, and the vanilla. Beat on low speed just until combined.
4. Pour filling onto the prepared crust. Bake about 25 minutes or until set in the center. Cool in pan on a wire rack for 30 minutes. Cover and chill for at least 4 hours or up to 24 hours.

5. For chocolate drizzle, in a small heavy saucepan heat chocolate over low heat, stirring until melted. Remove from heat and beat in enough of the 2 to 3 tablespoons milk to make drizzling consistency. Spoon chocolate into a small plastic bag; seal bag. Using scissors, snip off a very small corner from bag. Pipe melted chocolate over the filling. If desired, sprinkle with peanuts. Cover and chill until chocolate is set.

*SUGAR SUBSTITUTES: Choose Splenda Brown Sugar Blend for the brown sugar and Splenda Sugar Blend for the granulated sugar. Follow package directions to use product amounts equivalent to 1/4 cup brown sugar and 1/3 cup granulated sugar.

PER SERVING: 145 cal., 8 g total fat (3 g sat. fat), 8 mg chol., 203 mg sodium, 13 g carb. (1 g fiber, 8 g sugars), 7 g pro. Exchanges: 1 starch, 1 lean meat, 1 fat.

PER SERVING WITH SUBSTITUTES: Same as above, except 137 cal., 10 g carb. (5 g sugars), 202 mg sodium. Exchanges: 0.5 starch.

Almond-Chocolate-Cherry Cookies

Carb. per serving 11 g or 10 g

SERVINGS 38 (1 cookie each)
PREP 30 minutes CHILL 1 hour
BAKE 10 minutes per batch

6	tablespoons butter, softened
3/4	cup granulated sugar*
1	egg
1	egg yolk
1	teaspoon vanilla
1	ounce sweet baking, bittersweet, or semisweet chocolate, melted and cooled slightly
1 1/3	cups flour
1/2	cup dried cherries
1/3	cup sliced almonds
1	recipe Chocolate-Almond Glaze *(below)*

1. In a medium bowl beat butter with an electric mixer on medium-high speed about 2 minutes or until smooth. Add granulated sugar and beat until creamy. Beat in egg, egg yolk, and vanilla until combined. Stir in melted chocolate. Stir in flour. Fold in dried cherries and almonds. Cover and chill dough for 1 hour.

2. Preheat oven to 350°F. Line cookie sheets with parchment paper; set aside. Shape dough into 1-inch balls. Place balls about 1 inch apart on prepared cookie sheets. Bake for 10 to 12 minutes or until centers are set. Cool on cookie sheet for 2 minutes. Transfer cookies to wire racks; cool completely.

3. Drizzle Chocolate-Almond Glaze over cooled cookies. Let stand until glaze is set. To store, layer cookies between sheets of waxed paper in an airtight container. Cover. Store in the refrigerator for up to 3 days or freeze for up to 3 months.

CHOCOLATE-ALMOND GLAZE: In a small saucepan combine 1/2 ounce sweet baking, bittersweet, or semisweet chocolate and 1 1/2 teaspoons butter. Heat and stir over low heat until melted and smooth. Remove from heat. Stir in 1/2 cup powdered sugar,* 1 tablespoon fat-free milk, and 1/8 teaspoon almond extract until smooth.

*SUGAR SUBSTITUTE: Use Splenda Sugar Blend. Follow package directions to use product amount equivalent to 3/4 cup granulated sugar. We do not recommend using a sugar substitute for the powdered sugar for the glaze. Makes 34 cookies.

PER SERVING: 74 cal., 3 g total fat (2 g sat. fat), 15 mg chol., 20 mg sodium, 11 g carb. (0 g fiber, 7 g sugars), 1 g pro. Exchanges: 0.5 starch, 0.5 carb., 0.5 fat.

PER SERVING WITH SUBSTITUTE: Same as above, except 76 cal., 17 mg chol., 10 g carb. (6 g sugars), 22 mg sodium. Exchanges: 0 carb.

Rosemary-Kissed Orange Thumbprint Cookies

Carb. per serving 13 g

SERVINGS 24 (1 cookie each)
PREP 30 minutes CHILL 1 hour
BAKE 14 minutes per batch

    1   cup flour
  $1/2$ cup cornstarch
    1   teaspoon snipped fresh rosemary
  $1/4$ teaspoon salt
  $3/4$ cup butter, softened
  $1/3$ cup powdered sugar
      Few drops almond extract
  $1/4$ cup orange marmalade
      Powdered sugar (optional)

1. In small bowl stir together flour, cornstarch, rosemary, and salt; set aside. In a medium bowl beat the butter with an electric mixer on medium to high speed for 30 seconds. Add the $1/3$ cup powdered sugar and the almond extract; beat until combined. Add flour mixture; beat until combined. Wrap and chill dough about 1 hour or until easy to handle.

2. Preheat oven to 325°F. Line two cookie sheets with parchment paper; set aside. Shape dough into twenty-four $1^{1}/4$-inch balls. Place balls 2 inches apart on prepared cookie sheets. Use your thumb to make an indentation in each cookie. Spoon about $1/2$ teaspoon of the marmalade into the center of each cookie.

3. Bake about 14 minutes or until edges are lightly golden brown. Cool for 1 minute on cookie sheets. Transfer cookies to wire racks; cool completely. If desired, sprinkle with additional powdered sugar.

PER SERVING: 105 cal., 6 g total fat (4 g sat. fat), 15 mg chol., 77 mg sodium, 13 g carb. (0 g fiber, 6 g sugars), 1 g pro.
Exchanges: 0.5 starch, 0.5 carb., 1 fat.

Lemon-Ginger Shortbread

Carb. per serving 18 g

SERVINGS 36 (2 cookies each)
PREP 25 minutes **BAKE** 20 minutes per batch

3³⁄₄   cups flour
  2   cups powdered sugar
¹⁄₄   cup chopped crystallized ginger
  2   teaspoons finely shredded lemon peel
1¹⁄₂   cups unsalted butter
  2   to 3 tablespoons lemon juice
    Finely shredded lemon peel (optional)

1. Preheat oven to 325°F. Line two cookie sheets with parchment paper; set aside. In a medium bowl combine flour, 1 cup of the powdered sugar, the crystalized ginger, and the 2 teaspoons lemon peel. Using a pastry blender, cut in butter until mixture resembles fine crumbs and starts to cling together. Stir in 1 tablespoon of the lemon juice. Form mixture into a ball; knead until smooth.
2. Divide dough in half. Place each dough portion between two sheets of parchment paper or waxed paper. Roll each portion to a 12x6-inch rectangle. Cut each rectangle into thirty-six 2x1-inch pieces (72 pieces total). Place on the prepared cookie sheets. If desired, prick the tops of the rectangles with a fork.
3. Bake for 20 to 25 minutes or until bottoms are golden brown. Transfer to wire racks; cool completely.
4. For icing, in a small bowl combine the remaining 1 cup powdered sugar and add enough of the remaining lemon juice (1 to 2 tablespoons) to make drizzling consistency. Drizzle shortbread with icing. If desired, sprinkle with additional lemon peel. Let stand until set.

PER SERVING: 147 cal., 8 g total fat (5 g sat. fat), 20 mg chol., 2 mg sodium, 18 g carb. (0 g fiber, 7 g sugars), 1 g pro. Exchanges: 1 starch, 1.5 fat.

Coconut-Almond Frozen Greek Yogurt with Hot Chocolate Drizzle

Carb. per serving 21 g

SERVINGS 11 (^{1}/3 cup and 1 tablespoon chocolate mixture each)
PREP 15 minutes FREEZE according to manufacturer's directions + 3 hours

- 24 ounces plain fat-free Greek yogurt
- ^{1}/2 cup low-fat buttermilk
- ^{1}/3 cup honey
- ^{1}/3 cup unsweetened shredded coconut, toasted
- ^{1}/3 cup sliced almonds, toasted
- 1 teaspoon coconut extract
- 4 ounces semisweet chocolate, chopped
- 6 tablespoons unsweetened almond milk
- Shredded coconut, toasted (optional)

1. In a large bowl whisk together yogurt, buttermilk, honey, the ^{1}/3 cup coconut, the almonds, and coconut extract until well mixed.

2. Freeze yogurt mixture in a 1^1/2-quart ice cream freezer according to manufacturer's directions. Transfer yogurt mixture to a freezer container. Cover and freeze for 3 to 4 hours or until firm enough to scoop.

3. For chocolate mixture, just before serving, in a medium saucepan combine chopped chocolate and almond milk. Cook and stir over low heat until chocolate is melted and mixture is completely smooth. Drizzle chocolate mixture over scoops of the frozen yogurt. If desired, garnish with additional toasted coconut.

TEST KITCHEN TIP: If yogurt is too hard to scoop, microwave on 50 percent power (medium) until soft enough to scoop, checking mixture every 30 seconds to avoid melting.

PER SERVING: 153 cal., 6 g total fat (3 g sat. fat), 1 mg chol., 44 mg sodium, 21 g carb. (1 g fiber, 19 g sugars), 7 g pro. Exchanges: 0.5 milk, 1 carb., 1 fat.

Raspberry-Chocolate Almond Ice Cream

Carb. per serving 18 g

SERVINGS 8 ($^1/_2$ cup each)
PREP 20 minutes CHILL 8 hours
FREEZE according to manufacturer's directions + 4 hours

- 2 cups unsweetened vanilla-flavored almond milk
- 3 egg yolks, lightly beaten
- $^1/_4$ cup honey
- 2 tablespoons cornstarch
- $^1/_4$ teaspoon almond extract
- $^1/_8$ teaspoon salt
- 1 cup fresh raspberries
- 2 ounces dark chocolate, finely chopped
- $^1/_3$ cup slivered almonds, toasted

1. In a medium saucepan whisk together almond milk, egg yolks, honey, and cornstarch. Cook and stir over medium heat for 6 to 8 minutes or until custard coats the back of a spoon (do not boil). If necessary, strain through a fine-mesh sieve into a bowl to remove any lumps; stir in almond extract and salt. Cover and chill for 8 to 24 hours.

2. Freeze chilled mixture in a $1^1/_2$-quart ice cream freezer according to manufacturer's directions. Stir in raspberries, chopped chocolate, and almonds. Transfer mixture to a 2-quart freezer container. Cover and freeze for 4 hours before serving.

PER SERVING: 142 cal., 7 g total fat (2 g sat. fat), 70 mg chol., 87 mg sodium, 18 g carb. (2 g fiber, 13 g sugars), 3 g pro. Exchanges: 0.5 milk, 0.5 carb., 1.5 fat.

243

Banana Buster Pops

Carb. per serving 18 g

SERVINGS 4 (1 pop each)
PREP 20 minutes FREEZE 30 minutes

- 4 teaspoons peanut butter
- 1 banana, cut into 12 equal slices
- 4 6- to 8-inch white sucker sticks or wooden skewers
- 2 ounces milk chocolate or semisweet chocolate, melted
- 2 tablespoons finely chopped unsalted dry-roasted or cocktail peanuts

1. Line a baking sheet with waxed paper; set aside. Spoon $1/2$ teaspoon of the peanut butter onto each of eight of the banana slices. Place four of the peanut butter-topped banana slices on the remaining four peanut butter-topped slices to make four stacks of two banana slices with peanut butter between and peanut butter on top. Place one of the remaining banana slices on top of each stack. Push a sucker stick or skewer all the way through the center of each banana stack.

2. Place melted chocolate in a shallow dish. Place peanuts in another shallow dish. Roll each banana stack in the melted chocolate. Use a thin metal spatula to help spread the chocolate into a thin, even layer over the stacks. Immediately roll in peanuts. Place on prepared baking sheet.

3. Freeze banana pops about 30 minutes or until firm. Serve straight from the freezer.

PER SERVING: 165 cal., 9 g total fat (4 g sat. fat), 3 mg chol., 38 mg sodium, 18 g carb. (2 g fiber, 12 g sugars), 4 g pro. Exchanges: 5 fruit, 0.5 carb., 0.5 high-fat meat, 1 fat.

Layered Frozen Chocolate Coffee Pops

Carb. per serving 16 g

SERVINGS 8 (1 pop each)
PREP 20 minutes FREEZE 12 hours

- 1 4-serving-size package fat-free, sugar-free, reduced-calorie white chocolate instant pudding mix
- 1¼ teaspoons instant espresso coffee powder
- 2 cups fat-free milk
- 8 5-ounce paper or plastic drink cups
- ⅓ cup fat-free sweetened condensed milk
- ¼ cup unsweetened cocoa powder
- ½ teaspoon instant espresso coffee powder
- ½ teaspoon vanilla
- 1½ cups water
- 8 flat wooden crafts sticks

1. In a medium bowl stir together pudding mix and the 1¼ teaspoons espresso powder. Add the 2 cups fat-free milk; whisk about 2 minutes or until smooth and thickened.

2. Evenly spoon the pudding mixture into the paper cups. Cover with foil and chill while preparing the second layer.

3. In a medium bowl whisk together the sweetened condensed milk, cocoa powder, the ½ teaspoon espresso powder, and the vanilla. Whisk in the water until combined. Remove foil from cups and carefully spoon the cocoa powder mixture evenly over the pudding layer.

4. Cover cups with foil again. Cut a slit in the foil over each cup and insert a wooden stick into each slit, pushing the stick down into the layers. Freeze at least 12 hours or until firm.

5. To serve, remove foil and tear away the paper cups or remove pops from plastic cups.

PER SERVING: 78 cal., 0 g total fat, 1 mg chol., 206 mg sodium, 16 g carb. (1 g fiber, 12 g sugars), 4 g pro. Exchanges: 1 starch.

Recipe Guide

See how we calculate nutrition information to help you count calories, carbs, and serving sizes.

Inside Our Recipes

1. **Precise serving sizes** (listed below the recipe title) help you manage portions.

2. **When ingredient choices appear,** we use the first one to calculate the nutrition analysis.

3. **Ingredients listed as optional** are not included in the per-serving nutrition analysis.

4. **Kitchen basics** such as ice, salt, black pepper, and nonstick cooking spray sometimes are not listed in the ingredients list; they are italicized in the directions.

5. **Test Kitchen tips and sugar substitutes** are listed after the recipe directions.

6. **Nutrition facts per serving and food exchanges** are noted with each recipe.

7. **Ingredients**
- Tub-style vegetable oil spread refers to 60% to 70% vegetable oil product.
- Lean ground beef refers to 95% or leaner ground beef.

Key to Abbreviations

cal. = calories
sat. fat = saturated fat
chol. = cholesterol
carb. = carbohydrate
pro. = protein

A Fresh Take on
Tuna Salad

Cooking fresh tuna steaks is like cooking beef steaks. The tuna stays moist and flavorful when cooked until pink in the center, but it dries out if cooked longer.

½ Plate
Nonstarchy Veggies: watercress, cabbage, jicama, radishes, onion

¼ Plate
Starch, Grain, or Other Carb: brown rice

¼ Plate
Protein: tuna, cashews

Asian Tuna and Watercress
Carb. per serving 27 g or 25 g

SERVINGS 4 (2 cups salad, ⅓ cup rice, 1 tuna steak, and 2 tablespoons dressing each)
START TO FINISH 45 minutes

- 3 cups watercress
- 3 cups shredded napa cabbage or Chinese cabbage
- 1 cup jicama, peeled and cut into matchstick-size pieces
- 1 cup sliced radishes
- ¼ of a medium red onion, thinly sliced
- ½ cup rice vinegar
- 1 tablespoon sugar*
- 1 tablespoon reduced-sodium soy sauce
- 4 teaspoons toasted sesame oil
- ½ teaspoon ground ginger
- ⅛ to ¼ teaspoon crushed red pepper
- 4 4- to 5-ounce tuna steaks, about 1 inch thick
- ⅛ teaspoon ground coriander
- 1⅓ cups hot cooked brown rice
- 2 tablespoons chopped cashews
  Lime wedges (optional)

1. In a very large bowl combine watercress, cabbage, jicama, radishes, and red onion; set aside.
2. For dressing, in a screw-top jar combine rice vinegar, sugar, soy sauce, 2 teaspoons of the toasted sesame oil, half of the ginger, and the crushed red pepper. Cover and shake well.
3. In a large nonstick skillet heat remaining 2 teaspoons toasted sesame oil over medium-high heat. Sprinkle tuna steaks with ¼ teaspoon *salt*, ¼ teaspoon *black pepper*, the coriander, and remaining ginger. Rub spices into tuna steaks. Add tuna to skillet.

Cook for 8 to 10 minutes or until tuna is browned but still slightly pink on the inside, turning once halfway through cooking.
4. To serve, toss watercress mixture with ¼ cup of the dressing. Divide watercress mixture among four serving plates. Spoon rice over the watercress, dividing evenly. Thinly slice tuna. Arrange tuna slices over the salad and rice mixture. Sprinkle with cashews. Pass remaining dressing. If desired, serve with lime wedges.

*SUGAR SUBSTITUTES: Choose from Splenda Granular, Sweet'N Low bulk or packets, or Equal Spoonful or packets. Follow package directions to use product amount equivalent to 1 tablespoon sugar.

PER SERVING: 321 cal., 8 g total fat (1 g sat. fat), 44 mg chol., 374 mg sodium, 27 g carb. (4 g fiber, 6 g sugars), 32 g pro. Exchanges: 2 vegetable, 1 starch, 4 lean meat, 1 fat.

PER SERVING WITH SUBSTITUTE: Same as above, except 310 cal., 25 g carb. (3 g sugars).

Meal Total (per plate): 321 cal., 8 g total fat (1 g sat. fat), 44 mg chol., 374 mg sodium, 27 g carb. (4 g fiber, 6 g sugars), 32 g pro. Exchanges: 2 vegetable, 1 starch, 4 lean meat, 1 fat.

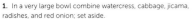

151

High-Standards Testing!
This seal assures you every recipe in this issue of *Diabetic Living® Meals by the Plate* has been tested in the Better Homes and Gardens® Test Kitchen. This means each recipe is practical, reliable, and meets our high standards of taste appeal.

Index

Page numbers in *italics* indicate illustrations

ⓖⓕ indicates gluten-free recipes